The Funniest Decade:
A Celebration of American Comedy in the 1930s

Garry Berman

BearManor Media

Orlando, Florida

The Funniest Decade: A Celebration of American Comedy in the 1930s
© 2020 Garry Berman. All Rights Reserved.

No portion of this publication may be reproduced, stored, and/or copied electronically (except for academic use as a source), nor transmitted in any form or by any means without the prior written permission of the publisher and/or author.

Published in the USA by
BearManor Media
1317 Edgewater Dr. #110
Orlando, FL 32804
www.BearManorMedia.com

Softcover Edition
ISBN: 978-1-62933-627-5

Printed in the United States of America

Table of Contents

Preface	ix
A Note About Radio Program Names	xiii
Introduction	xv
Chapter One: 1929	1
Chapter Two: 1930	35
Chapter Three: 1931	71
Chapter Four: 1932	87
Chapter Five: 1933	131
Chapter Six: 1934	163
Chapter Seven: 1935	197
Chapter Eight: 1936	215
Chapter Nine: 1937	241
Chapter Ten: 1938	255
Chapter Eleven: 1939	267
Chapter Twelve: 1940…and beyond	285
Legacy	293
Notes	297
Bibliography	315
Index	319

Acknowledgments

Many thanks to the following individuals for their encouragement and assistance in preparing this book: Bill Parisho, Bill Cassara, Steve Cox, Martin Grams, Michelle Morgan, and my publicist, Jennifer Vanderslice of Moonglow PR. Thanks also go to the Burlington County, N.J. Library, and the Cherry Hill, N.J. library.

A special, but unfortunately posthumous thank-you goes to the late George Bettinger, entertainer and broadcaster, who invited me to be a guest on his online podcast twice, to help me promote my books and chat about old-time show business and comedy. He gladly encouraged me to speak about this very book, long before I had even completed it, just in case any agents, publishers, and/or comedy fans might have been listening in and taking notes.

The photos on these pages are from the author's collection, unless otherwise noted. Most of the photos were originally issued to publicize or promote films and radio programs, produced by major film studios and broadcasters.

Preface

Researching and writing of this book has been much like coming full-circle for me. When I was 13 or 14 years old, I suddenly discovered the great film comedians of the 1930s, what I now refer to as the Golden Decade. I had known about them from an even earlier age, but, perhaps with a fresh onslaught of their films being shown on New York TV stations (often in the middle of the night) in the mid-1970s, I truly began to sit up and take notice—and laugh like crazy. At first, the Marx Brothers, with their sheer anarchy, wordplay, and eccentric, larger-than-life characters, quickly became my favorites, by the slimmest of margins over the unique relationship between Laurel & Hardy and the groaning, put-upon curmudgeon, W.C. Fields.

I took an interest in other comedians of the era as well (what teenage boy, of any decade, wouldn't love the Three Stooges?). As movie theatres in New York began running special Marx Bros. and Laurel & Hardy festivals, I begged my parents to drive me the ten miles from our suburban New Jersey home into Manhattan, so I could attend the screenings. They were welcome to accompany me to watch the films, which they did on occasion. More often, they simply dropped me off at the Carnegie Hall Cinema or Bleeker St. Cinema for a few hours and killed some time elsewhere in the city. It didn't matter to me, as long as I got to see the films and laugh along with like-minded fans. And, to my parents' credit, they agreed to chauffeur me to such cinematic indulgences on a fairly regular basis.

My parents also once ordered a set of LP records by the Longines Symphonette Society, as advertised on TV. Each record, narrated by Jack Benny, highlighted a different aspect of radio's "Golden Age" of the 1930s and 1940s. From these, I came to know Fred Allen, Burns & Allen, and other legends (those albums still occupy a space on my record shelf). My parents also bought me books about the comedians, so I could learn more of the clowns who had invaded my very psyche (being an early teen at the time, I didn't even know I *had* a psyche). Then came the syndicated reruns of Groucho's *You Bet Your Life* quiz show, airing every weeknight at 11:00.

There was also the re-release of *Animal Crackers* at the Sutton Theater, after the film had been out of circulation for the previous twenty years, due to copyright entanglements.

With all of this, the age of 14, I was well on the way to becoming a comedy "expert" of sorts, or so I thought. There was much more for me to learn and enjoy, especially from the Golden Decade, and there still is.

* * *

My goal in researching and writing this book has been to piece together a chronology of American comedy throughout the 1930s, *not* to provide a complete biography of each and every comedy performer mentioned on these pages, nor to list and critique every single comedy film, radio broadcast, and stage production in America throughout the 1930s. Even if I had the resources and budget to do so (a full-time staff would have been nice to have throughout this undertaking), chances are the finished product will still trigger cries from assorted entertainment historians, archivists, and aficionados, pointing out how I've neglected to include a particular film, broadcast, or performer that *must* be included in order to make this project truly complete. I do feel, however, that the abundance of classic comedy created throughout the 1930s deserves to be arranged and organized into a chronology, to put all of these creative milestones into a context that demonstrates how this particular decade saw a virtual explosion of the art form.

A note about radio program names

Radio in the 1930s became a means for retailers and manufacturers of consumer products to buy blocks of airtime on which to advertise to a mass audience. These companies and businesses hired advertising agencies to create the programs most likely to appeal to listeners, thus insuring a captive audience for many a long-winded commercial message, in between the creative content–or even as *part* of the creative content–extolling the sponsor's wonderful products or services. So, programs that listeners most commonly would refer to as *The Jack Benny Show* or *The Burns & Allen Show* were technically named after the sponsors themselves. For instance, Rudy Vallee's popular variety program was actually *The Fleishmann Yeast Hour*, or *Fleishmann's Hour*. Eddie Cantor's show was *The Chase & Sanborn Hour*, even though it was known colloquially as *The Eddie Cantor Show*.

However, the sponsors for most programs would often come and go in fairly rapid succession, while the stars and content of the show itself would remain basically the same, perhaps with an occasional change in format, in order to start a new sponsorship with a clean slate. One example is Fred Allen's first program, which was originally *The Linit Bath Revue* (named for a beauty powder manufactured by the Corn Products Company), but which morphed into the *Salad Bowl Revue* (sponsored by Hellman's mayonnaise), and had still other sponsors, all within a year's time. Eventually, Allen decided to forego the program's title as an umbilical attachment to the sponsor, and chose *Town Hall Tonight* as the name, partly to appeal more to rural audiences. Smaller towns, he reasoned, all had town halls to serve as meeting places for community events, which was the feel he was going after for his program. Regardless of the sponsor, he was, of course, still the star, offering his unique brand of comedy for his avid listeners.

For reasons such as this, and to help avoid unnecessary confusion, this book will, whenever possible, identify various radio programs by the *stars* they featured, rather than by their often-changing sponsors.

Introduction

It can be argued that the term "Golden Age," in any context, has become an overused cliché. Yet this book presents the argument that the entire decade of the 1930s proved to be the true Golden Decade of American comedy. This ten-year span produced the finest films, radio programs, and stage performances by the most talented comedians ever to make audiences laugh. There has never been quite a decade for comedy as there was throughout the 1930s. What a joy it must have been not only for comedy mavens at the time, but for the nation as a whole, as Americans struggled through the disaster of the Great Depression.

In film alone, the comedy titans of the movies—Laurel & Hardy, The Marx Brothers, and W. C. Fields—all reached their creative peaks within this relatively brief period, as did Mae West, The Three Stooges, and all of the comedy film series produced by the Hal Roach Studios, which, in addition to Laurel & Hardy, included the Our Gang (a.k.a. The Little Rascals) series, Charley Chase, Thelma Todd, and still more. It is a testament to the quality and timelessness of the film comedians of the Golden Decade that they are still celebrated today, albeit often viewed on devices they themselves couldn't have dreamed of over 80 years ago. We can also add to this list a few teams that are less-remembered today, such as Wheeler & Woolsey, Clark & McCullough, and the Ritz Brothers, but who found great popularity in the Golden Decade, and whose work can still be found, with just a bit of searching online or elsewhere. The 1930s also saw the birth of the "screwball" comedy, in which comic actors (as distinguished from *comedians*) played somewhat eccentric characters who tended to get entangled with each other in clashes of romance and/or social standing. The trend created some of Hollywood's best-loved stars, the foremost being Carole Lombard and Cary Grant.

Radio grew steadily throughout the 1920s, and became a mass medium by decade's end (the NBC network was formed in 1926, and CBS two years later). It became a truly major entertainment force throughout the 1930s, as it welcomed the arrival of seasoned vaudeville comedians like Jack Benny, Eddie Cantor, Ed Wynn, Fred Allen, George Burns & Gracie Allen, Edgar Bergen, Bob Hope, and Abbott & Costello, to name just a few. Most began as guests on variety programs, hosted by the likes of Rudy Vallee and Kate Smith, before being awarded shows of their own. The stage comedians who specialized in talking scrambled to find their niche in front of the microphone, hoping to become stars in a medium where tens of millions of listeners could hear them at once, rather than just one theatre audience at a time. There were a few skeptical holdouts in the early years, but their wariness of radio wasn't strong enough to keep them away for long.

At the same time, the likes of Bert Lahr, Fannie Brice, Jimmy Durante, Beatrice Lillie, and the aforementioned Wynn were performing regularly in stage revues and/or "legit" Broadway comedies, on their way to becoming entertainment legends. None were limited strictly to the stage, and all took their respective plunges into radio and films, with varying degrees of success.

What accounted for this burst of such comic creativity in the 1930s? To answer this question, we could choose to take a scholarly (i.e. more pretentious) route, in which we might look for the convergence of various sociological, economic, and political forces of the decade for our answer. We can explain it as a reaction to the troubled times of the Depression, Prohibition, and upheavals in Europe. Or, we can consider a simple but easily-missed fact about the comic personalities celebrated on these pages. To wit:

Introduction

One reason so many comedians hit their creative peaks in the 1930s can be found, in part, upon close inspection of their birth dates. In examining the decade spanning the years between 1888 and 1898, we can see the fairly astonishing revelation of how many legendary comedy stars, writers, and directors were born within a mere ten years of each other, and were of similar ages when they produced their finest works on film, radio, and the stage, throughout the Golden Decade.

Here then, is a chronology of their birth dates (some names might not yet be familiar to you, which this book is meant to rectify):

Bobby Clark - June 16, 1888
Robert Woolsey - August 14, 1888
Harpo Marx - November 23, 1888
Charlie Chaplin - April 16, 1889
George S. Kaufman (playwright/screenwriter) - November 16, 1889
Edgar Kennedy - April 26, 1890
Stan Laurel - June 16, 1890
Joe E. Brown - July 28, 1891
Groucho Marx - October 2, 1890
Chic Johnson - March 5, 1891
Fannie Brice - October 29, 1891
Hal Roach (director/producer) - January 14, 1892
Oliver Hardy - January 18, 1892
Eddie Cantor - September 21, 1892
Ole Olsen - November 6, 1892
Jimmy Durante - February 10, 1893
Mae West - August 17, 1893
Harold Lloyd - April 20, 1893
Charley Chase - October 20, 1893
ZaSu Pitts - January 3, 1894
Jack Benny - February 14, 1894
Beatrice Lillie - May 29, 1894

Fred Allen - May 31, 1894
Billy Gilbert - September 12, 1894
Jack Pearl - October 29, 1894
Shemp Howard - March 11, 1895
Bert Wheeler - April 7, 1895
Gracie Allen - July 26, 1895
Bert Lahr - August 13, 1895
Buster Keaton - October 4, 1895
Morrie Ryskind (playwright/screenwriter) - October 20, 1895
George Burns - January 20, 1896
Moe Howard - June 18, 1897
Bud Abbott - October 2, 1897
George Jessel - April 3, 1898
Leo McCarey (director) - October 3, 1898

Of course, this 1888–1898 range can be stretched a bit in either direction of the timeline, to include still more comedy stars who created their most celebrated work in the 1930s, such as W.C Fields, Will Rogers (both born in 1879), and Ed Wynn (born in 1886). Extending the opposite end of the timeline, we find the births of Stooges Larry Fine (born in 1902), and Curly Howard (born in 1903), as well as Hal Roach star Thelma Todd (born in 1906), and the Ritz Brothers (born between 1903 and 1908).

What's the significance of this? Look at it this way: As of 1930, just about all of the individuals listed above, as well as others included throughout these pages, were between roughly 32 and 41 years old; old enough to have already had at least a decade's worth of experience in comedy—be it in films, onstage, or both. Many of these individuals had already known each other quite well by 1930, having crossed paths at movie studios, or by performing around the country in vaudeville on the same bills. Even with their years of experience at the dawn of the Golden Decade, they were also young enough to have their creative energies running at full throttle. Of course, they all had their occasional failures along the way, but this energy nonetheless led to an immense volume of brilliantly conceived and performed comedy for films, radio, and the stage throughout the ten-year span of 1930–1940.

Where did all of these comedians come from? Geographically speaking, they came from all over the U.S., from metropolitan hubs to small rural towns, although the preponderance of them grew up on the east coast, most notably in the New York City, Philadelphia, and Boston areas. Most were the offspring of European immigrants, especially Jews from Eastern Europe and Russia, whose families had fled war, poverty, religious persecution, or all three simultaneously.

A great many comedians discussed on these pages had adopted stage names for themselves quite early in their respective careers. Some did so because their given names simply didn't sound right for show business. So, William Claude Dukinfield became W.C. Fields, John Florence Sullivan became Fred Allen, and Arthur Stanley Jefferson became Stan Laurel. Others, especially those from Jewish families, felt a need to present themselves as less "ethnic" to vaudeville theatre managers—and, by extension, to their audiences. There were exceptions, though. Fania Borach became Fannie Brice; not as blatantly Jewish-sounding, yet Brice used a Yiddish accent for much of her act (even though she didn't speak Yiddish), and drew from her Jewish upbringing and culture without apology.

Some entertainers were given their nicknames by others. The Marx Brothers—eldest brother Chico (Leonard), Harpo (Adolf, later Arthur), Groucho (Julius)—were nicknamed by a fellow vaudevillian, Art Fisher, during a poker game, as he dealt the cards to each brother. Younger brothers Milton and Herbert became Gummo and Zeppo.

Joseph Keaton was nicknamed "Buster" when he was a toddler, by his godfather Harry Houdini (who, by the way, was born Erich Weiss), upon witnessing the young boy topple down a flight of stairs, get up, and brush himself off with nary a scratch.

Other comedians of the Golden Decade went through name changes as well. Their stage names, followed by their given names, include:

Eddie Cantor - Edward Israel (or Isadore) Iskowitz
Mae West - Mary Jane West
Charley Chase - Charles Parrott
Jack Benny - Benjamin Kubelsky
Jack Pearl - Jack Perlman
Joe Penner - Jozsef Pinter
Three Stooges - Moe (Moses Horwitz), Shemp (Samuel Horwitz), Curly (Jerome Horwitz), Larry Fine (Louis Fineberg)
Bert Lahr - Irving Lahrheim
Ted Healy - Ernest Lea Nash
George Burns - Nathan Birnbaum
Bud Abbott - William Alexander Abbott
Lou Costello - Louis Francis Cristillo
Ed Wynn - Isaiah Edwin Leopold
Milton Berle - Milton Berlinger
Ritz Brothers - Harry, Jimmy, and Al Joachim

The great comedians of the day, regardless of the names they were known by, were still subject to the changing nature of show business itself. As the arrival of sound films thrilled audiences, it created repercussions in the world of the stage. Vaudeville, which had existed virtually unchanged for the previous fifty years by offering strictly live entertainment, began suffering in the late 1920s from the powerful draw talking movies held for the public's imagination and excitement. Radio dealt another, perhaps even greater blow to vaudeville. After all, unlike a stage show or film, radio was free, and people didn't need to leave their homes to be entertained by their favorite performers. This was no small thing once the Depression hit the nation's pocketbooks. Vaudeville was nonetheless determined to hang on and remain relevant, despite increasingly unfavorable odds.

The official arrival of "talkies" in the movies occurred on October 6, 1927, with the premiere of *The Jazz Singer*, starring Al Jolson. While it was by no means the first sound film to be released, it did boast the biggest name in all of show business at the time. It was mostly silent, and Jolson spoke a total of about 280 words—but he sang as well, and hearing such a star sing his heart out on the screen made the difference.

Talkies struck the film industry like a thunderbolt—a thunderbolt that could now actually be heard. Talking films were still getting the kinks out between 1927 and 1929, and some, like *The Jazz Singer*, were not all-talking so much as *some*-talking (*The Lights of New York* was the first all-talking feature, premiering in July of 1928). Many theatres in the U.S. and Europe needed to equip themselves for sound films, which didn't happen overnight. However, movie audiences for the most part had little inclination to stay with silent films, when they could hear as well as see their favorite stars. There certainly were those silent film diehards who didn't necessarily welcome sound, feeling that the movie industry should have left well enough alone. Talkies, some said, were too chattering, and too noisy, but their objections quickly fell upon deaf ears.

A consequence of the unstoppable popularity of motion pictures allowed movies to incrementally grab bigger and bigger shares of the entertainment rosters in America's vaudeville houses. By the early 1930s, most vaudeville houses across the country had succumbed by including films to the roster of live acts on each bill. By late 1932, the Palace Theatre in New York, the last major all-vaudeville theatre remaining in America, also added movies to its daily bill, effectively driving the fatal stake into the heart of vaudeville as an institution.

This combination of circumstances set the stage for comedy entertainment in the 1930s, the first decade in which comedians had a genuine choice of three forums in which to work: the stage, talking films, and radio. Many tried their hand at all three. Some fell short of successfully achieving the show business trifecta, especially in the early days of the decade, when comedians as a species were still getting acquainted with both radio and sound films. Still, a surprising number of them found continued success in all performing venues. This in itself was quite a feat, considering the different demands each placed on its performers (and, it should not be overlooked that a brand new medium, television, had begun to capture the imagination of both the public and show business community throughout the 1930s).

This was also the decade in which the modern-day comedy writer was born, quickly becoming many a comedian's lifeline between stardom and unemployment. *The New York Times* noted in October of 1932 that "with the accelerated pace at which the entire entertainment world has come to speed of late, the coiner of gags has become a mogul of mass production. With stage, motion picture and radio entertainers clamoring for new material with which to be louder and funnier, he is the man to whom they turn for grist to feed their mills. They take it as he gives it out. Hark to the lay of the gagster!"

Such was the state of comedy throughout the Golden Decade. With comedians crisscrossing between three available performing venues, the result was an extremely busy decade in the comedy world—and the funniest.

There are those less–devout observers who might look at comedy from this era and wonder why it was considered so funny at that time, whereas today much of it might seem just silly, slow, or simply unfunny compared to contemporary styles. It can be argued that whether a work is on film, or exists as a sound recording of a radio program, much of the material that provoked fits of laughter among audiences in the 1930s might not have quite that strong an effect when experienced now. Does this mean that the comedians of the time weren't *really* all that funny, or that audiences back then laughed too easily at jokes or gags that weren't so wonderful to begin with? Who's the better judge—audiences then, or audiences now?

Of course, there is no correct answer, and while some comedians of the 1930s might have had a style that was right for the time, but hasn't aged especially well in the decades since, there are others who are still, to this day, undeniably funny.

Steve Martin once reflected on the lasting value of any comedy style, even after it may have been deemed obsolete. "Unlike as in most of the arts," he wrote, "greatness in comedy is not necessarily judged by its ability to transcend generations. Comedy is designed to make people laugh now, not three generations later...But just because it isn't funny now doesn't mean it wasn't funny then."

Silent comedy legend Harold Lloyd offered a similar take on the sentiment: "It is sure that some jokes that made our grandparents laugh do not seem especially funny to us," he wrote. "But on the other hand, many of the same joke situations that convulse us today—on the screen, radio or television—also made our grandparents, and their grandparents before them, rock and roll with laughter."

So there.

Garry Berman
September, 2020

1929

Why does a book about comedy in the 1930s begin with the year 1929? Aside from offering you, the reader, eleven years for the price of ten (more bang for the buck), the events and trends in entertainment throughout 1929 made it a major transition year in show business, and determined to a great degree what was to follow in the coming decade.

Looking at 1929, and the 1920s as a whole, we can see how the one major form of public entertainment, i.e. vaudeville, had begun a steady decline, due greatly to two newer forms, radio and talking pictures, both of which were on the rise.

As 1929 began, the movie industry's transition from silent to sound was still underway. The process took place in stages. Some new films released earlier in the year were released as silent, incorporating only music and sound effects via synchronized discs (or, eventually, as a separate audio strip on the film itself). Other films were released in both silent and sound versions, bearing in mind that movie theatres throughout the country, and around the world, were still being fitted for sound systems, one by one. As the year began, Western Electric was already busy installing sound picture equipment in theatres across the country at a rate of about 250 a month. By the end of February, there were over 1,200 theatres equipped for sound, with another thousand waiting for their conversion.

Other countries, including those in Western Europe, lagged far behind this pace, necessitating film studios to continue producing both sound and silent versions of films, in an effort to collect as much profit as possible during the transition phase. Overall, the number of sound comedies released throughout the year grew steadily.

Surprisingly, the man credited with bringing us both motion pictures *and* sound recordings didn't think much of combining the two to produce talking films. In 1929, Thomas Edison said of talkies, "Without great improvement people will tire of them. Talking is no substitute for good acting we have had in the silent pictures." Edison's assessment notwithstanding, those on the creative side of the movie business knew that keeping up with the changeover to sound was essential to their survival.

Even the most talented of the film comedians, having already mastered the art of making silent two-reelers and features, had to face the new reality as they stood on the doorstep of the new decade. They simply didn't know what talkies would do for, or *to*, their established comedy, because now they would need to flesh out their screen characters with voices, speech patterns and rhythms, and funny dialogue—all things they did not need to consider in front of the camera before. Some adapted to sound well, and even looked forward to the new challenge; others, not so much (we'll examine them on a case-by-case basis as we move along through the decade).

Not all of the silent film comedians whose careers were to falter in the sound era could blame their decline solely, if at all, on the arrival of talkies. The new sound revolution presented them with the opportunity to further enhance their established characters through dialogue. Whether or not they could do so successfully was another story.

Of course, as we mentioned earlier, *The Jazz Singer* wasn't the first sound film. It was, however, the first feature film to include some spoken dialogue released by a major studio, and starring a top star.

Who then, was the first *comedian* to appear in a sound film? We can go back to 1923, nearly a full five years before *The Jazz Singer* was released, to consider experiments conducted by inventor and radio pioneer Dr. Lee De Forest. He, along with Theodore Case, had been developing the method of including a sound strip onto film, which they called Phonofilm.

On April 15, 1923, after having given demonstrations in the previous weeks to the press and the Engineering Society, De Forest premiered a total of eighteen one-reel films for public viewing at the Rivoli Theatre in New York. Some of those short films featured singers, musicians (such as famed black composer-performers Eubie Blake and Noble Sissle), and spoken recitations ("Casey at the Bat"). Also shown were *A Few Minutes with Eddie Cantor*, during which Cantor, who was starring in *Kid Boots* on Broadway at the time, recited bits of his comedy monologue of the day, while also squeezing two songs into the eight-minute running time. Also noteworthy among this film roster is a poolroom routine by the legendary vaudeville comedy team Weber & Fields. Luckily, both Cantor's and Weber & Fields' films still survive, and provide us with an invaluable record of their stage work at the time. Comedian/singer Phil Baker also appeared in a Phonofilm that year, so you have a choice for the answer to the question of which comedian was the first to appear in a talkie. Or, perhaps we can call it a tie.

Hal Roach, the legendary comedy producer who figures quite prominently on these pages, (for good reason), kept pace with the sound revolution, despite some early uncertainties about how sound would affect film comedy as a whole.

Roach had been working as an actor, stagehand, and whatever film-related position he could find when, in 1914, he was able to establish his own production company with money from a family inheritance. His limited budget required him to rely greatly on various locations around Los Angeles, but his dedication to comedy attracted the best in the business, both in front of and behind the camera. The first comedy star he created was Harold Lloyd, who, during his years with Roach, was to become one of the most revered and highest grossing film stars of the 1920s.

Roach created Our Gang comedy series in 1922, with the first short titled, appropriately enough, *Our Gang*. This one-reeler would be the first of over 200 short subjects comedies starring the gang (later known as "The Little Rascals" for TV syndication). He said he first got the idea of a film featuring kids after finding himself mesmerized watching a group of kids playing in a vacant lot one day. He felt there was ample comic potential in the idea, and created Our Gang.

Our Gang as the subject of a 1929 children's photo book by Eleanor Lewis Packer. Author's collection.

The Our Gang short *Noisy Noises*, released on February 9, 1929, is another example of American film comedy in transition from silent to sound. While it doesn't qualify as a true talkie, it was the studio's early attempt to blend sound with visual action. Roach began sending his distributor, Metro-

Goldwyn-Mayer (MGM), films with music and sound effects tracks recorded onto accompanying discs. Film historian and critic Leonard Maltin noted, "the original sound effects and discordant musical instruments (not requiring the same kind of precise synchronization that dialogue did) were probably quite convincing, even startling, for 1929 audiences in the unique position of straddling movies' silent and sound eras."

Once the recording of sound films became more practical—not to mention commercially viable—breaking into talking pictures became an irresistible goal for vaudeville comedians. Groucho Marx began noticing a change about halfway through 1929. "The vaudeville actors talk differently," he reported at the time. "In the old days they'd grab you and tell you what a riot they were in Findlay, Ohio and how they wowed them in Des Moines. Now, all you hear is, 'We don't know what to do—Vitaphone wants us to make a short, but Movie Tone is after us to do a full-length.'"

May 23 - *The Cocoanuts*, starring the Marx Brothers, premieres in New York (August 3 in wide release).

Of course, Groucho and his brothers were not immune to the lure of talkies either, appearing on the silver screen that August in *The Cocoanuts*, adapted from the Kaufman-Ryskind 1926 stage play, set in a Florida resort hotel.

The brothers were stage veterans when the play opened, having previously played the vaudeville circuits before starring in the revues *Home Again* and *I'll Say She Is*. Famed comedy playwright George S. Kaufman agreed to write *The Cocoanuts*, but asked his younger friend and fellow writer Morrie Ryskind to collaborate with him. Ryskind agreed, but felt unworthy of co-author credit, and asked that his name not appear with Kaufman's (to this day, the book of the play is almost always credited as a Kaufman solo work). Working with Kaufman, Ryskind said, "was quite an honor. I was just young and coming up at the time but Kaufman was a big man in the theatre. *The*

Cocoanuts was basically George's idea…when I was called in, he already had the outline. So, we began working together on that."

The plot features Groucho as a hotel manager trying to make his fortune from the Florida land boom, while contending with stolen jewels, and Harpo and Chico as trouble-making guests. As always, Zeppo is reduced to straight man (and, by his own admission, not a very interesting one at that). Songs were provided by none other than Irving Berlin, but no true hits emerged from his contributions. The play ran for 276 performances. Ryskind then adapted the stage show book into a screenplay, making *The Cocoanuts* one of the first feature-length sound comedies ever made.

During the filming at Astoria Studios in Queens, the brothers had to divide their days between shooting the film by day, and then hurrying back to Manhattan to appear at night in their stage hit, *Animal Crackers*, also written by Kaufman and Ryskind. Producer Sam Harris, who brought both *The Cocoanuts* and *Animal Crackers* to Broadway, had struck a deal with Paramount to adapt each production for film.

Even the finest prints of *The Cocoanuts* today look ragged, and reveal almost amateurish production values (French director Robert Florey often didn't bother to re-shoot flubbed lines and missed cues), but it's a fascinating look at the Marxes in transition from stage stars to movie stars. Highlights include the classic Groucho-Chico "Why a duck?" scene, in which Chico insists on confusing Groucho's use of the word "viaduct" by asking "Why a duck? Why-a no chicken?" Another impressive scene is an impeccably timed sequence with the brothers running through adjoining hotel rooms, slamming and opening doors with split-second precision. Other treats include Chico inadvertently sabotaging Groucho's land auction, and quite a daffy parody of the opera *Carmen*, which is especially fun because it literally comes out of nowhere.

1929

Print ad for *The Cocoanuts*. Author's collection.

The brothers with Basil Rysdale, the film's put-upon detective. Author's collection.

In those early days of talkies, filming with sound was not without its difficulties for those behind the camera. The primitive microphones were so sensitive that cameramen needed to be encased in small, hot, stuffy booths with their cameras, to keep the whirring of the mechanism from being picked up on the soundtrack. Even the crackling of a piece of paper could ruin a scene. A look at the "Why a duck?" scene reveals how the map Groucho and Chico examine needed to be soaked in water first, resulting in a quiet but noticeably limp sheet spread out before them.

Charles LeMaire, costume designer for the film, explained that measures also had to be taken to silence the actors' clothing:

"When your favorite heroine is pressed against the bosom of her lover, and he whispers 'I love you, darling,' there can be no movement of her elaborate garden frock that results in a rustle, for this slight noise may register far above his voice. Therefore, in designing a costume, I have to take into consideration the fact that taffetas, metallic cloths, crystal beads, and beaded fringes are absolutely taboo…But there are substitutes--soft materials, laces, transparent chiffons, and shimmery silk velvets of the finest texture which also photograph beautifully."

May 4 - Hal Roach Studios releases Laurel & Hardy's first all-talking film, *Unaccustomed as We Are*.

While it's a matter of continuing debate which Laurel & Hardy film was their first as a true team, by the end of 1927 they were acknowledged and billed as such. Both comedians had been working separately for Roach, and occasionally appeared in the same films, but not together. Stan originally signed with the studio in March of 1923, was let go after his one-reeler series failed, then returned to Roach in May of 1925. Ollie signed on in February of 1926. As the two comedians began sharing scenes together, they developed an on-screen chemistry, especially evident in their first true effort together, *Duck Soup* (no relation to the later Marx Brothers feature). Roach and director Leo McCarey were astute enough to notice, pursue, and develop the smooth rapport between Stan and Ollie. The first film billed as a "Laurel & Hardy" film was 1927's *Putting Pants on Phillip*, although they had not yet blossomed into their now-familiar screen characters.

By 1929, Hal Roach Studios was the top comedy film studio in the business, with the best of its creative output still to come. By the time *Unaccustomed as We Are* was produced, Stan and Ollie had developed their familiar characters and attire, creating the symbiotic working relationship that would come to be envied by other comedy teams of the time, and of those teams to follow. Put simply, Stan and Ollie were the perfect film comedy team, the best that ever was.

The two were the first major silent film comedians to take the plunge into sound successfully, and felt little need to be intimidated by the new facet of their work. They planned to use dialogue sparingly anyway, without forcing it on either themselves or their audience, even though fate had given them the voices that perfectly matched their characters' mannerisms and body language: Ollie was ever the dignified, if sometimes pompous, dominant half, who spoke with a slight, gentlemanly Southern accent, while Stan was childlike, accident-prone, and, more often than not, willing to follow Ollie's lead.

It quickly became obvious that sound brought a certain reality into films. Objects and people fell, moved, or were thrown at a speed more closely resembling reality than they did in silent films. The pacing of the action with sound had a slightly different feel, since the cameras needed to crank at a steady speed to accommodate the soundtrack. Still, a bit of tweaking made Laurel & Hardy's transition to talkies a smooth one, thanks in part to Roach's title writer, H.M. Walker, who provided them with dialogue that fit their screen characters snugly. Even better, their sound films, beginning with *Unaccustomed as We Are*, found ways to use sound itself as a means to enhance their comedy.

Despite Roach's stated intention to keep dialogue sparse in his talkies, *Unaccustomed as We Are* plays almost like a television sitcom episode, with considerable (and necessary) dialogue throughout. The short opens with Stan and Ollie arriving at Ollie's apartment for dinner, even though Ollie hasn't bothered to give his wife (Mae Busch, in her first of many roles as Ollie's shrewish spouse) advance warning. She expresses her displeasure in no uncertain terms before storming out, leaving the boys to prepare dinner for themselves. The dialogue, especially in the exchanges between Ollie and his neighbor across the hall, Mrs. Kennedy (the delightful Thelma Todd, playing Edgar Kennedy's wife), pokes fun at the art of polite conversation, as each character ends every sentence with a deliberate "…Mr. Hardy" or "…Mrs. Kennedy."

One clever gag, possible only in a sound film, comes when, during his wife's ranting, Ollie puts on the phonograph in an attempt to diffuse the tension. She soon finds herself yelling in time to the music before snapping out of it.

Another example of how the film utilizes sound comes with a running gag of lighting a match in Ollie's kitchen as it quickly fills with gas from the oven. First we *hear* an off-screen explosion from the kitchen, then immediately see

Ollie flying into the living room, accompanied by a puff of flame from the force of the blast. The sound of the blast allows us to know what happened a split second *before* we actually see the result. Later, in the closing shot of the film, we see Stan bid Ollie goodbye in the hallway, and then step out of view at the top step of the stairs. We then hear a long series of thuds and crashes, knowing that poor Stan is tumbling his way down to the first floor. By reversing the technique used with the gas oven gag, here we *see* Stan take that first step, but then only *hear* the result.

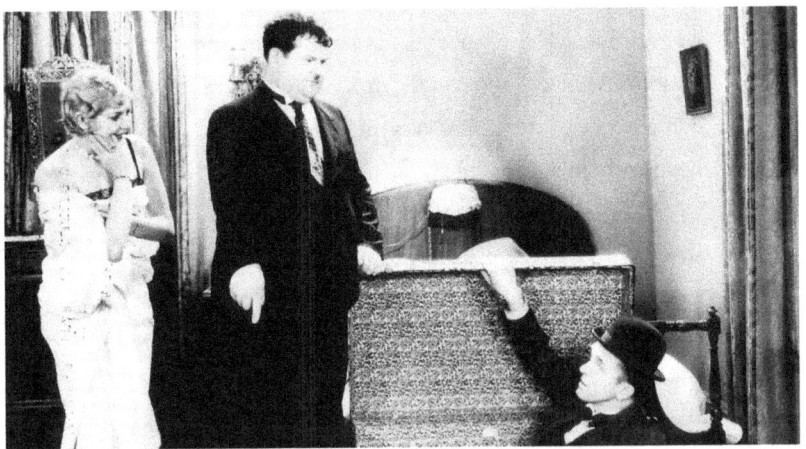

Thelma and Ollie look on as Stan tries to hide from Thelma's jealous husband. Author's collection.

As Stan once explained, "I thought then that there was nothing really funny about a guy falling downstairs. There's pain connected with it and that's never funny. I realized, of course, that you can take away the sting by not having the man really hurt, but there's nothing real about that. In that scene we removed the pain by having the camera stay looking at the top of the staircase. The sound effect of the fall lets the audience visualize its own scene, and that just made it funnier to them."

Despite containing so many gags that cleverly use sound in this very first Laurel & Hardy talkie, Roach himself expressed his skepticism of overusing sound in some contexts, while also demonstrating a sharp instinct for audience psychology:

"There has been too much sound in pictures anyway. We at first injected everything we heard, but that is unnatural…For example, when we are making the pictures we sometimes must halt our operations because an airplane is overhead. This is a natural noise and there is no reason to believe that an airplane should not be flying at that moment, but in the theatres an audience will associate the sound as a significant part of the plot and will expect something to come of it…The noises we do add artificially, however, mean twice as much and are doubly effective. For example, in a Laurel and Hardy comedy one of the comedians hits the other over the head with an automobile jack. The sound version of this blow is a great 'Bong!' which someone offstage struck on a gong. This brought roars of merriment from the audiences and taught us the value of adapting the methods of sound cartoons to comedies."

Roach's main comedy competitor, Mack Sennett, had already seen the peak of his own career as a comedy producer by this time. His career continued on a downward slope as Roach's fortunes were still rising. Sennett was, like Roach, unsatisfied with the way many new sound comedies were relying too much on dialogue and not enough on traditional visual gags. "I'm going back to the fundamentals of the silent screen comedy and I'm going to stay there," he declared in 1930. "The development of screen comedy does not lie along the lines of dialogue humor. We know that now."

Such stubbornness and defiance became part of Sennett's undoing in the sound era. Roach was wise enough to allow dialogue to enhance his roster of screen characters, without cheating the audience of top-rate sight gags. Within just a few more years, Sennett's departure from the movie business would leave Roach at the top of the comedy mountain.

On a side note, *Unaccustomed as We Are* doesn't carry a music track, which, after one has become familiar with Roach comedies, is conspicuous by its absence. The light, jazzy background music that would become so closely identified with most Hal Roach productions, was composed mostly by LeRoy Shield and Marvin Hatley. Both men's music would begin to appear within another year, although the earlier Roach talkies used a similar-sounding, bouncy music to match the comedy. Laurel & Hardy's theme song, "Dance of the Cuckoos" (or, "The Cuckoo Song"), written by Hatley, would first be used for the titles for *Blotto* in 1930. Shield's background music would also became prominent in Roach films beginning that year, and listening to it at length today (thanks to YouTube, vinyl, and CD issues of his scores), it is impossible to imagine the Roach comedies without the delightful enhancement the music contributed. Many of the catchy numbers run only a minute, or even less, but they've become part of a musical mix that, to this day, immediately identifies a Roach short even if the viewer is looking away from the screen. Shield's tune "Good Old Days," first used for the 1930 Our Gang short *Teacher's Pet*, became the theme song for that series, and his song "Beautiful Lady" was used as the theme music for the ThelmaTodd-Zasu Pitts series, which began in 1931.

Hal Roach posing in front of his studio's administration building, at the dawn of the sound era. Courtesy of Steve Cox.

Incidentally, *Unaccustomed as We Are*, and the first Our Gang talkie, *Small Talk*, began production on the same day, March 25. Just a week later, the studio began filming another sound short, *Hurdy Gurdy*, directed by Roach himself, with the story by Leo McCarey. It was filmed from April 2 through April 6, and released on May 11.

Hurdy Gurdy takes place mostly on the back balconies of a New York tenement house, with its inhabitants of various ethnic groups (Edgar Kennedy as an Irishman, Max Davidson as a German Jew) gossiping about one particular tenant (Thelma Todd) and her constant need to have ice delivered to her apartment. It isn't revealed until the final few minutes that she is keeping a circus seal in her bathtub, and needs the ice to keep her companion happy.

May 18 - Roach Studios releases the first Our Gang talkie, *Small Talk*.

Small Talk, was the 89th Our Gang short to be filmed, with a cast including Bobby "Wheezer" Hutchins, Mary Ann Jackson, Joe Cobb, and Allen "Farina" Hoskins.

Arguably, the most inventive Our Gang sound comedies, boasting the series' funniest cast members, date from this period, with Jackie Cooper, Norman "Chubby" Chaney (replacing Joe Cobb), Farina, Mary Ann, Wheezer, and a young Matthew "Stymie" Beard (fans of the series wouldn't meet a *very* young George "Spanky" McFarland until 1932).

The 1930 short, *Pups is Pups*, featuring Wheezer and his gang of wayward puppies who run to answer any ringing bell they hear, was selected for the National Film Registry in 2004.

Even the young actors' somewhat stilted recitation of their dialogue and occasional awkward pauses gives this particular cast a certain charm that the later, more polished cast members lacked. Moreover, few actors in film history, be they child or adult, have mastered the wide-eyed, head-bobbing "surprise take" as perfectly as Mary Ann or Wheezer (although June Marlow, as their beloved teacher Miss Crabtree, was no slouch at that, either). It is to Hal Roach's credit as a talent scout that the gang's ever-evolving cast changes occurred as seamlessly as they did, as younger players arrived with their own distinct personalities, to replace older cast members who had outgrown the film series.

Miss Crabtree (June Marlow) drives the gang to school in *School's Out* (1930). Author's collection.

Sound films boosted business for the studio. "When we were making silent comedies," Roach said, "our foreign distribution amounted to 25 per cent of our total production. Now that we have sound our foreign business has jumped to 50 per cent of our product. This is accounted for by the fact that we have begun making our films in the languages of other countries."

To accomplish this, a short would be filmed as many as three times: in English, then in Spanish and French, with the young stars reading the foreign languages phonetically to each other. Supporting actors who were already conversant in each language were brought in to replace the originals for each version.

"In comedies, the accent doesn't matter so much; it's the action," Roach explained at the time. "We teach our actors the few essentials of the language, and they are able to pronounce the 'si' or 'oui' as perfectly as any Spaniard or

Frenchman. If there is any part of the story that should be interpreted to the audience, and there is hardly a plot and sub-plot in most slapstick affairs, we introduce a minor character who speaks the language like a native and who conveniently talks the plot into the film."

Roach instituted language classes on the lot, twice a week, in Spanish and French. Most of the actors, including the Our Gang kids, attended. "It is not very difficult to teach children phrases in unknown words because then they are instructed to repeat the same words in English it means just as little then. For example, when we ask a child to repeat, 'How do you do, sir?' during the course of a picture it means as little to him as if he were to say 'Como esta usted?' or 'comment allez-vou.' With the child it is simply a trick of memory. But too often that memory is liable to fail, and we have to start all over again."

It took about twenty percent longer to film each Roach comedy in each language, amounting to about five extra days on each version than shooting in English only. The pictures are also considerably slowed down. "Formerly," he continued, "there were approximately forty scenes in each reel of a feature in comparison with ninety to more than a hundred in a reel of comedy. With sound there are about sixty scenes in each reel of comedy."

Despite Roach's good intentions to please his international audience, the process proved too time-consuming and costly to maintain, and was abandoned after little more than a year.

June 20 - MGM releases *Hollywood Revue of 1929*.

The sound revolution continued to gain steam virtually daily throughout 1929 and, by the end of the year, the film industry's transition from silence to sound was just about complete. MGM wanted to make its official jump into the sound era with a big splash, so, in June, the studio corralled all of its contract players before the camera in this all-talking, all-singing (and seemingly endless) feature. The film is basically a vaudeville presentation, which is a somewhat ironic approach, considering how sound films, in conjunction with radio, would be largely responsible for vaudeville's demise.

1929

Producer Irving Thalberg, not yet thirty years old but moving up the ranks at MGM, felt the film needed a popular, sophisticated host to segue from one act to the next. Jack Benny's agent Sam Lyons suggested that Thalberg see Benny perform his act at the Orpheum in Los Angeles. This was a number of years before Benny began to cultivate his public persona as a cheapskate and self-delusional ladies' man. He was known on the vaudeville circuits as a clever if low-key monologist, with an appealing presence, but no "schtick" per se. After seeing Benny in action, Thalberg asked him to be master of ceremonies for the film.

The long roster of acts varies in entertainment appeal, and the film as a whole moves at fairly turgid pace. But there are bright spots and novel performances. Buster Keaton makes his first appearance in a talkie here, and Laurel & Hardy (who were included due to MGM's distribution deal with Roach Studios) are on hand as well. Keaton doesn't speak in his segment, but performs a comic Egyptian-style dance in costume, which must have somewhat confounded his longtime fans. Laurel & Hardy's turn involves Ollie attempting to perform a magic act, with assistant Stan predictably making a mess of things and unintentionally sabotaging the "magic." Another notable feature is the debut of the song "Singin' in the Rain," performed twice, once for the film's grand finale.

"After he saw the first day's rushes," Benny later recalled, "Thalberg was so excited that he signed me to a five-year contract starting at $850 a week, with raises every six months. Imagine—me a movie star! I couldn't believe it. After a while I did believe it. I dreamed of a career in the movies. Let other vaudevillians mess around with this silly radio business—I wanted to be where the glamour was."

Thalberg later raised Benny's salary to $1,000 a week. However, according to the comedian, the producer also refused to loan him out to other studios, even when there didn't appear to be any desirable roles in MGM pictures for Benny. His next film for Metro, *Chasing Rainbows*, was a flop. *The Medicine Man*, a melodrama with Benny providing occasional comic relief, was made by low-budget Tiffany Pictures, and released through MGM in June of 1930.

In it, Benny plays the host of a traveling medicine show, offering his audiences a spiel full of exaggerations about a miracle tonic (viewing the film today, an unintended laugh-getter is his heavy white face makeup and lipstick, still common for actors in films at the time).

Impresario Earl Carroll called Benny to offer him a co-starring role in the new edition of *Vanities* for $1,500 a week, upon which Benny had to haggle with Thalberg to be let out of his contract. By the time *The Medicine Man* was released, Benny was already with the *Vanities*, standing out as one of the "clean" performers in a show that received a great deal of criticism at the time for its vulgarity.

Benny was just one of many vaudeville comedians who first appeared on sound film in 1929, even before making their better-known forays into radio. The list includes Fred Allen, George Burns & Gracie Allen, and Will Rogers—all of whom already had years of vaudeville experience behind them (and whom we'll discuss in more detail shortly).

August 19 - *Amos & Andy* premieres on the NBC network.

Radio was still a fairly young mass medium in 1929. The first commercial station in the country, KDKA in Pittsburgh, went on the air on November 2, 1920. Six years later, on the evening of November 15, 1926, NBC officially launched the first radio network in the nation, consisting of twenty-four stations, and ushering in a new era of mass communication. It did so with a four-hour gala event broadcast from several locales across the country, and heard by invited guests via loudspeakers in the grand ballroom of New York's Waldorf-Astoria hotel. The program boasted an eclectic line-up of participants. An opera singer transmitted her performance from Chicago. Weber & Fields reunited to perform one of their popular vaudeville routines. There was also a remote by Will Rogers from Independence, Kansas. With the birth of the NBC network, and the formation of CBS the following September (originating as the Columbia Phonographic Broadcasting System, with fifteen affiliates), radio became more than a smattering of stations each with a limited broadcast range. No longer just a fad, radio became a national obsession.

In 1929, comedy on radio wasn't heard with any regularity, especially in network broadcasts. *Amos & Andy*, created and performed by two white writer-performers Freeman Gosden and Charles J. Correll, originated in 1926 as *Sam 'n' Henry*, airing locally in Chicago on WGN. The two title characters, both black, had moved to Chicago from the South, struggling to make ends meet with their moving company.

Gosden and Correll soon expressed their desire to record each program on phonograph records to distribute to other stations around the country, which would have made it the first example of syndication on radio. Their request was denied, causing them to leave WGN in early 1928. They signed with WMAQ in Chicago, which was owned by the *Chicago Daily News*, and was agreeable to the syndication idea. However, WGN still owned the rights to the *Sam 'n' Henry* name, so the characters, and program title, became *Amos 'n' Andy*. One problem was solved, but another still remained. The new program's home, WMAQ, was a CBS affiliate, but the station's executives couldn't convince the CBS to take the show onto the network. Seeing the program's fast-growing popularity, the NBC Blue network then offered the team $100,000 for the program, leading to its debut episode on August 19 (although it didn't begin airing coast-to-coast until November). The two characters were re-located from Chicago to Harlem, where they'd run the Open Air Taxicab Company.

Gosden and Correll worked intensely on a tight schedule, being responsible for writing each daily 15-minute episode, and performing it live. While they worked meticulously on each script, being careful to write out the dialogue in precise "negro" dialect and pronunciation, they didn't rehearse before going on-air. "We couldn't do that," Correll told an interviewer, "because of the fear of going stale. We have lived with our characters so long that we can assume the roles on a moment's notice. We fall into them naturally because we have studied their traits and their mannerisms; that is, we know just how Amos feels about everything, and how Andy is certainly always ready to make the best of an opportunity to rest and spout off." They recorded each episode alone, sitting on opposite sides of a table in the studio, except for announcer Bill Hay, and did not allow an audience or guests to witness their performances.

Gosden and Correll portrayed what would come to be regarded by many, including civil rights groups, as offensive black stereotypes. Even so, the program—sometimes referred to as the first situation comedy—quickly became immensely popular, so much so that it has been said the entire country practically ceased all activity to listen to Amos, Andy, Kingfish, and the other characters get themselves into both business and romantic predicaments.

Some early measurements of the show's ratings estimated 40 million listeners. Jack Benny recalled, "They even had Pepsodent Toothpaste for a sponsor. They were on five nights a week. I remember you could walk down a street on a warm evening when the windows were open and hear their voices."

In the program's first year on the network, *Radio Revue* magazine offered considerable insight into how and why the program's characters were being portrayed as they were: "In order to get material for their act…the two men spend much time among Negroes, studying their accents and natural witticisms and picking up ideas for situations. The Open Air Taxicab idea is a counterpart of a real situation they discovered in one small city and many of their stories or droll remarks have been picked up in New York's Harlem or in the negro section of Chicago."

The article also attempted to offer some justification for the perceived negative stereotypes of urban black people on the show. Despite its own good intentions, *Radio Revue*'s explanation includes some terms that today would be considered, at the very least, cringe-worthy:

"So fair and deft have been their characterizations of the southern Negro transplanted to the north that never have there been protests from the colored race about the programs. In fact, many of their most ardent admirers are of the same race as the characters in the radio program."

George Burns, a diehard vaudevillian if there ever was one, saw the popularity of *Amos & Andy*, and of radio in general, as more of a threat to vaudeville than films were, citing that stage presentations in vaudeville and burlesque had, to that point, managed to co-exist with movies. Radio, though, was a different animal. "For the first time people didn't have to leave their homes to be entertained," Burns explained. "The performers came into their house. Gracie and I knew that vaudeville was finished when theaters began advertising that their shows would be halted for fifteen minutes so that the audience could listen to *Amos & Andy*. And when the *Amos & Andy* program came on, the vaudeville would stop, they would bring a radio onstage, and the audience would sit there watching radio."

It wasn't only vaudeville theatres that would succumb to the program for fifteen minutes each night for the benefit of their *Amos & Andy* fans. When movie theatre managers across the country began to notice a drop in attendance while the show was on the air, they also felt little choice but to broadcast the show in the theatre, in order to get and keep customers in the seats.

Within a year of the program's national debut, the team signed a contract with RKO studios to appear in the film *Check and Double Check*. Gosden and Correll were to split a quarter of a million dollars for the film, while continuing their broadcasts from the studio lot via a special hook-up to the radio network.

Ad for *Check and Double Check*. Courtesy of Steve Cox.

Check and Double Check was to be their only film; while it made money from curious fans who wanted to see their favorite radio stars on the screen, many were surprised, and apparently disappointed, to discover that the duo were actually white men performing in blackface. The film as a whole, despite the appearance of a young Duke Ellington and his band, was not a very high quality affair, and ticket sales dropped after a brief time. The team was not asked back for another film, either by RKO, or any other studio.

September 15 - *Rio Rita*, featuring Wheeler & Woolsey, premieres.

The 1927 Broadway musical *Rio Rita*, produced by Florenz Ziegfeld, ran for 494 performances, and first paired Bert Wheeler and Robert Woolsey for the story's comic subplot. Upon repeating their roles for RKO's film version, the two made such a positive impression on audiences that the studio offered them a contract to appear as an official team.

They would star in twenty-two features throughout the next eight years, beginning with *The Cuckoos* in 1930 (based on Clark & McCullough's stage show *The Ramblers*), and continuing until Woolsey's death in 1938.

The two proved so popular in their first year on the screen that in 1931 RKO attempted to get twice the bang for the buck by splitting up the act, to have each star in his own film. The experiment was not a success, and the team reunited as partners from that point on. In fact, it was reported in *The New Movie Magazine* in early 1933 that the team had formed their own corporation, called the Bobert Corporation "to protect them from murdering each other or leaving each other flat." It was the first time in entertainment history that a team had "protected itself from the prevalent form of *teamitis temperamentum*—and it should work!"

In some ways, Wheeler & Woolsey were the quintessential 1930s movie comedy team. That's not the say that they were necessarily the funniest, but they were extremely popular, and made good money for RKO. Unlike most double-acts of the time, which comprised of the straight man and the comedian, the team didn't stick to that standard formula. Wheeler's ongoing character was that of the somewhat naïve, dreamy-eyed romantic, often pursuing their longtime onscreen cohort, Dorothy Lee. Woolsey shined as his smart-alecky friend who always seemed to have a plan for making money, or for getting out of whatever predicament in which they'd find themselves entangled. And each could toss off his fair share of sharp one-liners at the other.

Print ad for *The Cuckoos*. Author's collection.

Hook, Line & Sinker was another early Wheeler & Woolsey success. Courtesy of Steve Cox.

A few other top teams of the time had also disposed of the rigid roles of straight man/comic, such as Olsen & Johnson, and, of course, Laurel & Hardy. Wheeler & Woolsey also consistently offered a good number of comic songs and/or dances in nearly every film. True, the Marx Brothers indulged in song & dance on occasion. Many of their films, such as *Animal Crackers*, *Horsefeathers*, and *Duck Soup*, include an opening musical number featuring Groucho, and nearly all had musical interludes by Harpo and Chico. The Ritz Brothers certainly specialized in their own brand of comic dancing and singing, but their material outside of their musical novelty routines was never memorable. Wheeler & Woolsey sometimes included their musical sequences as a break from the comedy, but often as a part of it. And they performed them with welcome abandon. They were talented singers (especially Wheeler) and fine dancers. What more could a Depression-era audience ask for?

1929

September 18 - Will Rogers' first talkie, *They Had to See Paris*, is released.

Rogers had spent years traveling the world in rodeos, circuses, and vaudeville, mainly performing tricks as a roper and lariat expert. Upon arriving in New York, his skills and cowboy image intrigued New Yorkers. He hit the big time in 1915 with his debut in the *Ziegfeld Follies Midnight Frolic* variety revue, held on the rooftop venue of the Amsterdam Theatre on 42nd Street. The following year, he joined the *Follies* proper, adding social and political commentary to his act.

As his friend W.C. Fields once recalled, Rogers' success playing the Amsterdam Roof venue earned many repeat customers, who soon became familiar with his routine. Consequently, with growing familiarity, the laughs got lighter over the span of a few weeks. "He talked the situation over with the most wonderful woman I have ever known in my life—his dear wife Betty," Fields said. It became obvious that Rogers needed to come up with new material at a steady pace. "Betty's sage counsel was to read the newspapers and talk of the topic of the day. That gave Rogers the impetus to his great fame and success. I was with him for years in the *Follies* and he did an entirely different monologue every night, a thing I have never known in my 37 years of trouping."

Eddie Cantor, one of Rogers' co-stars in the 1917 *Follies*, wrote in his memoirs, "He'd added a monologue to his [rope trick] act, and he wasn't satisfied to joke; the jokes must have substance. Every morning he read the papers, the *Morning World*, *The New York Times*, the *American*, the *Tribune*. Then he'd sit down at his little portable typewriter and peck out his commentaries on the news. He'd never had much education...but he had a built-in shrewdness and he worked at it, edited it, until it became 99.9 per cent pure wisdom."

While still in New York, Rogers tried his hand at silent films, but it was Samuel Goldwyn who lured him to Hollywood in 1918 for top money. Rogers would later spend 1923 and 1924 starring in films at Hal Roach Studios, but silent films proved too restrictive for his increasingly verbal brand of comedy. After forty-eight films, he left the industry, but when talkies arrived, he returned to make *They Had to See Paris*.

In the story, oil is found on his land in Oklahoma, making him very wealthy indeed. His wife insists on a trip to Paris, but the two of them, plus their daughter, stand out as hicks in the sophisticated city, becoming the quintessential fish out of water. *Photoplay* magazine proclaimed, "The real Will Rogers steps before the microphone and you'll have to forgive him for all of those silent efforts. He's great!…This is big entertainment, with Rogers giving some of our first rate emotional actors a run for their Saturday night remittance."

Variety was also happy to see Rogers as a talking comedian on film, concurring that silent films just weren't for him: "Will Rogers in pictures without dialog was as Senator Borah with his tongue cut out. Speaking in *They Had to See Paris* he is completely the man who has made a fortune out of being strictly and ridiculously American. His first talking picture is a certain moneymaker…and Rogers gets all the laughs."

The review also reported "more sure laughs whenever Rogers tackles French," and especially liked a shot in which Rogers stands in the middle of his new, massive chateau, looks around, and begins to bellow train calls.

Rogers' subsequent films, including the follow-up *They Had to See London*, made him a truly big-time film personality. He seemed to appear everywhere as a performer, but radio became the most comfortable fit for him, as was writing his syndicated newspaper column.

September 22 - Beatrice Lillie opens at New York's Palace Theatre.

Toronto-born Lillie spent most of her early life with her family in England, where she grew up performing with her mother and sister in music halls. In 1920, she married Sir Robert Peel, technically making her Lady Peel when she wasn't performing. She debuted in America in 1924 in French impresario Andre Charlot's revue, where she won highly favorable notices. Specializing in song parodies, in which she would either sing a "straight" dramatic song with considerable comedic flourish and facial expressions, or, conversely, sing a nonsense song with mock sincerity and angst. She also didn't consider herself above doing an old-fashioned pratfall or other bits of visual business, even while immaculately attired in a formal evening gown, with her jet black hair slicked back in a short bob. Her biggest successes came in a number of London and New York revues, many of which included Noel Coward's best-known songs, such as "Mad Dogs and Englishmen." She first performed at the Palace in November of 1928, where the city audiences appreciated her sophisticated, but accessible, parodies and comedy sketches (unsurprisingly, her style didn't fare as well in middle America). J. Brooks Atkinson, theatre critic for *The New York Times*, wrote years later that Lillie "overwhelmed the audience, not by broad strokes, but by gleams and grimaces. Her mind was hard, and it was always far ahead of the audiences. It hated sentimentality, pretentiousness, and buncombe."

Her acclaim continued with her appearances at the Palace at different points throughout 1929. As *The New York Times* reported during one of her brief runs there. "The unique Beatrice Lillie, of whom there is positively only one, is at the Palace Theatre this week, and considerable should be the rejoicing thereat…that she is a success is to put it mildly."

The piece continues, "In a poisonous red wig and an evening gown, Miss Lillie starts her antics with a devastating travesty of concert singers here, there and everywhere—a bit of mimicry which probably reaches its high spots with the number called 'The Roses Have Made Me Remember What Any Nice Girl Should Forget.'"

Lillie, being a stage specialist, would appear on film only a handful of times in the 1930s and later decades, making the permanent film record of her comedy rather limited, although she was a frequent guest on radio, and several of her on-air performances have been saved. For the most part, however, she has virtually vanished from the public's consciousness, and into the mists of entertainment history.

Atkinson also noted, "The standard musical show was the most comfortable home she ever had, and it was a privilege to visit her there."

He concluded his remembrance of her talents by dubbing Lillie "the most intelligent comedienne Broadway ever had."

October 8 - Burns & Allen release the short *Lamb Chops*.

Shortly after Will Rogers broke his own personal sound barrier on film to find success in talkies, George Burns and Gracie Allen did likewise, albeit with a more modest first effort than a full-length feature.

Burns & Allen circa 1930. Courtesy of Steve Cox.

1929

The couple formed their comedy team in 1922. Burns at that time was having marginal success with his vaudeville act, which at one point included a trained seal as his partner. Gracie was born into a show business family but was also struggling when a friend introduced her to George. Burns later recalled, "When we first started, I had all the funny jokes and Gracie had the straight stuff, but even her straight lines got laughs." He quickly picked up on the audience's enchantment with Gracie, and re-wrote the act this time giving her the jokes. But there was still a bit of trial and error before the act hit its stride. Burns learned from audience reaction, for instance, that they wanted her sweet and innocent, not sarcastic.

"She had a funny delivery…It took a good year to get her into character. That doesn't mean it took a year to do a good act, but it took a year to get the wrong words out of Gracie's mouth…I just timed the jokes for Gracie…[her] sense of concentration was so marvelous that she didn't know there was an audience." The couple married in 1925.

They actually tested the waters in talkies before ever performing on radio, performing "Lamb Chops" for the cameras at the Warner Bros. studio in New York, before leaving for a tour of the United Kingdom.

This film debut actually came by default; Jack Benny's agent, Arthur Lyons, asked Benny to fill in for Fred Allen by doing a 10-minute comedy short at Astoria Studios, for $1,800. Allen had first ventured into film a few months earlier, in April, with the one-reel *The Installment Inspector*, also filmed at Astoria. Benny, however, wasn't available to do a short film at the time. Upon hearing this, Burns volunteered himself and Gracie for the gig. It helped that the director, Murray Roth, was an old friend of Burns from the Lower East Side of New York.

"Gracie didn't want to do it," George recalled. "She wasn't a movie actress, she said, then suggested, 'You go and do it.' I told her the truth. 'Listen, kiddo, if I go out there and I say, 'How's your brother?' and you're not standing next to me, that short is going to be a lot shorter than they think.'" Gracie reluctantly agreed to do it.

"The set was a living room," George explained. "That was fine for Fred

Allen, but all wrong for us. We did a flirtation act, we were supposed to be bumping into each other on a street corner. The theater audience knew we were supposed to be outside because we wore hats. Life was easier then—you wore a hat, you were outside. So we had a problem. It's hard to be surprised when you bump into someone in your living room, and we couldn't perform without our hats."

The opening shot has the couple walking into a room, with Gracie searching all over for something. George points to the camera and explains, "The audience is right there," after which they launch into their "Lamb Chops" routine, written by ace comedy writer Al Boasberg (it was added to the National Film Registry at the Library of Congress in 1999). The film was a hit with audiences, at a time when many shorts, like *Lamb Chops,* were little more than filmed vaudeville acts.

Paramount was pleased with the short and signed the team to do four more, at $3,500 per film. From that point on, Burns & Allen took to films quite well. "In the next two years we made a total of fourteen short films," George said. "They were really just skits. I wrote most of them. I had to do something. The plots were very basic: Gracie was a nurse and I was a patient. Grace was a salesclerk and I was a customer…"

Performing on film was all well and good, but George still harbored misgivings about that other medium, radio, which he correctly saw as an immediate threat to his beloved vaudeville. He and Gracie paid attention to what was happening, and decided to adopt the "if you can't beat 'em, join 'em" approach. Since theirs was a talking act anyway, George realized that he and Gracie were perfect for radio. "Both of us could stand in front of a microphone and read out loud. Gracie had a terrific voice, and I had Gracie. And that's all it took."

The two first performed on radio later in 1929, but not in America. While touring England for several months with their stage act, they accepted a number of invitations to perform part of the act on the air. "In those days radio stations would use five minutes of comedy to break up the orchestra music," George explained. "So one day we did five minutes in London, the next day we did the same five minutes in Liverpool, the day after that we did the same five minutes in Southampton. We were always smart enough to stay one day ahead of our reviews."

October 12 - Harold Lloyd's *Welcome Danger* is released.

One example of how the transition from silents to talkies affected film comedy can be found with Harold Lloyd, one of the "Big Three" silent film comedians, along with Charlie Chaplin and Buster Keaton. As was the case with so many comedy stars, Lloyd's career in front of the camera began in earnest at Hal Roach studios. Soon after Roach opened his studio in 1914, he put Lloyd at the top of his roster of comedy stars. "At first I made pictures for Roach," Lloyd recalled, "and Roach had complete control. Later on [in 1924] he came to me and said, 'Harold, you don't need me anymore. I've got so many pictures of my own to do, we might as well just go our own way.' Which we did, and it was I think the most amicable way that any two people could have parted."

Lloyd's first sound feature film, *Welcome Danger*, wasn't originally produced to be a sound film at all. He had completed the filming and editing, and began showing it to preview audiences in 1929, when he took a good look at how the movie business was undergoing the sound revolution. "When we previewed it for about the third time," he said, "there was a one-reeler sound comedy on the bill and they howled at it. It had the punkest gags, but [the audience was] laughing at the pouring of water, the frying of eggs—it didn't matter what—the clinking of ice in a glass. We said, 'My God, we worked out hearts out to get laughs with thought-out gags and look here: just because they've got some sound, they're roaring at these things." He realized it was time to make the transition, and revamped the film by re-shooting major portions with sound, as well as dubbing in dialogue and sound effects for other scenes, all costing almost one million dollars.

Sound also forced the silent slapstick comedians to test their abilities as speaking comic actors. In Lloyd's case, he demonstrated a knack for it immediately. Roach expressed his opinion that "Harold Lloyd was not a comedian, but he was one of the best actors around. He *played* a comedian."

Photoplay's review of *Welcome Danger* proclaimed, "This is the film that converted Harold Lloyd to talkies. It should. His voice is excellent, and Barbara Kent boosts her assets a thousand per cent. Story is about a young botanist who is mistaken for a famous sleuth and forced into detective service. Being afraid of a mouse, he would 'welcome danger!' Not a gag of any age is omitted, but we wager you will laugh continuously."

Variety was also pleased: "Even talkers haven't stopped the begoggled comedian from digging up a lot of new gags, and working up situations for all they can stand…When the big comedy sequences begin to build up and he goes hectic with his pantomime and slapstick his voice arises to the occasion and the audience will be likely to forget or overcome any disappointment over it in other spots."

November 20 - *The Rise of the Goldbergs* debuts on NBC.

Following the radio debut of *Amos & Andy* by three months, *The Rise of the Goldbergs* was considerably more honest in its depiction of ethnic characters. While white performers Gosden and Correll obviously could only imitate the dialects and attitudes of their black characters, the Jewish Goldberg family members and their Old World sensibilities, accents, and outlook were performed by a Jewish cast, led by the show's creator and sole writer, Gertrude Berg.

Berg loved writing and performing from an early age, but her most of her early written work never saw the light of day. Having married while studying playwriting at Columbia University, she graduated and settled into life as a housewife, but continued writing. She first created the character of a Jewish saleslady for a script in 1928, but this initial attempt met with disinterest from radio stations. Refining the idea and creating a fictional family matriarch based on her grandmother, a Russian immigrant ("Old ladies are my hobby," she explained), Berg peddled her scripts to every radio outlet she could find, but

1929

encountered still more rejections. She was told a program with Jewish dialects just wouldn't pass muster with the listening public, and would probably even offend many.

Finally, upon pitching the series to NBC, and then having to wait for a slow, deliberately-made decision, she was given the green light for the program.

The Goldberg family consisted of Mollie, her husband Jake, son Sammy, and daughter Rosie. Casting the roles proved a challenge, as Berg listened to countless auditioning actors. Finally, stage veteran James R. Waters secured the role as Jake, with Rosalyn Silber and Alfred Corn becoming Rosie and Sammy.

Gertrude Berg and Eli Mintz in the TV incarnation of *The Goldbergs*.

Berg had just turned thirty when the program debuted, although the character of Molly was presented as being almost two decades older. The fictional family lived in a New York tenement, with neighbors frequently calling to each other through their open windows ("Yoo hoo, Mrs. Goldberg!"). Characters of extended family members and friends further enriched the stories, as the series quickly gained popularity.

The program began as a weekly, 15-minute show on November 20, 1929, and would become daily in 1931. The title was shortened to *The Goldbergs* upon the program's move to CBS in 1936.

A review in *The New York Times* noted that *The Rise of the Goldbergs* was "an accurate portrayal of the life of many New York families is indicated in letters received from listeners, who declare that the story might be their own. The dialect, too, has been praised, especially by Jewish listeners."

Throughout the program's history as a radio show, TV program (one of the first sitcoms on television, premiering in 1949), a film, and even a Broadway play, Berg wrote over 10,000 scripts, all in longhand, and with few revisions made to their original drafts. She put in full, eight-hour days writing, creating a four-month backlog of scripts for the program. In the early 1930s, especially for a woman with no previous entertainment experience and two children at home, Berg's accomplishment was nothing short of remarkable.

"It is gratifying that the peoples of every race liked it," she told a journalist. "I would not have written it had I not thought it was a true picture of the lives of every family."

1930

New Year's Day of 1930 brought with it the usual revelry across the nation, celebrating both the new year and new decade. On New Year's Eve, crowds gathered in Manhattan's Times Square to see the illuminated ball drop from the roof of One Times Square. Admiral Byrd sent a New Year's message from Little America in Antarctica.

In the meantime, no fewer than twenty speakeasies and nightclubs throughout the city found themselves raided by federal prohibition agents. That night, over forty owners and employees were arrested, but the patrons were not disturbed.

Herbert Hoover was president, busy dealing with the after-effects of the stock market crash just two months earlier.

As the new decade began, a survey by the Metropolitan Life Insurance Company determined that one-third of the homes in the United States were receiving radio programming. The number of radios had grown from an estimated 60,000 in 1922, to over 9 million in 1929, but other estimates ran closer to 12 million. The listening audience nationwide was estimated at 41 million.

January 14 - *Strike Up The Band,* **starring Clark & McCullough, opens on Broadway.**

Vaudeville's days may have been numbered as the world welcomed the new decade, but comedy on the "legitimate" stage, in the form of Broadway and Off-Broadway revues and musical comedies, was still thriving. The calendar year opened with a bang for musical comedy on Broadway, led by comedians Bobby Clark and Paul McCullough in *Strike Up the Band*. The two men had been childhood pals and, in 1900, developed their acrobatically-infused comedy sketches, venturing into both small-time show business, and big-time circuses (including Ringling Brothers, for whom they worked for a five-year stint). Over time, their act's comedy content began to outweigh the tumbling, and by the early 1920s they were top stars in burlesque before continuing their success on Broadway. They were easily identifiable, with Clark's greasepaint eyeglasses, oversized cigar, walking stick, and his rapid-fire stream of wisecracks; McCullough, sporting a derby, furry overcoat, and bushy (fake) moustache, served as Clark's passive accomplice.

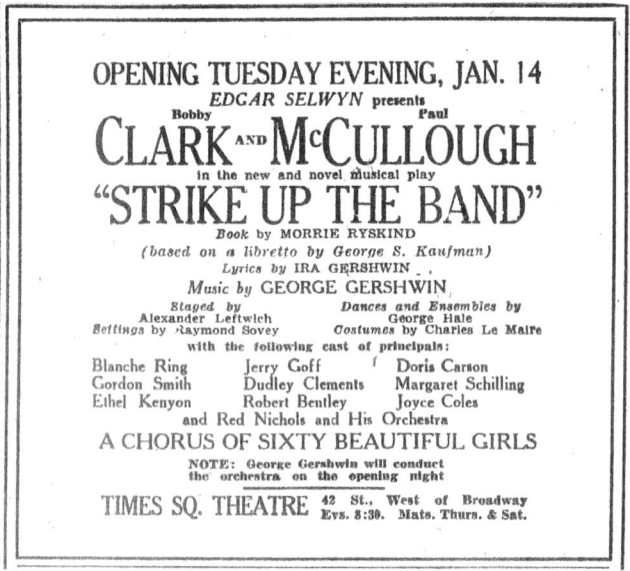

Newspaper ad for *Strike Up the Band*. Author's collection.

1930

The original 1927 version of *Strike Up the Band* boasted a libretto by George S. Kaufman with songs by George and Ira Gershwin. The dark satire of war had the United States declaring war on Switzerland, stemming from an issue involving imported cheese. It proved unsuccessful in its Philadelphia try-out run, but Morrie Ryskind later revised the script, giving it a happier ending, while the Gershwins removed some songs, and added others.

The finished product received reviews such as this from *The New York Times*:

> "When you have such a stage full of comedians as Bobby Clark and Paul McCullough can supply in themselves, you are in no position to distribute the usual gratuities carefully. They are the most expansive buffoons we have—Clark, with his broad shoulders, gleaming smile, murderous walking-stick and inspired cigar; McCullough, gazing with rapt admiration and astonishment at the master and playing the foil better than anyone else. Some of their clowning is familiar without being any the less funny…[they] still beam and still sing loud. In fact all that keeps Bobby Clark singing in the low register is his fear that on the high notes his eyes might pop out. As it is, his cigar pops out continuously and his walking stick bounces back and forth with the most surprising elasticity."

Variety said of the duo, "Bobby Clark and Paul McCullough as 'two men about town' are on high with the comedy throughout...*Strike Up the Band* started like a wow and it is in the hit class." The show ran through June, for a total of 191 performances.

J. Brooks Atkinson, writing for *The New York Times* in 1928, expressed his appreciation for stage comedians appearing in Broadway productions in which they were required to produce their comedy magic on a nightly basis:

"Nothing is more fascinating and nothing more futile than speculating upon the insane art of the hired buffoons who night after night make the impossible come true in the theatre. People of a practical instinct may patronize them as triflers in a serious world. But most of us will at least admire or envy the comedians who we do not actually love, for they perform no negative service, such as giving us relief through laughter. They are supermen. They create comedy through excess of the life we are all leading."

Atkinson then went on to invoke the names Clark & McCullough, the Marx Brothers, and W.C. Fields as examples of those who, at the time, were all plying their trade to audiences on Broadway.

Incidentally, there is a surviving bit of rare footage, shot by Movie Tone newsreel cameras, capturing a rehearsal of *Strike Up the Band*, shot from the wings, with Gershwin himself playing the title song as the dancing girls practice their steps. In some obviously pre-arranged dialogue, Clark & McCullough enter from off-stage, to be met with Gershwin's admonition about their tardiness. After Clark tosses off a few one-liners, they launch into a rousing version of the show's "Mademoiselle in New Rochelle" before the film abruptly ends (as of this writing, this clip is available to view on YouTube).

Concurrently, over at the Palace Theatre in Manhattan's Times Square during the first week of January, the bill included Jack Benny, George Jessel, and Burns & Allen, with headliners Clayton, Jackson, & Durante to appear later in the month.

Performing at the Palace, for any entertainer, carried with it an almost supreme significance, which should become clear with a brief history of its early days.

Showman Tony Pastor's original idea of presenting a family-oriented variety program in the 1860s was later refined by Benjamin Franklin Keith and partner Edward Franklin Albee, as they dubbed the variety format "vaudeville." The name derives from one of two possible French sources, or possibly a combination of the two: Val de Vire (Valley of the River Vire), or most probably, the phrase "voix de ville" or "voices of the town", referring to street singers and performers.

Keith and Albee's first vaudeville show to be labeled as such, opened in Boston in 1882. In 1894, the team opened their next venue in the city, the ornate Colonial theatre. The theatre set a standard of opulence among the bigger vaudeville houses throughout the country, where ordinary customers, in such lavish surroundings, could feel as privileged and "important" as wealthy patrons, but were charged a modest admission fee. In addition, Keith devised the two-a-day format for the big-time houses, in which a full bill of entertainment acts was presented twice a day, and a more continuous three-a-day format for the small-time theatres. By the turn of the century, there were 2,000 vaudeville theatres in North America, and the number continued to rise.

The bill for the Palace Theatre's opening week. Author's collection.

Keith's Palace in New York opened on March 24, 1913, with a bill that included a young Ed Wynn, performing his sketch "The Court Jester." Before long, the theatre became *the* venue to which virtually all vaudevillians aspired to perform. Located on Broadway and 47th Street, at the northern end of Times Square, it became the Mecca of vaudeville. "The Palace Theatre was the goal of every act in America," Fred Allen wrote, "An act that had played the Palace was booked by any theater manager sight unseen. A Palace program, with an act's name on it, was a diploma of merit." George Burns agreed. "To me, playing the Palace Theatre on Broadway meant you were a star. Of all the thrills I've had in show business, playing the Palace for the first time was the most exciting."

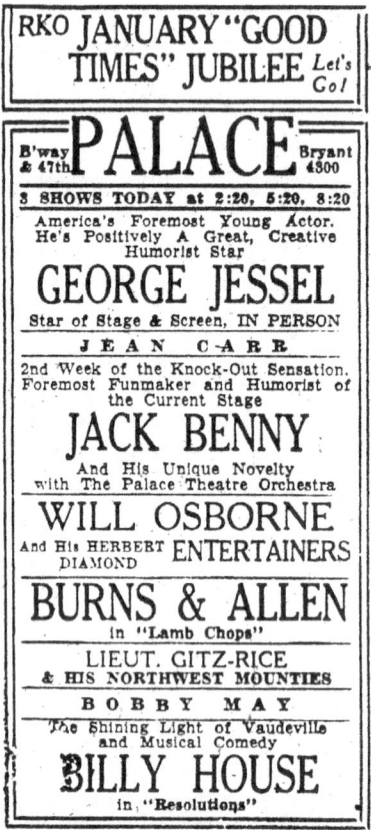

A January, 1930 all-star bill. Author's collection.

1930

With Burns & Allen, Jessel, and Benny on the same Palace bill in January of 1930, Palace patrons got their money's worth. *Variety* said of Benny, "He has the regular skeleton of his standard easy-going chatter routine, pleasantly stuffed with newer sassy sayings and gossip. Benny is one of those rare light comedians who drift in and out with the knowledge that what they have to say is funny but doesn't really matter. The few who have the knack aren't bothered by one-night jumps."

Billboard reported, "Jack Benny combined his own act with a corking potpourri of clowning and melody, in which he has the support of Lou Forman and his house orchestra, who work on the stage for the occasion… Amusing burlesques of [Rudy] Vallee and Ted Lewis helped raise the laugh score considerably higher. Mrs. Benny, who is not new to the Palace mob, sang a chorus of 'Love Me' and she easily made the grade."

The same review also looked favorably upon Burns & Allen, reporting that the couple "appealed mightily in a well-bolstered version of their Al Boasberg skit, 'Lamb Chops,' being preceded by few kind words and characteristic clowning by Jack Benny. Miss Allen's handling of her dizzy daisy part is performing at its very best. They do appealing song-dance businesses between slices of the mirthful crossfire. "

As for Jessel, who years earlier had won over audiences with his routine of a telephone chat with his unseen/unheard mother (a forerunner to similar phone routines by Myron Cohen, and, in the 1950s, Bob Newhart, and Shelley Berman), he was among the growing number of big time vaudeville stars who continued to reach for yet another, higher rung on the show business ladder, even higher than that occupied by the *Ziegfeld Follies*. The common goal for many comedians was to star in a legitimate Broadway production or revue. For those who made the attempt, the success rate was impressive. In Jessel's case, it was he, not Al Jolson, who starred in the original Broadway version of *The Jazz Singer* in 1925 (Jolson got the film role after Jessel demanded too high a fee).

A 1928 *New York Times* review of Jessel's act declared that he was, "beyond question, a smart and vaudeville-wise entertainer… Most of his comedy is funny—especially some of the lines that he employs in a telephone speech with his mother—and he knows how to dispense other sort of elementary sentiment that brings direct returns from his auditors. He is, in sum, a showman, and his act is deservedly among the played-up items of the bill."

For his Palace run with Benny and Burns & Allen, Jessel opened with the "Hello, Mama" phone routine, followed by songs, jokes, and even a dash of drama, before closing with the sentimental tune "My Mother's Eyes." "He came on to a deafening ovation," *Billboard* reported, "and this clamor was intensified at the bows."

Two weeks later, Clayton, Jackson, and Durante would offer an entirely different act altogether. Their mishmash of songs, jokes, and knockabout slapstick, which often included the virtual destruction of their onstage piano, made for one of the most raucous comedy acts in the business at the time.

The New York Times described the trio:

> "The madcap Durante and company lend their immediately high spirits to a rendition of that unique dance known as 'the hot potato,' to buffoonery, both vocal and physical, that they have made familiar in the course of their vaudeville, night club and 'Show Girl' activities, and, in conclusion, to their hilarious proving of the proposition that wood has ever been one of the greatest civilizing forces known to man. As usual, their act is sublimated nonsense, but, as usual, it offers, in the frequent moments when Mr. Durante has the floor, some shrewd comment on human foibles and pretentions."

February 14 - Our Gang stars in *Love Business*.

How appropriate it was to release this genuinely hilarious short on Valentine's Day. Directed by Robert McGowan, it's arguably the finest two-reeler featuring the cast at that time, with priceless dialogue supplied by H. M. Walker, and acted to perfection by the young performers.

1930

In the story, Jackie Cooper and Chubby Chaney are vying for the affections of their teacher, Miss Crabtree, who has moved into Jackie's house as a boarder. Mary Ann and Wheezer, as his siblings, are present to tease him about his crush on the lovely schoolmarm, but Mary Ann asks the teacher for assurance that she isn't actually in love with Chubby (whom Mary Ann has her sights set on). Of course, just when Jackie is able to get Miss Crabtree alone for an intimate chat, repeating his highest compliment to her ("You're even prettier than Miss McGillicuddy"), Chubby arrives with candy and flowers. He also has a host of memorized sweet-nothings to whisper in Miss Crabtree's ear, courtesy of love letters he "bought off of Wheezer," written to the siblings' mother years before. Jackie does his best to sabotage Chubby's declarations of affection, while Miss Crabtree finds it all quite amusing (although she does give each of the rivals a lingering kiss on the lips that could certainly be deemed unacceptable—or worse—by today's social norms). The mother, overhearing the familiar passages from her old love letters, interrupts the love fest, and the jig is up.

Roach Studios' promotion for Our Gang. Author's collection.

The Our Gang kids were treated pretty much as royalty on the Roach lot, and given virtually free run of the studio during their time off from school. A classroom and tutor were provided for them on the lot itself. Roach was quite protective of his young actors, and even once went to court to obtain an injunction against a father who considered his child's acting income as his own. On the lot, one parent of each actor was required to be on hand during filming, but studio also had rules against interfering behavior by parents, and these were expected to be strictly obeyed. There were no favorites, and the kids' onscreen nicknames were given to them by the production crew.

The search for the Gang's cast additions/replacements was ongoing, but parents arriving unannounced with their aspiring child actors were turned away. All had to first submit photos, after which studio agents would respond to those kids whom Roach wanted to see for a screen test. Parents and children were then brought to the studio, at Roach's expense. The lucky ones would become stars, even while some were still learning how to read and write!

February 18 - Ed Wynn's *Simple Simon* opens on Broadway.

Wynn had already been a comedy star for nearly thirty years by 1930. He traveled the country in vaudeville, both as a solo act and with a number of partners and patter routines, the most popular being a dialogue sketch he wrote called "The Freshman and the Sophomore," and later spent two seasons with the *Ziegfeld Follies*. Upon enthusiastically supporting the Actor's Equity strike of 1919, he found himself blacklisted by the major producers in New York. This forced him to produce his own reviews through the 1920s, including *The Ed Wynn Carnival*, *The Perfect Fool*, and *The Grab Bag*. In the early days of 1930, Wynn joined forces once again with his old boss Ziegfeld to create his new show, *Simple Simon*. Guy Bolton, longtime collaborator with P.G. Wodehouse and Jerome Kern on many hit shows, was brought in to co-write the book. It was billed as "a musical extravaganza in two acts and thirteen scenes" (Bolton would go on to co-write *Anything Goes* with Wodehouse in 1935).

The plot of *Simple Simon* centers on Wynn as Simon, a Coney Island shopkeeper who sells books and newspapers, but prefers to read only fairy tales because he does not like to read bad news. One day he falls asleep in front of his shop and dreams that his fellow merchants from Ferrymen Alley are fairy-tale characters (Cinderella, King Cole, Jack and Jill, Snow White), and that he is the hero in each of their fables.

Print ad for *Simple Simon*. Author's collection.

The show contained gags that were designed to entertain both younger and adult audiences. "For every hickery-dickery-dock," Wynn said, "there was going to have to be something sort of sophisticated, like a bottle of Scotch." And he meant it: at one point in the show, a live horse would appear from the wings with a flask conveniently secured to its hip. But, because children as well as adults were encouraged to see the show, Wynn would refrain from smoking his ever-present cigar onstage.

Brooks Atkinson's review in *The New York Times* was typical of the notices

Wynn received not only for *Simple Simon*, but for his earlier stage offerings throughout the 1920s, and for those to follow:

> "...It is Ed Wynn's field day, and quite properly. For amiable and droll and delightful as the Perfect Fool has been in the past, he has never seemed so indisputably great as he does this time in the full ripeness of his art—not merely an expert musical stage comic, although it is essential that he should always be that, but an artist who lifts his tomfoolery into the realms of fantasy...The Perfect Fool has become one of the two or three great comedians of the day."

Meanwhile, other stage comedy stars whose popularity was on the rise at this time included Bert Lahr and Joe E. Brown.

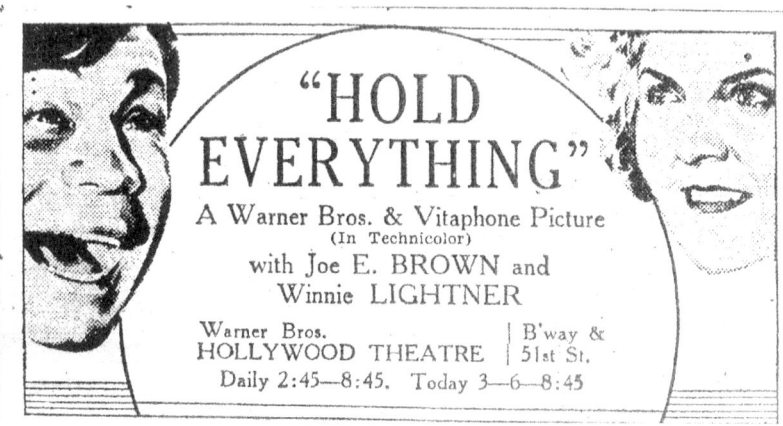

Print ad for *Hold Everything*. Author's collection.

Lahr had graduated from burlesque to the legitimate stage with a bang. He stole the show in the 1928 Broadway musical comedy *Hold Everything*, as a young boxer, giving audiences fits of laughter with his eccentric clowning, facial expressions, and vocal sound effects that combined to create what was quickly becoming his trademark behavior. But when it came time for Warner

Brothers to produce a film version of the show, producer Vinton Freedly would not release Lahr from his contract, preferring to keep him around for the touring edition. Joe E. Brown was then cast in Lahr's role for the film.

Lahr was angry enough for having been shut out of the film, but, to add insult to injury, it did not go unnoticed by audiences and reviewers alike that Brown seemed to mimic a few too many of Lahr's mannerisms for comfort. This incensed Lahr still further, as did the positive reviews for Brown.

Variety praised *Hold Everything* as the best Warner Brothers comedy since talkies took over, and the best filmed musical comedy of all to that point. "...The basic point of the picture is Brown. On the strength of this effort he of the wide grin grabbed himself a long and sweet starring contract with Warners. Which should make it an event for Bert Lahr. The latter has now made two people—himself and Brown."

The piece went on to ponder the ramifications of Brown's performance.

> "What [Brown's] work in this film is going to do to Lahr when he goes on the road with his show is a big problem —for Lahr. Brown is doing everything Lahr did in the same show unto the 'gong, gong, gong,' voice inflections on lines and mannerisms. Brown must have seen 'Hold Everything' on the stage 18 times to lift as minutely as he screens here...Brown is plenty funny and the public will think Lahr is doing a Brown when they see him... There are those who can and will contend that Lahr is not the originator of the style which he has developed."

The question of just who is entitled to stake a claim on any given comedy technique has rarely been a cut & dry issue. Copyrighting the actual words of a sketch, play, or screenplay can ward off bogus claims of authorship, but that doesn't include the rights to *how* those words are spoken or performed. For every act, joke, comical character, or bit of slapstick that may look new when a particular comedian performs it, something very similar, if not identical, can likely be found, delving back in time, by another performer. The *Variety* piece on Lahr and Brown goes on to trace Lahr's basic "pansy Dutch" shtick to a 1920 burlesque revue *Folly Town*, written by future radio gagman Billy Wells (the production also included Lahr's future *Wizard of Oz* co-star, Jack Haley). The lineage is then followed further back still, to comedians Solly Ward and Sam Bernard. "Lahr is still really doing the same character today with variations, and Brown hasn't missed an imprint in following the Lahr tracks. It's practically a cinch that this picture is going to ruin Lahr's golf for the summer."

Lahr's temper and insecurities were legendary among his show business contemporaries, and the circumstances prompted him to write a letter to *Variety* shortly after *Hold Everything* was released, in which he accused Brown of deliberately "lifting" his mannerisms point for point. His anger may have been equally directed at Vinton Freedly, but Brown caught the brunt of it in public.

The famously volatile Bert Lahr in a cheerier pose. Courtesy of Steve Cox.

Lahr nevertheless made another positive comic impact on theatre audiences in early 1930, with the show *Flying High*, in which he played an aviator attempting a new record flight. Unlike *Hold Everything*, however, he was allowed to repeat his role for the film version, and *Variety* praised his performance, including the facial expressions and sounds, which had become familiar, but no less welcome. One gag in the film, taking place during a doctor's exam and playing on the idea that Lahr was taking a swig of liquor from a urine specimen bottle, was deemed "strictly for adults" but funny just the same (and not nearly as graphic as the description implies).

The problem remained that film-goers who hadn't yet seen him on the stage in *any* production, would most likely find his mannerisms in *Flying High* looking suspiciously like Brown's in *Hold Everything*. Lahr feared that moviegoers would suspect him of copying Brown, rather than the other way around.

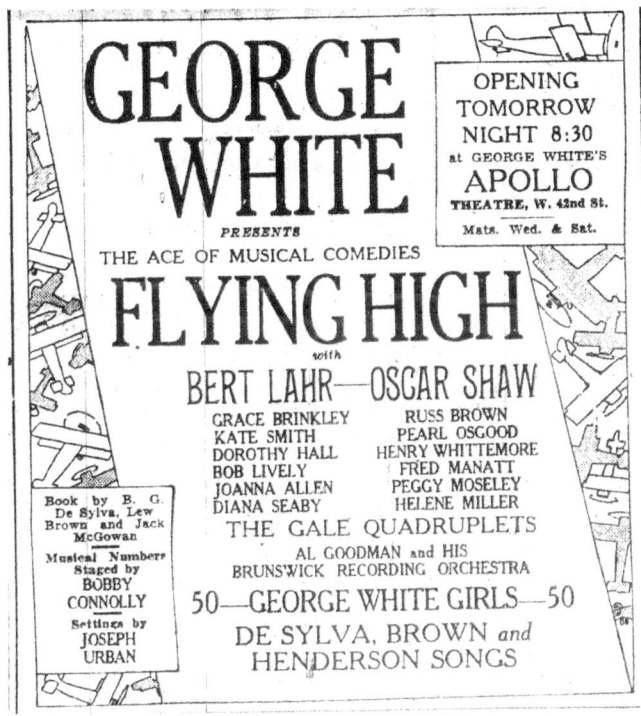

Print ad for *Flying High*. Author's collection.

Photoplay also reported on the situation, with a touch of dramatic flair:

"War broke out between two famous comedians not long ago. So far no peace treaty has been signed, and a smack on the nose may come any day…Mr. Lahr charges, with some show of justice, that Mr. Brown has lifted many of his mannerisms, 'unique expressions' and bits of business. This imperils, says Mr. Lahr, his future in the talkies…So there's a big mad on, and I'd like to be around when they meet. Mr. Lahr is one of the funniest men in America. And I have a hunch he is in strict training for his meeting up with Mr. Brown."

Brown chose not to directly address Lahr's accusations and resentment, hoping his peer would eventually simmer down, but Lahr would hold onto his grudge for years. Fortunately, each comedian's career was already secure, with or without comparisons between them, but Lahr's habit of accusing other comedians of stealing his style and/or material would not fade over time.

March 22 - Buster Keaton releases his first sound feature, *Free and Easy*.

By 1930, it had become obvious that talking pictures were here to stay. Depending on the comedian, that could be a welcome or intimidating concept. For the more visual stage comedians who specialized in sight gags and slapstick, silent films presented them with an opportunity to expand upon their routines and build simple scenarios around them, utilizing both interior sets and exterior locations. Re-takes could be shot whenever necessary, as well. However, for silent comedians who had never before needed to create or recite dialogue in their films, sound posed a considerable challenge.

We've already seen how Laurel & Hardy proved to be naturals for talkies from the get-go, and how Harold Lloyd recognized the need to convert *Welcome Danger* to sound, but how were other major silent comedy stars faring in the early years of the sound era?

1930

Unlike his friend and professional rival Charlie Chaplin (whom we'll discuss shortly), Buster Keaton felt no anxiety about making the transition to talkies. He welcomed the arrival of sound, knowing that even a sound comedy could be comprised primarily of slapstick anyway, and adding dialogue wouldn't hurt the visual gags. There was no reason why Keaton couldn't continue just being Keaton, as long as dialogue wouldn't usurp the visual comedy he was such a master at creating.

It was not sound that threatened Keaton's career, but rather the callous treatment he received from the monolithic MGM studios, which took over his contract in 1928, and which quickly stifled his ability to control his material. Upon joining MGM, he made his last two silent films, *The Cameraman*, and *Spite Marriage* (which he wanted to be a sound picture), but found his ideas and working techniques immediately at odds with the studio. By the time *Free and Easy* was released, Keaton's aggravation with his new employer had already been simmering.

A true legend among legends: Buster Keaton. Courtesy of Steve Cox.

He was taken aback by the studio's approach to comedy filmmaking. "New York stage directors, new York dialogue writers, and the musicians union all moved to Hollywood," he recalled. "So the minute they started laying out a script, they're looking for those funny lines, puns, little jokes…everybody at Metro was in my gag department. They'd laugh their heads off laughing at dialogue written by all the new writers. They were joke-happy. They don't look for the action. They're looking for funny things to say."

He spoke to MGM *wunderkind* executive Irving Thalberg, who was fast-building on his reputation by approving and supervising the production of hundreds of films, a good number of which received their share of box office success and industry awards. Keaton asked to have his scripts prepared in such a way that would allow for long stretches in which his own visual gags could pick up the action, with little or no dialogue at all. Thalberg insisted that Keaton work with the writers from the scenario department, resulting in way too much interference from people who didn't possess a fraction of Keaton's innate talent for creating visual comedy.

Ad for *Parlor, Bedroom and Bath.* Courtesy of Steve Cox.

1930

"They were picking stories and material without consulting me," Keaton said, "and I couldn't argue them out of it. I'd only argue about so far, and then let it go."

Not one to pursue confrontation, his unhappiness with the studio led him to skip work at times, resulting in reprimands. His drinking increased. His marriage to actress Natalie Talmadge also began to fall apart.

Keaton also disliked the scripts for the pictures that followed *Free and Easy*, such as *Parlor, Bedroom and Bath* and especially *The Sidewalks of New York* (which, ironically, became his highest grossing film). He had to obey orders, though, or face suspension. As if it weren't bad enough that the studio had robbed him of his creative freedom, he then found himself placed in an arranged onscreen "marriage" to Jimmy Durante.

A scene from *The Sidewalks of New York* (1931). Courtesy of Steve Cox.

As Keaton struggled to save his career, which had been riding high only a year before, his close friend and mentor, Roscoe "Fatty" Arbuckle, was attempting to recover from his own harrowing, personal tragedy.

Once a rival to Chaplin as the world's most popular film comedian, Arbuckle was a broken man at the dawn of the 1930s, due to the horrendous ordeal he experienced throughout the previous decade.

In 1921, one of Hollywood's most notorious scandals involved the death of a 26-year-old girl, Virginia Rappe, in Arbuckle's San Francisco hotel room during a party. As a result of a lurid sequence of events, with evidence strongly suggesting a frame-up, Arbuckle was accused of sexually assaulting Rappe, whose internal abdominal injuries lead to her death. He stood trial three times, with each trial a sensational media event. Two ended in a hung jury, the third in acquittal. Despite this, his personal reputation was forever tarnished, leaving him with virtually nowhere to go from that point on. Despite his exoneration, Roscoe "Fatty" Arbuckle, who at the height of his career was earning $1,000 a day, found himself living as a pariah for the following decade.

He found some jobs directing, but he had to do so under the alias "William B. Goodrich" (also known by the rather cynical abbreviation, "Will. B. Goode"). "It was Mack Sennett who took the first chance," *Photoplay* reported. "He gave 'Fatty' a job directing and gagging. But even Sennett had Arbuckle use another name." Arbuckle only stayed a few months, as his increasing depression, mood swings, and alcoholism made him difficult to work with.

He then found work with RKO in late January of 1930, as a writer in the scenario department. He worked uncredited as a gagman on the Wheeler and Woolsey feature comedy *Half Shot at Sunrise*, but left the studio just six months later. *Photoplay* reported, "[RKO] kept it very, very dark. If Fatty happened to get into a photograph taken on the set he was working on, while acting as gag-man, the negative was destroyed. The studio adopted a rigid hush-hush policy on Arbuckle's presence while he worked there as a comedy adviser."

He returned in 1931, working for RKO Pathe as director and writer on the *Traveling Man Comedies* series, starring Louis John Bartels.

1930

Roscoe Arbuckle. Author's collection.

In *Photoplay*'s March issue profile, titled "Just Let Me Work," the author of the piece, James Ellis, sadly reported that Arbuckle was doing his best to resist feelings of bitterness.

> "When we say that, we mean that Fatty is resigned. He has lost his fight; he has lost his illusions. And of hope, he retains only a vestige. That hope is the one thing he has never given up. It is the hope that someday, somehow, he may once again return to the screen—*on* the screen! …It's because he can never forget the place he once held in the hearts and affections of movie-goers. He wants that place back."

In Arbuckle's own words, "All I want to do is to be allowed to work in my field. It isn't for money. I'm not broke. I never have been broke. I don't want anybody sobbing or whining over me. I've no resentment against anybody for what has happened. My conscience is clear, my heart is clean. I refuse to worry. I feel that I have atoned for everything."

He also claimed to have harbored no ill will to those who continued to consider him guilty of *something* that horrific night ten years earlier. "People have the right to their opinions," he said. "The people who oppose me have the right to theirs. I have the right to mine—which is that I've suffered enough, and been humiliated enough. I want to go back to the screen. I think I can entertain and gladden the people that see me. All I want is that. If I do get back, it will be grand. If I don't—well, okay."

Arbuckle's words did not go unnoticed by the public. In the May issue of *Photoplay*, editor/publisher James R. Quirk reported on having received two thousand letters in support of Arbuckle, while pointing out a glaring hypocrisy. "But the good club women and organized professional performers who stoned him into oblivion show no signs of putting into practice the precepts they mouth so glibly on Sabbath morn."

Two months later, Quirk wrote of a letter Arbuckle sent to *Photoplay* (presumably after the original Ellis article appeared, although Quirk didn't specify). In an odd and heartbreaking contradiction to his earlier remarks, Arbuckle reportedly claimed in his letter, "I have no desire to return to the screen as an actor. In the dark hours of my life it was a consolation to know that I had given happiness to millions of people. There doesn't seem to be much chance of happiness for me. No man can live and be happy without work, and all I want is to be permitted to use whatever talents and training I have in the writing and direction of pictures under my own name." Quirk then stressed his own desire to see any producer make a stand on Arbuckle's behalf, and put Arbuckle's name back on the screen as a writer or director. "Then let us see if the relentless moralists and professional reformers would have the audacity to attempt to overrule American Fair Play!"

Arbuckle didn't know it at the time, but he wouldn't need to wait much longer before seeing a glimmer of light at the end of a long, dark tunnel.

As for other silent comedy stars entering the sound era, Harold Lloyd continued the success of *Welcome Danger* with his second talkie, *Feet First*. "He has bridged the chasm between silent and audible pictures, without losing—or gaining—a single point," *Picture Play* said. "He remains an institution, the same in technique, in laughing appeal, that he was some ten years ago. He stands alone. And for that reason, he stands apart. In his new picture, *Feet First*, he is at his best. An amusing, carefully worked out film, his is perhaps the most truly American sense of humor one sees on the screen today."

Harry Langdon, on the other hand, had considerably more trouble, even before the industry's transition to sound, due in part to the character he created for himself in silents. His rather eerie baby-face—enhanced with ample white pancake make-up—and childlike mannerisms, now necessitated him to take on a similarly young voice to match. With sound adding an extra dimension of reality to film, the sight—and sound—of a grown man looking and speaking like a shy child can come across as somewhat disturbing. He signed with Hal Roach Studios in 1929 for a series of sound shorts, but they didn't catch on with the public. Roach himself concluded that Langdon just wasn't as an effective comedian in talkies, and by the end of 1930, Langdon would part ways with the studio.

July 22 - R.K.O. drops use of the term "vaudeville"

In an ominous development, the Radio-Keith-Orpheum chain announced that it was to discard the term "vaudeville," and that its stage shows were to be known henceforth as 'R-K-O Varieties." The new term was intended "to emphasize the distinction between the performances in which actors appear behind the footlights and the screen programs, which are also part of the bill in most variety theatres." This was a result of an increasing number of vaudeville theatres adding movies to their bills, thus muddying the once-pure waters of exclusively live stage performances.

The winds of change for vaudeville were magnified that much more at the Palace. Throughout the country, vaudeville had been suffering from stale acts, smaller audiences, and theatres that had undergone conversions to accommodate films. Even sadder, many had closed altogether. The Palace itself was losing $4,000 a week in 1930. As show business reporter and historian Able Green explained, "The great showplace found itself caught in a web of its own contradictions. It had helped wreck vaudeville by raising salaries to astronomical heights. Now it sought headliners in vain…The headliner shortage compelled the Palace to hold acts for two and four weeks, and to repeat them frequently…but that didn't add up to a year's salary."

The theatre began to call for headliners from radio, Hollywood, musicals and night clubs, but nothing seemed to work in keeping vaudeville audiences interested. Only movies could save the Palace, but, philosophically, the very idea sent shivers throughout the entertainment business.

For the vaudeville comedians, however, there were new outlets of comedy to explore, especially on radio and in films. The only problem was that most vaudevillians didn't know anything about making movies, or performing in front of radio microphones. In a way, even the brightest performers essentially needed to learn their art all over again, and re-apply it to the popular culture's new technologies.

August 22 - *The Golf Specialist*, W.C. Fields' first talkie, is released.

When Fields joined the ranks of comedians taking the plunge into talkies, he was already fifty years old, and had made eleven silent films, beginning with the one-reeler *Pool Sharks* in 1915. That short was ostensibly shot to preserve his famous stage billiards routine, but the use of unconvincing special effects pretty much defeated the purpose of displaying his skills.

As for his silent features throughout the 1920s, they didn't go over especially well with audiences. Negative reviews almost always exempted Fields from the critics' displeasure with the overall product, as he smartly included a good number of his tried-and-true stage routines that had won acceptance years before in front of live audiences.

The content of *The Golf Specialist*, except for an opening scene in the lobby of a golf course clubhouse, consists of his routine first performed in the *Ziegfeld Follies* of 1915, in which constant distractions and interruptions delay his tee shot. Fields first committed the sketch to film in the silent features *Her Majesty's Dilemma*, and *So's Your Old Man*, and would do so yet again, in his most polished version, for the 1934 feature *You're Telling Me*.

The bulk of *The Golf Specialist* was filmed in one day at Ideal Studios in New Jersey. Monte Brice is credited as director, but Fields pretty much directed it himself. It was released by RKO.

Photoplay reported, "W.C. Fields, noted stage comedy star, is another entrant in [RKO's] rush of short laughers. This is a screen amplification of the howling golf act he's done on the stage for years, and it's an excellent job. Laughs are continuous for twenty-three minutes. Fields is just swell."

With sound now enabling him to embellish his bits of business with his own brand of dialogue, ad-libbed asides, throwaway lines, and miscellaneous utterances, *The Golf Specialist* signaled the true beginning a film career that would solidify Fields' status as arguably (but not *too* arguably) the greatest film comedian of the 20th century.

September 6 - Marx Brothers release the film version of *Animal Crackers*.

The brothers' second feature was adapted by Morrie Ryskind from the 1928 play he co-wrote with George S. Kaufman, and which ran on Broadway for 191 performances. The look of this filmed version is much improved from that of *The Cocoanuts*, and the comedy sequences themselves are at least as memorable. Groucho's dialogue in particular (as his most famous character, Captain Jeffrey T. Spaulding) reaches new heights. Joe Adamson, in his book *Groucho, Harpo, Chico, and sometimes Zeppo*, writes that the dialogue in *Animal Crackers* "reaches a level of literacy and wit that future Marx films can't hope to rival."

The plot, such as it is, takes place at a weekend party on the Long Island estate of Mrs. Rittenhouse (Margaret Dumont), during which a famous painting is unveiled and promptly stolen, leading to a search throughout the grounds of the mansion.

The brothers effortlessly wreak havoc at the party. Author's collection.

Highlights include the classic opening Kalmar & Ruby number "Hooray for Captain Spaulding," in which Groucho arrives still in his explorer's gear and carried on a reclining sedan seat by four tribesmen. Also memorable is his pun-filled monologue recounting his African adventures, which includes the oft-repeated line "One morning I shot an elephant in my pajamas. How he got in my pajamas I don't know," and the even better (and racier) line, "We took some pictures of the native girls but they weren't developed. But we're going back again in a couple of weeks…" Chico, at the piano, attempts the song "Sugar in the Morning," but can't remember the finish, so he plays it over and over, like a phonograph needle stuck on a record. We're also treated to a chaotic bridge game between Harpo, Chico, Margaret Dumont and Margaret Whiting, which manages to turn into an all-out brawl. Closing the film is

Harpo's famous knife-dropping scene, in which a drawer-full of stolen silverware slowly but surely cascades from his coat sleeve.

Aside from features, comedy in the form of two-reelers was becoming omnipresent on movie screens. *One*-reelers, roughly ten minutes long and used as filler in between features, consisted mostly of filmed vaudeville acts by singers, dancers, and various novelties. Many acts, however, became fearful of a drop in demand for their live performances, once a film of their material could be distributed to countless theatres across the country. "This turn in the market on shorts," *Variety* reported, "has directly hit hundreds of vaude acts that a year ago would have been considered ideal for shorts purposes."

Consequently, some performers began to demand top dollar from film producers, even though the additional exposure ultimately boosted their name recognition and popularity. Times and tastes were changing fast. Throughout the second half of 1930, one-reelers of non-comedy acts had begun to give way to the more popular *two*-reelers by comedians. Even better were those offering some semblance of a storyline. *Variety* continued:

> "Where six months ago it looked as though two-reel comedies would go out… producers are favoring this type of 'filler' more than ever before…Comedy is so high in demand that anything without some comedy is faced with getting thumbs down for shorts use, according to producer and distributor sources…
>
> Where producers can find sufficient original material, either contributed or written by staffs, to fill out program needs, the rank and file of vaude turns will be disregarded. Only exception now seems to be good comedy material and 'names' from vaude…The lean toward two-reel product seems to be in line with comedy demands and easy sale of slapstick. Also, it is claimed producers can develop more plot in two reels, something audiences are demanding."

A random sampling of two-reelers making the rounds in the autumn of 1930 would include those by Mack Sennett silent film veterans Lloyd Hamilton and Andy Clyde, continuing their work for their boss, but now in talkies. Audiences at the time also saw Harry Langdon, ably assisted by aspiring comedy starlet Thelma Todd, in *The Fighting Parson* for Hal Roach (as we mentioned earlier, Langdon's stay at Roach Studios would be a brief one). Roach was also overseeing the Our Gang series, its newest entry being *Bear Shooters*. And, of course, Laurel & Hardy were going strong, with the autumn releases of *Pardon Us* and *The Laurel & Hardy Murder Case*. And, vaudeville star Jack Benny was trying to find his niche at MGM with the short, *The Rounder* (several months before making his first radio appearance).

* * *

Meanwhile, comedy on radio was still getting its artistic bearings in 1930. With the rare exceptions of duos Amos & Andy and the countrified Lum & Abner, comedians had been accustomed to working in front of live audiences. Back in 1922, WJZ in Newark was conducting experimental broadcasts, and arrangements were made with Ed Wynn to perform his hit revue *The Perfect Fool* on the air in the station's studio. The broadcast was the first musical variety show with a full cast to be broadcast on radio. When Wynn decided he couldn't perform nearly as well in an empty studio, he quickly gathered a makeshift "audience," consisting of whoever was in the building at the time, to sit and watch the proceedings, and laugh whenever a joke struck their fancy. As radio continued to establish its own methods and rules for broadcasting, such live audiences became *verboten* at the time.

In 1930, there was either no studio audience present to react to a comedian's on-air jokes, or, even stranger, if there *was* a live audience in attendance, the guests were instructed not to laugh out loud or applaud at any point during the broadcast. Just imagine sitting in the studio audience of your favorite current late-night TV talk show, and being asked *not* to laugh audibly at the jokes by the host or the guests for the entire show. As difficult as it may be to fathom now, comedians, in the first few years of network radio, had only a cold, silent studio in which to perform their material, having to time their jokes to the laughter of audiences in their heads. It seemed as if radio was no place for the comic whose stock in trade was to rattle off a series of jokes and hope listeners at home would laugh at what they heard.

Thus, there was no way for comedians to time jokes so that listeners at home could laugh at one line before a performer continues with the next. The editorial board of *The New York Times* (those well-renown experts on comedy) took notice, and offered a methodical solution that any number-cruncher would love: "Players and directors need a table of statistics or some scientific basis for judging the comic content and reaction of their material. At present they must guess at the whole thing, but the time may not be far off when an analysis of comedy will be provided for every funny skit for the radio or the talkies, which are having the same sort of trouble."

Thankfully, change was on the horizon. George Burns recalled, "I think as soon as the sponsors began allowing people to come into the studio to watch the broadcast, radio began changing. Instead of working in small rooms, we began broadcasting from theaters. Going to a radio show being broadcast became an event, like going to see big-time vaudeville on Saturday night. On a few occasions we even broadcast from the stage of a vaudeville house we'd played in a few years earlier." Tickets were usually given away, but whenever the team alternated between a stage show and radio show at the same venue, they'd give anyone who bought a ticket to the live show a ticket to the broadcast. "That way we packed two houses," Burns explained.

November 17 - *Sweet & Low*, featuring Fannie Brice, George Jessel, and James Barton, opens on Broadway.

Fannie Brice had first made a name for herself in smaller burlesque revues around New York, before joining the *Ziegfeld Follies* in 1910. She was barely 19 years old at the time, but was already known as a comic dancer and accomplished comedian, who delivered her comedy with an exaggerated Yiddish accent onstage (although she did not speak Yiddish), and had a gift for making contorted facial expressions.

A beautifully serene portrait of young Fannie Brice. Author's collection.

A decade later, she earned further praise for her heartfelt and dramatic renditions of popular torch songs. Her showstopper was the ballad "My Man," which she introduced to Ziegfeld audiences in 1921. She valued the ability to create a dramatic moment on stage, such as by singing that signature number, as she did the ability to generate belly laughs. "People like to feel miserable," she told *The New Yorker* in 1929. "You make them laugh, they will forget you, but if you make them cry, they will never forget you."

One of her many fans was one-time *Follies* co-star W. C. Fields, who succinctly described her thusly: "Comical dancer, comedienne, did burlesque dances, sang character songs in Yiddish and other dialects. She was a fine dramatic actress, believe it or prove your ignorance."

Sweet and Low ad. Author's collection.

As for *Sweet and Low*, Brice's talents were in fine company. *The New York Times* informed readers:

> "…[the show] leans heavily on its stellar trio. And for them—particularly for Mr. Jessel—it is more or less of a field day. With the individual talents of the three stars you are doubtless well acquainted. Miss Brice, as you know, can inject a genuine touch of simple pathos into a banal Broadway ballad or make a comical song seem better than it actually is. Here she does both. Mr. Jessel, as you know, is at his best when his is brashly humorous, and considerably less good when he grows sentimental. Here he does not grow sentimental. And Mr. Barton for all his all-round skill as an entertainer, is primarily a

dancer, and a dancer who has few peers. Here he does not dance enough."

The revue ran for nearly 200 performances.

Brice made her most indelible mark as a comedian with the creation of her character Baby Snooks, an inquisitive child who would gently badger her "adult" friends with questions and quips not often heard from the mouths of babes.

Here she explains how the Baby Snooks character developed:

"When I was in vaudeville in 1914, one of my songs was 'Poor Pauline.' It made such a hit that I began to sing it in different ways, as an opera singer would do it, as an Italian organ grinder would do it, and so on. Finally, one night at a party, I did it as a baby in a high chair. That's how Snooks was born…She came to life again when we were talking about numbers for the stage show *Sweet and Low*. Moss Hart wrote the Snooks skit for this production, after that I did a show called *Crazy Quilt* with Phil Baker and the late Ted Healy, for which that great comedy writer, Dave Freedman, did a Snooks skit. Thus began an association which continued until Dave's death, and it provided much of the material I have recently used for Snooks' radio program."

Brice wasn't in favor of meticulous rehearsals. "Some comedians work out every detail of their business in putting over a song or an act," she said, "and I think it is a most admirable method, because it relieves one of the tyranny of moods. But I can't do it. My comedy, to be successful, must be spontaneous. Whenever it isn't, the feel of the audience tells me so and I throw out that particular piece of business and work out something else to use in its stead."

Brice as Baby Snooks. Courtesy of Martin Grams.

December 22 - W.C. Fields stars onstage in *Ballyhoo*.

Having tested the waters in the world of sound pictures with *The Golf Specialist* earlier in the year, Fields returned to the Broadway stage. *Ballyhoo* was based on the experiences of C.C. Pyle, a promoter of sorts, known for several unusual business ventures, including a cross-country foot race, and a new professional football league that never got off the ground. His reputation was a tad shady, and the writers of *Ballyhoo*, Harry Ruskin and Leighton Brill, had Fields in mind when they went to work writing the book. The show was produced by Arthur Hammerstein.

According to Fields historian (and grandson) Ronald J. Fields, the production was loosely constructed to allow the comedian ample room to insert some of his favorite stage business borrowed from his earlier outings, such as scooting around the stage in a tiny motorized car, as he had done in the *Follies*. He also juggled, reprised his pool table gags, and starred in a few set pieces loosely connected with the plot. As Ronald Fields described, "the piece seemed like a playground for all of W.C.'s wild antics…The show was all his, plot be damned."

The comedian got good reviews, but the show as a whole did not. *The New York Times* concluded, "Although Mr. Hammerstein has assembled a large company and a wide assortment of scenery, *Ballyhoo* is a fairly dull musical production. Excepting W.C. Fields: When Mr. Fields strains every muscle to squeeze into the driver's seat of his unweened automobile and then tries to close the door, music hall comedy may here be reported as fundamentally sound."

Newspaper ad for *Ballyhoo*. Author's collection.

The show lost money in the first three weeks, partly due to troubles with unionized stagehands, the poor state of the economy, and other factors. Hammerstein reluctantly closed the production in early January. Fields offered to continue on without pay, while the leads in the cast agreed to a salary cut. Negotiations led to the solution that the cast would self-produce the show, without Hammerstein's involvement. Fields was especially determined to fight for the show's survival, due mostly to the fact that he was dominant figure in the production. The book was even re-worked to present him, in Hammerstein's words, as "a specialty artist, and not a character."

The effort helped keep the show in production until the end of February, 1931.

1931

January 30 - Chaplin's *City Lights* premieres.

It was no secret at the dawn of the sound era that Chaplin, unlike most of his fellow silent film comedians, had been expressing considerable resistance to making sound films. He vowed to continue making silents at his own expense, even if it cost him millions of his own money. This attitude led to a bit of head-scratching among his peers.

Al Jolson, for one, wanted to see Chaplin enter the sound era. "If Charlie Chaplin doesn't make talkies, he won't make anything," he told a reporter. "The talkies are not spoiling the art of pantomime…in certain parts of a play you can be a pantomimist, and the same is true of talkies. Talking adds to the effectiveness of pantomime…"

"I think Chaplin's great," he continued. "Why not become greater by doing what the public wants him to do?...I think he'd better get to like [talkies] or he'll find out the public don't like him…His trouble is he has an inferiority complex on talkies, because he's been such a success as a pantomimist."

But Jolson was no doubt unaware of the extent of Chaplin's anguish behind his defiant façade. The silent comedian saw sound films as a threat to his very career. With talkies here to stay, he was finding it increasingly difficult to justify his non-talking films, even as he hoped they would survive the advent of sound. "I was determined to continue making silent films," he later wrote, "because I believed there was room for all types of entertainment. Besides, I was a pantomimist, and in that medium I was unique and, without false modesty, a master."

Seeing sound pictures changing the film business at such a rapid pace had him truly torn between the past and future of the industry. "Occasionally I mused over the possibility of making a sound film, but the thought sickened me, for I realized I could never achieve the excellence of my silent pictures. It would mean giving up my tramp character entirely. Some people suggested that the tramp might talk. This was unthinkable, for the first word he ever uttered would transform him into another person."

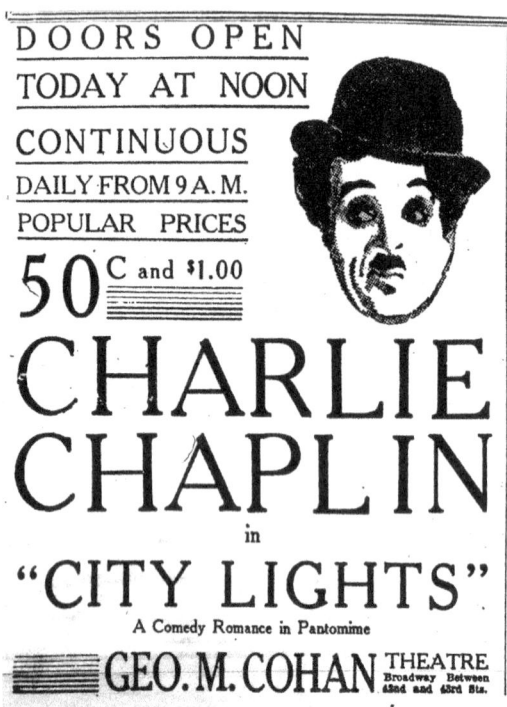

Print ad for *City Lights*. Author's collection.

1931

In *City Lights*, the Little Tramp befriends a blind girl as she sells flowers on the street. She mistakes him for a millionaire. Coincidentally, the tramp saves the life of a millionaire about to commit suicide, thus beginning a comical on-again, off-again friendship. While keeping the blind girl company during her illness, he reads about a possible cure for her blindness, and convinces the millionaire to pay for the necessary (and successful) operation.

Later, the tramp discovers the girl running her own flower shop. Upon seeing him outside the window, she doesn't realize who he is at first, but, seeing the state of him, hands him a flower out of kindness. She then recognizes the feel of his hand and clothes, and asks, "You?" to which he nods. The closing shot of his face, a mix of joy for her, and shame for himself, has deservedly become a classic.

The week leading up to the film's premiere, several of the top movie studio bosses (Adolf Zukor of Paramount, Harry Warner of Warner Bros., Nicholas Schenk of MGM, et. al.) were asked about Chaplin's somewhat daring decision to release a silent film in 1931. The question was put to them whether the expected success of *City Lights* might influence Hollywood's transition to sound, or spur any second thoughts regarding a place for silent films as the industry continued moving forward. To the man, each studio head expressed an admiration of Chaplin's visual comedy talents, with most of them calling him the greatest pantomimist of the past decade, but each also remained firm that *City Lights* was not going to influence or reverse the progression of movies away from their previous, mute existence.

After nearly two years of production, Chaplin released *City Lights* amid much praise from audiences and those in the movie business. Nonetheless, he was fighting a losing battle with progress.

June 6 - Thelma Todd and ZaSu Pitts star in *Let's Do Things*, for Hal Roach.

Todd was a ridiculously beautiful blue-eyed blonde from Lawrence, Massachusetts who, while training to become a schoolteacher, happened to win the Miss Massachusetts beauty pageant. Almost simultaneously, she was accepted to Paramount Studios' new school for aspiring actors in New York. According to Todd biographer Michelle Morgan, a friend of Todd's had actually applied to the studio's program on Thelma's behalf, being sure to include a number of flattering photos of her. She was accepted to the school *before* winning the Miss Massachusetts contest, contradicting the common version of the story that she used the victory to jump-start her acting career. Before long, she was playing various supporting roles in silent comedies (such as Ed Wynn's only silent film, *Rubber Heels*) and dramas (the original version of *The Maltese Falcon*), before Roach signed her to begin her comedy career in earnest.

Beginning in 1929, Roach, put Thelma in a number of shorts starring his biggest solo personality, Charley Chase, for his own series of sound comedies for the studio. Director Leo McCarey recalled, "I had so many ideas for gags that [Roach] gave me an actor named Charley Chase and he let me direct him. I was fortunate enough to draw a very clever fellow. He was a big help to me and I hope that I reciprocated to him. And our pictures were extremely successful."

Chase and Todd were essentially a team in all but official billing, and demonstrated terrific comedy chemistry. Many of the film plots were variations of Charley's attempts to win Thelma over, with complications or misunderstandings getting in the way. Among the best of these are *Looser than Loose*, and especially *The Pip from Pittsburgh*. In the latter, Charley tries to get out of a blind date, until he discovers it's the gorgeous Thelma. *Photoplay* said, "Two tried and true troupers, Charley Chase and Thelma Todd, manage to get a good deal of fun out of a slim script."

Just when it seemed that the two would soon be officially billed as equal co-stars, Roach decided he wanted to pair Thelma with another female, ZaSu Pitts, to create a female team as a counterpart to Laurel & Hardy, with Thelma playing as an energetic go-getter, and ZaSu as her accident-prone pal with a sullen face.

Roach had previously experimented with a female comedy duo when he paired Anita Garvin with Marion Byron (Garvin was nearly six feet tall, provided an amusing physical contrast to the petite Byron), and the two showed promise as a team, especially in the Roach silent short *A Pair of Tights*, a true silent comedy classic. Their teaming, unfortunately, lasted only for three shorts.

ZaSu Pitts (pronounced "Zay-Su," a combination of her aunts' names, Eliza and Susan) had made a name for herself primarily as a dramatic silent film actress, but it was her forays into comedy that began winning audiences over. In the mid-1920s, she became a favorite of director and German émigré Erich von Stroheim, who cast her in his 1924 silent film *Greed*, which was to become both his greatest achievement and greatest failure (its initial running time of nearly ten hours was whittled down to two, leaving the public with a mess of a heavily-edited version to see). Much to von Stroheim's chagrin, ZaSu's comedy roles had begun to overshadow her dramatic efforts. "The average person thinks she is funny looking," he lamented. "I think she is beautiful, more beautiful than the famous beauties of the screen, for I have seen in her eyes all the vital forces of the universe, and I have seen in her sensitive mouth all of the suppressions of humankind. I've seen her lifted to the heights of great acting." He then revealed his distaste for comedy when he added, "Art must weep when ZaSu Pitts plays a comedy role. She should not be in comedy for she is the greatest of all tragediennes."

While ZaSu's versatility as an actress enabled her to gain acceptance in both dramas and comedies, her dual talents ironically worked against her with her role as Frau Baumer in the 1930 film *All Quiet on the Western Front*. She played her role as mother of the lead character in an appropriately serious manner. However, during the film's first preview, her initial appearance onscreen prompted "loud and totally unwarranted guffaws from the audience…ZaSu hadn't done a single thing that even a master of ceremonies could call funny, but because she had been playing comedy rules for some time her mere appearance on the screen was the signal for loud mirth. The public knew that she was apt to do something funny at any moment and they weren't going to be caught without their laugh muscles limbered up."

Producer Carl Laemmle was so horrified by the reaction that he hastily had all of ZaSu's scenes re-shot with Beryl Mercer as her replacement. "So," warned *Photoplay*, "if you heard that ZaSu Pitts was in *All Quiet* don't be surprised if she looks like Beryl Mercer. It is Beryl Mercer and this is why."

Teamed with the vivacious, if somewhat bossy Thelma onscreen, ZaSu—with her sad eyes, put-upon demeanor, and gently fluttering hands as she spoke—provided a perfect contrast as the more cautious and socially awkward of the two. "I really don't know when I first began waving my hands," she told an interviewer. "I mean, I never noticed it was funny until an audience laughed at it. My hands have always waved around—sort of without me, if you know what I mean. And that 'oh dear…' The first time I said that was in my first talkie, *The Dummy*, and I've been saying it ever since. Sometimes I swear I'll never say it again. I'm so tired of me on the screen. I started out to be a tragedienne. But my hands and voice and my face were too much to work against."

ZaSu and Thelma sharing a bed (a la Laurel & Hardy) in *Let's Do Things*. Author's collection.

Roach was so enthusiastic about the new team that he directed *Let's Do Things* himself, as he did for other top-notch entries in their series, *Pajama*

Party and *On the Loose*, until his duties as studio chief prompted him to leave the directing to others. *Variety* noted that *Pajama Party* is an "old fashioned two-reeler idea, but with the sex angle reversed. Two women do the comedy and take the falls...a first rate team with all the requirements. [They] could continue indefinitely as a combination for two reelers. They make the old gags sound slightly different."

The team would make 17 two-reelers together (like Laurel & Hardy and most of Roach's all-stars, the two used their real names in their films, a charming custom which no doubt created a greater personal connection with audiences). Many of the scenarios involve ZaSu getting pulled into Thelma's plans without time to object.

The series as a whole also benefitted from ever-reliable Roach supporting players such as Billy Gilbert, Charlie Hall, and the wonderful Garvin (whose hilarious performance in the short *Show Business* very nearly steals the film right out from under Thelma and ZaSu).

The Todd/Pitts shorts, however, do not boast the impressive consistency and clever gags found in nearly every Laurel & Hardy release. This was mostly because the girls' films went through a series of directors, and did not enjoy the advantage of having a genius like Stan as a full-time gag man/director/editor. Still, the films are highly enjoyable, and the novelty of having a female comedy team with such a high profile in the business didn't hurt matters.

Thanks to a generous contract allowing Thelma to appear in films other than those for Roach, she kept busy with a number of high-profile appearances at the time. She served as the object of desire for the Marx Brothers in both *Monkey Business* and *Horsefeathers* Whereas the team's other female foil, Margaret Dumont, was called to play the somewhat stuffy, often bewildered dowager role for the brothers, Thelma fit in nicely with the team, while also providing some much-appreciated sex appeal.

She also appeared in still more Laurel & Hardy shorts throughout the early 1930s (*Another Fine Mess, Chickens Come Home*) and shared memorable scenes with Buster Keaton in his 1932 feature *Speak Easily*, for which he was reluctantly partnered with Jimmy Durante. Thelma also shines in a silly but wonderful dance routine with Wheeler & Woolsey and Dorothy Lee in *Hips Hips Hooray* (1934).

Patsy Kelly takes over for ZaSu. Author's collection.

ZaSu Pitts left Roach studios in mid-1933, when negotiations to renew her contract broke down. She went elsewhere to pursue both comic and dramatic roles, but regretted leaving her close friend Thelma. Roach replaced Pitts with Patsy Kelly, a Brooklyn native who provided a brash, wisecracking New York character to the series. Patsy later confessed to being somewhat unprepared for all of the slapstick she would be expected to perform on camera. However, as a sharp contrast to ZaSu's meek, awkward screen character, Patsy proved to be another good fit for Thelma. The two would continue the series with twenty-one shorts together.

September 13 - Eddie Cantor debuts as host of the *Chase & Sanborn Hour*.

Cantor's popularity had been steadily rising with his stage work in vaudeville, as a *Ziegfeld Follies* regular, in the Broadway musicals *Kid Boots* and *Whoopie!*, and in film hits, both silent and talkies. He was nothing if not versatile, being comfortable with comedy, and as a song & dance man, but was known first and foremost for his boundless energy. He could rarely sit still—or stand still—in front of a radio microphone, and punctuated his words with a multitude of facial expressions, highlighted by his bulging eyes and big smile.

He had been a guest in February on *The Fleishmann Hour*, hosted by singer Rudy Vallee, who often used the show as a springboard for up & coming entertainers, as well as stage veterans who had yet to experience performing on radio. It seemed as if everyone who would soon become a radio star got their first exposure via Vallee: Joe Penner, Olsen & Johnson, Burns & Allen, Edgar Bergen, and many more. *Radio Dig*est would write of Vallee, "He has stepped over to Broadway and brought in any number of shining names from the marquees of the Great White Way. Dramatists, singers, comedians, have all helped to make his program highly entertaining; and Rudy himself with his inimitable radio voice gives the flavor to the cake."

Eddie Cantor. Courtesy of Martin Grams.

Cantor's popularity as a guest on the show led to his own program later in the year.

Even with his established credentials in show business, Cantor was not without his critics, especially among his fellow comedians. True, he was versatile, but as George Burns put it, "There was no continuity to Eddie's character. In his first joke, he'd claim to be so cheap that when he lost a one-dollar bill he tried to have George Washington declared a missing person; in his next joke, he was so generous that when he got mad a somebody, instead of giving them a piece of his mind he gave them the whole thing. Whatever Eddie did, it worked. For almost three years he had the highest-rated show on radio."

As it was in vaudeville, his on-air performance was one of constant movement. His detractors sneered that he naively equated perpetual motion with giving a true comedy performance. Ed Wynn referred to him as "a man with no talent whose idea of entertainment is rolling his eyes and moving his hands in circles." Others, like Fred Allen, were just as disapproving, pointing out how Cantor "wore funny costumes, pummeled his announcer with his fist and frequently kicked his guest star to obtain results."

Milton Berle also concurred, offering a sober assessment of Cantor's almost desperate efforts to keep the laughs coming at any cost: "Eddie Cantor had to fight for his laughs. Unlike some comedians who are ready to garner laughter a minute after birth, Cantor wasn't born a funnyman…He had a desire to be funny, the urge to provoke laughter. The equipment was missing. He wished himself into comedy. Many comedians need writers, but Cantor NEEDED writers." Natural ability or not, Cantor's manic performances burned into the memories of those who simply couldn't take their eyes off him, even when he was supposed to remain stationary behind the microphone stand.

Chico Marx's evaluation of Cantor was more succinct: "Eddie's a great performer. He's not really a funny man, but he's a great performer." Future comedian Jerry Stiller, who, as a child, once sat in the audience of Cantor's show, could attest to Chico's backhanded compliment, with this description of how a Cantor broadcast proceeded once the star bounded onto the stage:

"His energy, his bulging eyes, his jet-black hair seemed to burst out of his body...Cantor started to sing. His body seemed to surge as if it had been hit by an electric current. His feet and hands were moving vertically and horizontally like piston rods. He looked like a puppet that had been given life and wanted us all to wonder at it...To call it a radio show was a misnomer. When Eddie came to a joke he'd roll his eyes, which meant for us to laugh. He nodded his head when a joke didn't go over, which meant laugh anyway. When the show ended, Eddie seemed exhausted, but he performed a few encores. He gave us a great show, a great evening."

As star of *The Chase and Sanborn Hour*, Cantor was the first radio comedian not only to perform in front of a live audience on a regular basis, but the first to encourage the audience to respond audibly while the show was on the air. As we mentioned earlier, studio audiences to that point were invited to view some radio broadcasts in person, but were instructed to remain silent for the duration of the programs, and to even suppress their laughter during comedy segments. Performers would stand on a stage facing the audience but with a thick sheet of glass, or "glass curtain," hanging between them. The logic behind this practice remains elusive, but broadcasters at the time apparently felt the distracting sound of audience laughter during a broadcast would confuse, even unnerve, those listening at home.

Cantor reasoned that listeners sitting at home would feel more involved in the proceedings if they heard the studio audience laughter, and thus would feel more inclined to laugh along while listening to the show. Others agreed.

"Keeping an audience under glass was one thing," George Burns explained, "but asking them not to react made working in front of them really tough. We would do great material and these people would sit there smiling loudly."

Cantor's encouragement of audience responses on the air didn't occur immediately. During his inaugural 1931 season, he lived with the glass curtain just like every other radio performer. Before each broadcast, an announcement from the J. Walter Thompson ad agency (which handled Chase and Sanborn) was read to the studio audience, requesting them to remain quiet.

During one broadcast, however, Cantor and announcer Jimmy Wallington acted a skit about two women truck drivers. Suddenly, Cantor succumbed to a spontaneous urge and ran down to his wife Ida and Wallington's wife seated in the front row, and grabbed their hats and fur scarves. He and Wallington wore them for the remainder of the skit. "The audience is howling," he recalled in his memoirs, "and there's no stopping them as we two clowns mince around in our finery. They keep on laughing until the show is over." Immediately after the show, a representative from J. Walter Thompson called the wary Cantor, who was expecting a stern reprimand, and surprised him with praise for enlivening the show with the audience's participation.

A dilemma arose among comedians like Cantor, who, as new radio stars, were still accustomed to including visual, kinetic gags in their stage performances. They hadn't considered how these would play on radio. While some comedians may have begun making an effort to help home listeners feel more a part of the laugh fest, they were often just as guilty of shutting them out by including visual gags that catered to the live audience in attendance. The antics for the benefit of their theatre-goers were obviously lost on the millions at home who had no use for funny faces and slapstick on a radio show. Consequently, the practice of throwing in visual bits of business created the risk of alienating radio listeners at home, who would often hear laughter without hearing any joke preceding it, such as during that first frenzied bit as Cantor snatched the hats and scarves.

Some comedians wore costumes, mugged for the studio audience, and insisted on including sight gags to keep the patrons sitting in front of them laughing along, thus eliminating the possibilities of dead air. As true vaudevillians, they needed to hear the laughter—not just for its spiritual uplift, but for its more earthly purpose of helping them with their timing. This in itself was a reasonable argument for allowing audience laughter on the air, but it became an annoyance to many, who wrote to magazines and newspapers complaining about the practice.

It took some time before the message sank in. In some cases, it took several years to fully adapt (when Ed Wynn was about to begin his program *Gulliver the Traveler* in early 1937, he announced, as part of a New Year's resolution, "I promise to remember I am performing for my listeners, not my studio audience.").

George Burns, despite his quibbling about Cantor's lack of a specific comedic approach, was indebted to Cantor for giving the Burns & Allen team their first big break on radio. After working with them for two months at the Palace, Cantor asked Gracie to appear on his show. "We agreed," Burns recalled, "as long as he let me write her material. The bit I wrote was a combination of old and new stuff, like everybody else on radio. I just rewrote part of our stage act; then I added some new material about the one thing everybody on radio liked to talk about—being on radio…"

After Gracie's appearance, she and George were asked to make a number of appearances on Rudy Vallee's show. "We were a bit hit. And when we left the studio that day there was only one thing bothering me: we had about another two hours' worth of tested material left, and somehow I had to figure out how to stretch it out over about twenty years."

September 19 - Marx Bros. release *Monkey Business*.

The Marx Brothers began 1931 performing as headliners overseas, in London's Palace Theatre, as part of *Cochran's 1931 Varieties*. Afterwards, and with their movie career kicking into high gear, they all settled in Los Angeles. The last few official days of that summer brought a dash of joy for their fans, with the release of the brothers' first film *not* adapted from a stage show.

The bulk of *Monkey Business*, co-written by the brilliant humorist S.J. Perelman, with Will Johnstone and Arthur Sheekman, takes place on an ocean liner, with the brothers as stowaways. They get mixed up with gangsters, as Groucho woos the gang leader's girlfriend (Thelma Todd). Many experts agree that, of all the Marx Brothers films, *Monkey Business* comes closest to being virtually plotless, giving it even more of a free-wheeling feel than their other efforts.

As Groucho's Depression-era crack in *Monkey Business* reminds us, "the stockholder of yesterday is the stowaway of today." Author's collection.

Highlights include Chico confounding Groucho in a pun-filled exchange involving geography, history, sailing, and Chico's unlikely ancestry. Harpo's diversions while on the run from the ship's steward include crashing a Punch & Judy show. With considerable grace, speed, and hilarity, he commandeers the show as he joins the cast of puppets, perfectly blending in, right under the steward's nose. Rarely has Harpo looked more in his element than while delighting a happily shrieking group of children with his interactions among his co-stars of the puppet show.

Groucho and Thelma Todd enjoy some flirting and a hearty rumba in her stateroom, and, later, all four Marxes attempt to leave the ship by imitating singer Maurice Chevalier singing "You Brought a New Kind of Love to Me" (Harpo's imitation is especially ingenious, as he lip synchs to Chevalier's version, playing on a small phonograph strapped to his back). There is also the inevitable high society party scene, complete with Groucho tossing off a fistful of one-liners, as well as musical numbers from Harpo and Chico.

November 2 - Ed Wynn's *The Laugh Parade* opens.

During a fairly traumatic tour of out-of-town rehearsals for his latest show, during which the laughs simply weren't coming from audiences, Wynn worked night and day on the material. Word got back to New York that *The Laugh Parade* was in trouble. Wynn even had to buy up remaining unsold tickets for opening night to ensure a full house. Much to his relief, though, the reviews from both the public and critics were immensely favorable. *Time* magazine said, "*The Laugh Parade* goes on its merry way without benefit of libretto or commonsense. At one point particularly does Mr. Wynn...rise to appreciable heights. This is when he imitates a juggler of the Tony Pastor era, complete with silk tights and handlebar mustache. For incidental music he requests the orchestra to play '"something in a jugular vein.'"

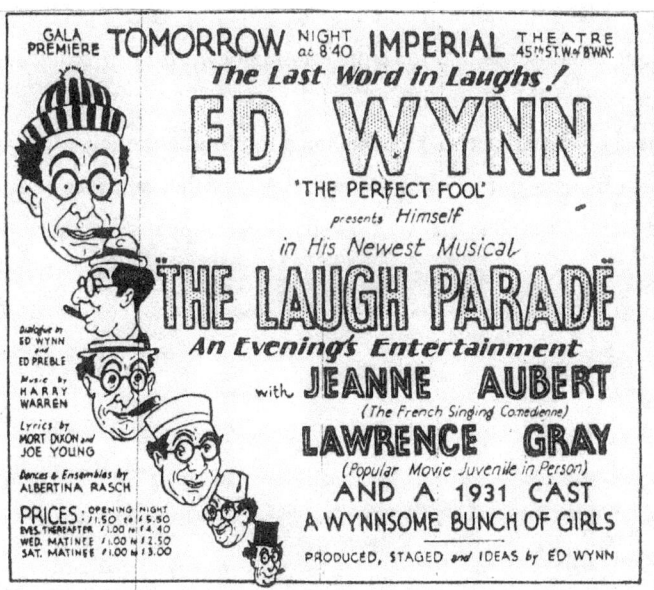

Print ad for *The Laugh Parade*. Author's collection.

Reviewing the show for *The New York Times*, Brooks Atkinson wrote of Wynn:

> "To me Wynn is immune from the law of diminishing returns. Although he is a formula comedian, he has a stage personality of such warmth and disarming simplicity that the repetition of lines, giggles, grimaces, costumes and crack-brained inventions seems hardly to matter at all…The foolish grin, the flabby chin, the arched eyebrows, the solemn spectacles, the witless flutter of hands—well, everyone knows them. It all makes a fantastic invention in the sphere of things that are silly."

Finally, critic John Mason Brown paid Wynn perhaps the ultimate compliment for any comedian. "While he is at work," Brown wrote, "Mr. Wynn succeeds—as almost no other major comic in our theatre succeeds—in wiping out all recollections of the everyday world outside the theatre and in making the laughter of the moment seem more important than life itself. He is the king of nonsense, and the emperor of idiocy…*The Laugh Parade* is well-nigh the perfect Ed Wynn show."

The show would become Wynn's longest-running production at a total of 231 performances, but he would soon find yet another new avenue opened to him during the run, one that would make him a truly national star.

1932

January 23 - Laurel & Hardy star in *Helpmates*.

This hilarious short further exemplifies how the team had not only made a virtually seamless transition to sound, but also how the comic creativity of their films at this time continued to run at a consistently high level.

In *Helpmates*, we first find Ollie sadly chastising himself in front of a mirror for throwing a wild party while his wife is away. After she phones to scold him for making her wait at the train station, he panics at the sight of the messy house, and calls Stan to ask his help in cleaning up. The rest of the film consists of the boys attempting to restore the house to order, only to create one mini-disaster after another. The gags come at a continuous pace, with little dialogue to intrude. When their tempers grow short, Stan and Ollie engage in some delightfully askew verbal combat.

> Stan: You know, if I had any sense, I'd walk out on you.
> Ollie: Well it's a good thing you *haven't* any sense!
> Stan: It certainly is!

Stan later puts the finishing touches on the house as Ollie leaves to pick up his wife. When he returns home (somber, with a black eye, and without the wife), and finds Stan amid the smoldering ashes of the house, he calmly resigns himself to his misfortunes.

Roach director Charley Rogers recalled the working methods of Laurel, Hardy, and Roach.

> "They were quite a bit alike, Babe and Hal. Stan was totally different from either of them. And yet there was a curious amalgam formed by the three of them that was pure gold coin. Roach had a terrific ability to spot talent. He knew what a good gag was but he usually let someone else work it out. He'd get an idea, talk it over with us, and then when it came to actually putting the gag on film, he'd say, 'That's the idea, boys. Work it out. Know what I mean?' Then he'd walk away and too many times we didn't know what he meant—not that that ever stopped us."

Typically, once a day's shooting on the Roach lot was over, Ollie would make a quick getaway to the golf course, while Stan would remain at the studio and work with his gagmen to create the brilliant visual gags that set L&H comedies apart from all others. Stan also closely supervised the editing, often working well into the night, making sure the timing of each gag was just right in the final print. He personified the film comedian who lived comedy twenty-four hours a day, and was in fact compensated by receiving twice the salary as his partner. Ollie had no qualms with that.

Agreeing with others on the Roach lot who remembered Ollie as a performer rather than creator, Rogers said, "He was good-natured, but by temperament somewhat easygoing. He was an artist to his fingertips once he got going, though. And when the shooting was over, back to the golf club. I don't know what would have happened to the Laurel and Hardy films if it hadn't been for Stan. He was the one who usually took an idea that Roach would have and bring it to life."

1932

Destitute Stan and Ollie, "victims of the Depression," find a wallet in *One Good Turn* (1931). Author's collection.

Roach's creative input occasionally came at inopportune times, such as while a scene was already being shot. He'd arrive and begin changing things around. Laurel & Hardy biographer John McCabe suggested that "perhaps in those days, the word used was not 'interfering' but 'collaborating.' It was a pleasant way of making a living. There was no regular schedule in the fullest sense of the word. An idea would be taken up and discussed without the fear that it had to be finished by a certain date. All hands joined in to create a fully and powerful comedy, and good ideas were welcome."

Even with sound, the emphasis for Roach and his creative employees was on visual comedy. The gagmen would search for ideas and dream up gags while sitting in on story conferences led by Stan and the director. Ollie rarely attended, trusting Stan and the team to whip up a workable story for the team.

As Leo McCarey, who directed seven silent films with the team, recalled,

"It's amazing how much thought went into what on the surface looked like low-down stupidity...Laurel was one of those rare comics intelligent enough to invent his own gags. He was remarkably talented. Hardy wasn't. That was the key to the Laurel-Hardy association."

McCarey's assessment of Ollie's talents seems a bit harsh, although he was careful to emphasize, that the pay disparity between Stan and Ollie was not because Stan thought he was twice as funny as Ollie, "but because he was doing twice as much work as Babe, and Babe agreed with him. When the end of the shooting day came for Babe, he'd be out on the golf course, but Stan would be starting almost another full day of working on gags and story with me or helping cut the picture."

Stan and Ollie, in their heyday. Author's collection.

In Ollie's defense, his superb talents as a performer are not to be underestimated. "I like to get a good reaction just the way any comedian does," he said, "but I have never really worked hard in the creation department. After all, just *doing* the gags is hard enough work, especially if you've taken as many falls and been dumped in as many mud holes as I have. I think I've earned my money."

Ollie is also commonly credited as being the first film comedian to break the "fourth wall" of film, i.e. reacting directly to the camera/audience in an exasperated response to a ridiculous comment, or act of clumsiness by Stan.

Ollie's greatest fan was probably Stan himself, who, while editing their films, usually found himself captivated and hugely entertained by his partner's performances.

Patsy Kelly admired the team from both a personal and professional perspective:

"…In addition to being two of the funniest men who ever lived, they were the kindliest. Not to like Laurel and Hardy you would have to be very much nuts, because they were absolutely wonderful, both off and on the screen. Stan was an absolute genius. How they helped Thelma Todd and me when we were making our pictures! They would come on the set, tear up our indifferent scripts, and give us all sorts of practical suggestions—do this, do that—and the results were wonderful. Everybody on the lot loved those two great, great men."

Stan and Ollie had gained the admiration and respect of their fellow comedians as well. When Ed Wynn was at MGM to film *The Chief*, he walked into the studio commissary one day and spotted the team. "One of them jumped up and said, 'Here's the master,'" Wynn recalled. "I looked at him as thought he was nuts because I thought *they* were the greatest."

Roach Studios, as a comedy factory, was churning out an impressively high volume of superior comedy in the early 1930s, although the Depression did inflict financial woes for some time. Despite tightening budgets, the comedians, writers, directors, and crew were there very much for their love of comedy, not just for their paychecks.

As Roach himself said in 1934:

"We all know it is easier to make an audience cry than laugh. So our players must have the instinctive comedy flair, must know all the tricks of bringing out the full humor of every word and situation. A comedy studio is the best place for beginners. Stage experience is not so necessary if the ability to do things and say things in an amusing manner is ever on tap. If I were starting in for a film career today, I'd go for comedy. It is the best training you can get for any kind of screen work."

Print ad for Sennett's comedies at Educational Studios. Author's collection.

Roach Studios, however, was not the only game in town for producing comedy, it was just the best.

Another independent studio that had been producing low budget shorts, starring familiar names, was the curiously-named Educational Pictures.

Actually, the name was perfectly appropriate for the type of films the studio originally produced. Founded in 1916 by Earle Hammons, the studio specialized in educational films for schools, travelogues, and other novelty shorts. Comedies, however, including those starring Mack Sennett stars such as Al St. John, Lloyd Hamilton, and Andy Clyde, proved to be more lucrative.

The studio joined the transition to sound films along with the rest of Hollywood, but initially used an inferior recording system, somewhat hampering its ability to keep up with the competition. Sennett released his first talkies at Educational, but he left by 1932, following Hamilton and others. A number of comedy stars came and went at Educational throughout the decade, including Harry Langdon, Buster Keaton (when each was on the downward slope of his top-tier stardom), the Ritz Brothers, Bert Lahr, Bob Hope, and many others.

Educational had its films distributed by Twentieth Century Fox, which cut off financing for short comedies in 1937, forcing Educational to search for a new companion company. Further financial difficulties led to bankruptcy and ultimately closing-up shop in 1939.

Most of the major studios produced their own short subjects throughout the decade, even as they served to distribute for smaller, independent companies. The 1930s saw the Big Seven studios (MGM, Paramount, Columbia, Warner Brothers, Universal, Fox, RKO) sign new comedians, as well as "refugee" veterans from the silent era, to star in two-reel shorts. The results were mixed.

Columbia Pictures, for instance, opened its short subject division in 1933. Some silent film comedian's from Mack Sennett's former roster sought refuge from obscurity at Columbia. The longest-running, and most popular series to come out of the studio starred The Three Stooges, beginning in 1934 (more on that later). The *Blondie* series, based on the comic strip and starring Penny

Singleton and Arthur Lake as Blondie and Dagwood Bumstead, began production at Columbia in 1938, and would produce a total of twenty-eight features starring the duo.

RKO also produced a good share of quality comedy films throughout the Golden Decade, taking on Wheeler & Woolsey for their two dozen features, as well as Clark & McCullough, who signed with the studio in 1930, and starred in twenty shorts, until McCullough's death in 1935.

RKO also brought on Edgar Kennedy in 1931, after he had made his mark at Roach Studios as a perfect foil for Laurel & Hardy, Our Gang, and other Roach series. At RKO, he began a seventeen-year run starring in six two-reelers a year, starring in The Average Man series, which provided a perfect outlet for his perpetually frustrated character and "slow burn" reaction to anything that interrupted his attempts to enjoy some peace and quiet at home. Kennedy biographer Bill Cassara astutely points out that The Average Man series, with its continuing characters from one twenty-minute installment to the next, was, in effect, the first talkie situation comedy series for film, and forerunner to sitcoms that were to become a staple of network television.

Edgar Kennedy, in his familiar role as the cop on the beat, chats with Stan and Ollie in *Night Owls* (1930). Author's collection.

Australian stage comedian Leon Errol, who once spent five celebrated years in the *Ziegfeld Follies*, joined RKO in 1934, and, like Kennedy, embarked on a nearly two-decade run of two-reelers (ending with his death in 1951).

MGM, notorious among comedy film historians for having been almost totally inept at producing quality comedy, especially with established practitioners of the art, nonetheless did offer a number of series from the likes of humorist Robert Benchley, who made his popular "how-to" style shorts on an irregular basis.

* * *

One of Mack Sennett's brightest former stars, the struggling Roscoe Arbuckle, finally took a major step toward redemption (not that he needed it as an innocent man) in February of 1932, when movie mogul Jack Warner contacted him to offer a deal, in which the comedian would appear in a new series of six Vitaphone two-reelers, to be distributed by Warner Brothers. Arbuckle would star, but not direct. That task was given to his old friend from the Sennett days, Alf Goulding. Considering Arbuckle's struggles to re-enter the movie business—including his slogging through his work as a scenario writer, and directing only if he used a pseudonym to mask his identity—Warner's offer came as a stunning surprise. Arbuckle was elated at the chance to work in front of the cameras again.

He knew better than to jump back onscreen expecting audiences to quickly return the love they had bestowed upon him in his heyday. Taking a more cautious approach, he took to the vaudeville stage, performing sketches, sometimes with a stooge as a foil, just to measure how the public would even tolerate his presence again. *Variety* caught up with his stage act at the Pantages in Hollywood:

> "Roscoe 'Fatty' Arbuckle is again hesitantly testing the duration of his ostracization…If this and other personal appearances, including a week as guest star

with the Moore theatre stock company in Seattle, it is found that agitation against him has subsided, he probably will be given a chance in features by one of several studios which are interested."

The review advised Arbuckle to play it extra safe in choosing his material, to ward off even the faintest possibility of offending someone, somewhere, as his tour continued.

A rather poignant ad for Arbuckle's return, performing his stage act at the Palace. Author's collection.

"Because of the many eagle eyes which will be fastened on Arbuckle it is best that he eliminate such targets for war-whoops as the cross-fire bit with the stooge about Pharaoh's daughter finding Moses in the bulrushes. For most of the cross-fire is fresh and clean."

As he attempted to gain a modest foothold as a film comedian once again, Arbuckle's dear friend Buster Keaton also found himself struggling with his own career, but under far different circumstances.

1932

February 6 - The first Keaton-Durante film, *The Passionate Plumber*, is released.

Since MGM held such little regard for Keaton's happiness, or his creative satisfaction with his work for the studio, the powers-that-be decided to team him with Jimmy Durante, who, of course, had already cemented his reputation as an energetic, talkative, if not especially well-heeled performer.

Durante was born in New York City, and grew up with little formal education (his endearing mispronunciations weren't always just an act). As a teen, his early, rag-tag career consisted mostly of playing piano in Bowery and Coney Island saloons and cabarets, where he earned the nickname "Ragtime Jimmy." Upon moving up the ranks to nightclubs, he at one time played for singing waiter Eddie Cantor.

Durante's likeable and energetic demeanor later made him a favorite in Harlem, playing venues such as Club Alamo and The Nightingale. His sense of humor, developed in part by reading his collection of magazines and other publications pertaining to comedy, helped spread the word among New York celebrities about his after-hours antics.

His surge to the big-time came upon forming a music-comedy trio with Eddie Jackson and Lou Clayton (as mentioned earlier, the three often played the Palace to raucous responses).

Durante's career was on the rise when he signed with MGM, just as Keaton's career had begun its decline. Not only had the studio robbed Keaton of control over his own material, but teaming him with Durante seemed a mis-fire from the start. "…As I see it," Keaton wrote, "there was no way to mesh, match, or blend Durante's talents with mine. Yet Jimmy would have been great in the pictures we did together if he had been allowed merely to do spots of comedy instead of playing a character all of the way through…"

The Passionate Plumber, based on the French stage play *Her Cardboard Lover*, takes place in Paris, with Jimmy as the chauffer for a wealthy young American woman, Patricia Alden (Irene Purcell). He's sent to hire Buster, a plumber by day and inventor by night, who would like to sell his new invention—a pistol with a spotlight attached to the barrel—to the army. Patricia only needs a bathtub pipe repaired, but Buster's house call leads him to become involved in her social life—specifically, her complicated love affair with a two-timing gigolo.

Keaton pointed out the basic clash of approach with Durante to working in films: Keaton was ever the perfectionist, carefully considering his onscreen character's traits and overall quiet affect, whereas Durante pretty much relied on the sheer force of his gregarious personality to produce laughs. "When you give me a Jimmy Durante, [he] can't not keep quiet," Keaton said. "He's gonna talk no matter what…and you can't direct him any other way."

The film is uneven to say the least, but Buster is given several moments to shine. Irene Purcell provides a good deal of the energy to the proceedings, and Jimmy is, well, Jimmy.

"Buster Keaton is leaning over backwards to give Jimmy Durante the breaks in *Her Cardboard Lover*," Cal York wrote in *Photoplay*. "So they can't say Buster is jealous of another comedian."

Indeed, he worked quite well with fellow comedian Cliff Edwards in *The Sidewalks of New York* (despite Keaton's personal disdain for the film itself), and it would have been interesting to see them paired again. However, with *The Passionate Plumber*'s success at the box office encouraged MGM to continue Keaton's partnership with Durante. Keaton would only grow unhappier. And it didn't help that he was going through a divorce and a deepening drinking problem at the time.

February 15 - Burns & Allen begin as regulars on *The Guy Lombardo Show*.

The year 1932 became a break-out year for comedy on radio, beginning with Burns & Allen, who received a good deal of attention and gained new fans by the week, with the team's increasingly frequent appearances on Lombardo's show. The sponsor, General Cigar Company, eventually offered George and Gracie a weekly featured role for the program's third season (two

1932

years later, with Lombardo moving to NBC, the team took over the CBS time slot in the re-named *The Adventures of Gracie).*

"Radio was made for performers who talked or sang," Burns explained. "It didn't matter what you looked like, or how you dressed—there was no costume budget in radio—only what your voice sounded like. Radio allowed performers to create any fantasy they wanted to."

Burns devised a deliberate method for producing scripts for the show. He and/or one of his writers would start with a basic idea, after which writers Al Boasberg and Eugene Conrad would each write a separate script. Upon receiving the two divergent scripts stemming from the original concept, Burns would choose the best passages from each, and dovetail them into one final script. A few years into the program's run, with the writing team comprised of Conrad, John Medbury, and Harvey Helm, Burns described his system: "The three script writers never see each other," he explained. "They are in keen competition, and I am told they always listen to the program to keep score on their own gags. This combination gives us three ideas instead of one to build on. Gracie never sees the script until the day of the broadcast." However, throughout two rehearsal sessions, she was invited to contribute phrases that would emphasize the dizzy nature of her on-air character.

During the program's early going, the creative team hit upon what they considered a typically kooky idea for Gracie. "We got this idea of Gracie's brother being missing," George explained, "and we thought we'd go on a few CBS programs and ask whether anyone had seen Gracie's brother. Until then, if you had your own show, you didn't make guest appearances on anyone else's. We were the first to do it. Eventually, the thing caught fire and we went on all the shows. Like, the phone would ring on some dramatic radio show about, say a submarine and Gracie would say, 'Is my missing brother down there?' We went right to the top of the ratings."

Alas, the running gag had unexpected repercussions.

A reporter discovered that Gracie had a real brother, George Allen, living in San Francisco, and working for the Standard Oil Company. As *Radio Digest* dramatically reported, "Like a pack of wolves, newspaper men descended upon George Allen, pulled the curtains of privacy from his quietly peaceful life. Photographers followed him wherever he went, recording—insanely, George Allen thought—every move he made." If they were expecting George to be anything like the nutty persona his sister had created for the public, they were sorely mistaken.

Gracie's convoluted descriptions of her fictional relatives had become the center of many Burns & Allen routines, but she had no idea that using her real brother's name in fictional settings would create such an uproar. While the 'search' was at its height, George Allen was besieged by vaudeville managers, offering stage contracts to the man who paled at the thought of facing an audience (just what his "act" would have been we can only conjecture). He was pointed out in public places, and made the butt of jokes. He sought escape from the press and the public however he could. He considered legally changing his name to Brown, and even took four weeks off work to escape the madness. Eventually, to spare the man's very sanity, the running gag was brought to a close.

March 1 - *Easy Aces* debuts on CBS radio.

Goodman and Jane Ace first went on the air in 1930 in a local 15-minute program. Goodman, a film critic for the *Journal Post* in Kansas City, began his career on the air reviewing films on his Friday evening slot, and reading comic strips to kids on Sunday mornings. The Aces' first broadcast was put together at the last minute, when the cast of the program to follow had not arrived at the studio in time. Goodman and Jane ad-libbed their conversation about their regular bridge game. They were an unlikely hit, and were given their own program, which Goodman fashioned into a domestic comedy of give-and-take between the spouses.

The tall, bespectacled, moustached Goodman wrote and directed each script, winning the praise of his fellow comedy professionals in doing so, but he created petite blonde Jane's on-air character to be the center of laughs, imbuing her with a vocabulary littered with malaprops and twists on the language, endearing her to listeners. A few gems heard coming from her mouth included "time wounds all heels," "I'm no shrieking violet," "He lives by the sweat of his frau," and "It's the gossip truth." They rehearsed each episode only once before broadcast, to retain spontaneity.

After a full decade on the air, the Aces remained popular without having made headlines or living a flashy lifestyle. They prided themselves for their very ordinariness. "They are never seen in night clubs," it was reported, "in fact, [they] have a passion for being anonymous. Goodman's list of 'nevers' of which he is quite proud, includes: Never have been stopped for an autograph, never have had a script returned for changes, never have won a radio popularity poll." Each year, on the anniversary of the program's debut, the Aces would publish an ad in a trade paper spoofing their modest showing in listener polls.

April 16 - Laurel & Hardy's *The Music Box* is released.

A true comedy masterpiece, borrowed in large part from their 1927 silent short *Hats Off*, devotes virtually two-thirds of the entire 30-minute film to Stan and Ollie, as piano movers, attempting to haul a piano in its crate up a dizzying outdoor flight of concrete steps. They encounter several obstacles, both human and otherwise (including a temperamental Billy Gilbert, complete with phony German accent), as they make their ascent. They even reach the top twice, only to end up with the battered piano back at the foot of the hill—once with Ollie still desperately clinging onto the crate.

The slapstick continues when they finally reach the summit for good and attempt to get the piano in the house. Once that's accomplished, they proceed to remove the piano from its crate (but not without causing considerable damage to the home). When homeowner Gilbert arrives and sees the piano, he flies into a rage. He *detests* pianos, he screams, and immediately begins to destroy it with an axe. His wife arrives to explain it was meant to be a birthday present for him. Gilbert apologizes and all is forgiven, until Stan and Ollie have him sign for the delivery. The fountain pen squirts ink in his face, reigniting his temper as he chases the duo out of the house.

Film Daily reported, "Getting the piano into the house creates more confusion and hilarity. It is up to the Laurel-Hardy standard, and should score easily."

At the time, most shorts, or two-reelers, ran about twenty minutes. A feature was commonly considered to be four reels or more. *The Music Box* seemed to take some audiences and critics by surprise with the more unusual three-reel length. *Motion Picture Herald* said of the film, "The combination of more than a little slapstick, as the pair know how to handle that comedic form, and numerous amusing lines well-spaced and well rendered, aid in making this an exceptionally amusing comedy…Unusually long for a comedy, it is worth the extra length."

Hollywood Citizen News offered, "A hilarious Laurel & Hardy comedy is the hit of the screen. In *The Music Box*, these two comic undergo the trials and tribulations of piano movers and you can readily imagine the slapstick antics they perform."

The film won the Academy Award for Best Comedy Short Subject. It would be the only Oscar the team would win (although Stan did receive an honorary Lifetime Achievement award in 1961). *The Music Box* was also added to the National Film Registry in 1997.

April 26 - Ed Wynn premieres as Texaco's Fire Chief.

The spring of 1932 continued to smile upon a number vaudeville pros beginning their rookie season on radio. By the end of the year, still more comedians would see their new-found radio careers launch them into stardom.

Wynn, a comedy stage star throughout the previous decade, enjoyed his greatest success to date with *The Laugh Parade,* just as Texaco was looking for a host for a new program to sponsor. The company's chief ad executive, George W. Vos, decided to experience *The Laugh Parade* by facing away from the stage, so he could assess Wynn solely by hearing him, to determine just how funny he could be on radio. Vos concluded that Wynn was funny even without his costumes, props, and sly facial expressions. Texaco then sent a man to visit Wynn, asking why the comedian hadn't gone into radio yet. Wynn wasn't any more interested in the inquiry than he was in many previous pleas to host his own radio program.

"You couldn't pay me enough money to go on the radio," he said, hoping that would kill the discussion.

"Money is no object," was the reply. "How much would you want?"

The question stumped Wynn for a moment. "I mentioned a price I considered prohibitive. I never thought anyone would pay me $5,000 for a single broadcast. I don't believe any one is worth that much. Imagine my embarrassment when he said that amount would be quite satisfactory."

He insisted, however, that he perform the show in make-up and costume, and in front of a live audience that was permitted to laugh out loud during the broadcast, putting another chink in the glass curtain, which would soon disappear from radio comedy programs. NBC also agreed that the program would be performed and aired from the New Amsterdam Theatre's new 675-seat rooftop venue, (which later became the NBC Times Square studio).

Wynn and McNamee perform a *Fire Chief* broadcast. Author's collection.

Even with his demands met, the anxious Wynn wasn't so sure how his radio listeners across the country might react to his new venture. "How can a man please twenty million people?" he asked rhetorically. "The answer is he can't. No man is that funny."

The positive reception by the studio audience helped him relax, as he wore a fireman's hat, coat, and assorted accessories for the benefit of those watching him perform live. He once explained, "I can't act funny unless I dress funny. I have to look the fool in order to play the fool." His mike fright, however, caused his voice to jump an octave, turning it into a cartoonish, high-pitched shriek. Listeners loved it.

Variety called the show's debut "a splendidly conceived and executed half hour…the program evidenced smart headwork behind the microphone giving both Texaco's new brand of gasoline and Ed Wynn a scintillating start. These 30 minutes are apt to become a model upon which future advertising broadcasts will be based, as everything it went after it probed for full worth." Wynn wrote most of each broadcast himself, calling upon his files of thousands of time-honored jokes. "It would be an impossibility for any comedian to create enough jokes to fill a weekly half-hour single-handedly," he said. "I don't create all my own jokes; most fellow comics of the air originate none of their own material." He also assigned his assistants, like Eddie Preble, to help plunder those files as well as contribute original jokes of their own.

May 2 - *The Canada Dry Program*, starring Jack Benny, debuts.

Benny credited Ed Sullivan with giving him his first break on radio in March of 1932 (although it wasn't Benny's first time in front of the microphone). Sullivan, then an entertainment/gossip columnist for the New York *Daily News*, had just begun his own program and asked Benny to be a guest. Benny addressed the radio audience with, "This is Jack Benny talking. There will be a slight pause for you to say 'who cares?'" The president of the ad agency for Canada Dry ginger ale enjoyed Benny's five-minute performance, and before long offered him his own show.

1932

Upon signing the contract, Benny wondered if he had agreed to do the impossible. He had obligated himself to do thirteen weekly episodes. "It can't be done," he decided. "There just aren't enough gags in the world to keep feeding out new ones every week. I wish I'd never signed up." His panic was somewhat alleviated with the help of writer Harry Conn, whom Benny paid $100 for each of the early scripts. As Benny's salary increased, so did Conn's, whose paycheck eventually reached $1,200 per script (when Benny received the offer to step in front of the movie cameras, he agreed only if Conn got the job of writing Benny's dialogue, for $1,800 a week).

Jack Benny. Courtesy of Steve Cox.

Benny's May 2 inaugural radio program on NBC reveals how awkward and nervous he must have been as host. Without a live audience—or at least an audible audience that was allowed to laugh out loud—many of the jokes were rather generic, and weren't timed particularly well. That in itself is shocking, considering how Benny's reputation as a master of timing would, in time, earn the praise of his comedy peers. His role at first was mostly to introduce several singing and instrumental performances (with George Olsen leading the orchestra), and to plug Canada Dry ginger ale. His cast of supporting characters had yet to be created.

The program went through a few changes of sponsors and networks, moving to CBS in October that same year (with a live audience), then returning to NBC in March of 1933.

Benny's radio career wouldn't take off in earnest until October of 1934, when General Foods, desperate to interest the public in the floundering new product called Jell-O, gave him free reign over the content and commercials of his show. The time slot, on the NBC Blue Network, Sunday nights at 7:00, was not considered desirable at the time, and the show was given thirteen weeks to prove itself. The program took on the now-familiar sitcom style format, with Benny opening with a few words, then getting interrupted by a cast member or two for some banter before proceeding with the comic story. Harry Conn is credited for including the other members of the program into the scripts, beginning with Benny's wife, Mary Livingstone.

The Jell-O sponsored show began with Mary and announcer Don Wilson in tow; singer Kenny Baker joined in 1935 (to be replaced by Dennis Day in 1939). Over the next several years, the cast solidified still further with additions of bandleader Phil Harris in 1936, Eddie "Rochester" Anderson in 1937, and Mel Blanc in 1939.

An often overlooked quality to Benny's comedy, as it continued to evolve at this time, was his willingness, even encouragement, to become the butt of jokes by his cast. While a good number of comedians thrived at poking fun at *others*, few, if any, made themselves the target of mockery. Benny was kidded about his cheapness, vanity, cowardice, you name it.

"Now the reason my character sustained over so many years," he explained years later, "well, because I played a character that included all of the faults and frailties of mankind. Every family had somebody like me. Either they had an uncle who was stingy, one who thought he was very sexy and he wasn't, so every family has that kind of a person."

And, of course, his silent reactions to wisecracks made at his expense became an art form unto itself, and one that no other comedian since Benny could match. The longer he would hold that take, the harder his audiences laughed.

George Burns, Benny's best friend for half a century, said, "No one was better suited for radio than Jack. Radio consisted of sound and silence. That was it. And while the rest of us were trying to figure out ways of using sound, Jack was smart enough to figure out how to use the silence. No one ever got more out of nothing than he did."

July 23 - Laurel & Hardy arrive in London for a British Isles tour.

The team's intended holiday with their wives, during which time Stan would visit his parents in Ulverston, Lancashire, quickly became an unofficial promotional tour, thanks to considerable persuasion by MGM. It wasn't unheard of for film stars at the time to be welcomed by adoring crowds in their travels, especially if it was work-related, such as attending premieres or receiving awards. But the sheer size and boisterous enthusiasm of the crowds for Stan and Ollie were downright intimidating. The two found themselves genuinely surprised, and even frightened, by the hysteria. At times, they were almost swallowed up by their British fans.

As Ollie described it, "Stan and I went abroad on what we thought would be a pleasure trip, but the next thing we knew we were making personal appearances for nothing, and that's no pleasure…"

The New York Times reported, "Nine persons went to hospitals and many others were less seriously hurt in a wild crush of several thousand at Central Station [Glasgow] today to greet Laurel & Hardy, the Hollywood movie team, who came to spend the weekend. Police were unable to control the mob and the comedians almost lost their coats when enthusiastic souvenir hunters tried to snatch buttons. Some persons were thrown over a stone balustrade by the crowding enthusiasts and others were run down by a tramcar. Laurel wept with emotion. Each of the comedians said he never had seen such a welcome."

Ollie further detailed his perspective of the experience:
"As our train wasn't due in Glasgow till half-past ten at night, we didn't think there'd be anybody to meet us. But there was a terrific crowd at the station. I'm not saying this to brag, but just to show you what we ran into. Those people meant well, but there was no holding them back. We never expected to reach the station alive, and when we finally did make it most of our clothes were torn off. They took everything we had on us for souvenirs, even Stan's wrist-watch, but it was returned the next day. After that experience we didn't dare leave the hotel together—it wasn't safe."

August 10 - *Horsefeathers*, **starring the Marx Brothers, premieres.**

The brothers' fourth film for Paramount stars Groucho as Professor Quincy Adams Wagstaff, who, in the opening sequence, takes the reins as president of Huxley College. His accompanying song, "Whatever It Is, I'm Against It," sets the tone for how seriously he intends to treat his new position. Chico, meanwhile, works in a speakeasy, Harpo is the town dogcatcher, and Zeppo plays a Huxley student who, believe it or not, is Groucho's *son*.

The plot involves gangsters (again), who plan to rig a football game between Huxley College and its arch-rival, Darwin, by kidnapping a couple of star players and replacing them with professionals. The brothers then attempt to foil the scheme, while at the same time taking turns pursuing the "college widow" (Thelma Todd). It all builds to a climactic football game, in which the

Marxes literally run amuck, with Harpo arriving on the field in a horse-drawn garbage wagon, resembling a Roman chariot.

It speaks to the brothers' stature as comedy stars to see them grace the cover of *Time* magazine's August 15 issue.

August 13 - *Speak Easily*, starring Keaton, Durante, and Thelma Todd, is released.

While the Marx Brothers were enjoying positive reviews and healthy box office numbers at Paramount, MGM continued its pairing of Buster Keaton and Jimmy Durante. Granted, they perhaps were not so much a "team" in the traditional sense, but their film characters always found themselves in each other's company for a considerable portion of each feature. As Keaton wrote in his memoirs, "From the time Jimmy and I were teamed up I heard rumors that Mr. Mayer was planning to build him up at my expense. This didn't worry me much, although I can't say I liked it. With my record of successful pictures, I felt I was a fixture at MGM. I couldn't imagine anyone there wanting to get rid of me." He reasoned with himself that his reputation as a top film comedian throughout the previous decade would stand him in good stead at the studio. "I had unshakable confidence in my talent and ability to hold the place that I had staked out for myself," he wrote.

In *Speak Easily*, Keaton plays Professor Post, a quiet-mannered and unworldly college professor who, to put it mildly, doesn't get out much. His sympathetic assistant writes a bogus letter which tells of the professor's inheritance of $750,000, enough for him to take a long vacation and see the world. As he begins his journey (somewhere in the mid-west), he meets a traveling entertainment group led by Durante, who is having trouble paying the troupe's debts. Keaton, who has struck up a friendship with the leading lady, Pansy Peets, offers to pay all fees to open the show in New York. But the show is still without real funding, and Durante does his best to stall the authorities until the opening night performance is over, hoping the show will be a box office hit. Keaton's constant onstage interruptions wreak havoc, much to the delight of the audience, and the show is saved.

Speak Easily does have its moments, especially when Keaton is allowed to be Keaton (which doesn't happen much until the slapstick-heavy final scenes). He's also quite amusing portraying the awkward and socially naïve professor. The film also benefits greatly from the presence of Thelma Todd, who was having her busiest year yet as a comic actress. She commands the middle third of the film, beginning with her sauntering entrance as an aspiring star, Eleanor Espere, on the prowl for a wealthy producer and/or sugar daddy. She literally strips to her lingerie to get herself a part in the show, the sight of which has Keaton and Durante toppling over themselves. The highlight of the film comes in a delightful sequence in which her attempt to seduce the uptight professor is undermined by both of them getting hopelessly inebriated.

After the third and final pairing with Durante in *What? No Beer!*, which Keaton referred to as "a 100 per cent turkey," MGM discharged him.

October - Jack Pearl introduces Baron Munchausen to radio listeners.

A man who referred to himself more as an actor than comedian, Pearl indeed found his niche in comedy as a performer in vaudeville and revues in the 1920s, mostly as a dialect comedian. He found semi-regular work on the radio show *Ziegfeld Follies of the Air* earlier in 1932, but that would provide just a taste of what would come later in the year.

As Pearl related the story, "I was in England on a vacation in August of 1932 when I received a cable from Billy Wells, the comedy writer, that he had a 'great idea.' Lucky Strike was looking around for a program. Well, Eddie Cantor and Ed Wynn were going big, so it was decided that it must be a comedy program." Wells was assigned to come up with a story idea. "One day, in a Broadway vaudeville house," Pearl explained, "he heard a blackface comedy team use the line 'Let's tell lies!' It gave him an idea. He talked it over with an advertising man who happened to have just been reading *Baron Munchausen*. That started it."

Pearl found some irony in being selected for the show. With the rise of Hitler in Germany, and the accompanying anti-Semitism of the regime, he said, "They needed a German comedian for the part, so I was picked. It's funny, isn't it—I'm Jewish."

By the end of the year, and continuing throughout 1933, Baron Munchausen was a smash on radio, with his outrageous and fanciful adventure stories, and his equal outrage when straight man Cliff Hall doubted the stories' veracity. Baron would angrily retort in his gargling accent, "Vas *you* dere, Sharlie?"

"I work hard at being funny," Pearl said at the time. "It may sound as if it were all done on the spur of the moment. It isn't. Few people know how hard a funny man works to get that way. Every intonation of the voice, every turn of phrase must be carefully thought out beforehand. Every gag is painstakingly executed."

October 23 - Fred Allen debuts the *Linit Bath Revue* on CBS.

The autumn of 1932 brought yet another vaudeville comedian to the microphone. Allen often denigrated his own career onstage as a magician, ventriloquist, and monologist, but he had indeed become quite popular with vaudeville audiences, and in revues such as *The Passing Show*. Indeed, he had just completed a two-year run in the revue *Three's A Crowd*, when, as was the case with so many of his peers, he was asked to host a radio program. This one would be sponsored by Linit beauty powder and bath products.

"In the early 1930s," Allen wrote, "when the Broadway comedians descended on radio, things went from hush to raucous. The theatre buffoon had no conception of the medium and no time to study its requirements. The Broadway slogan was 'It's dough, let's go!' Eddie Cantor, Jack Pearl, Ed Wynn, Joe Penner and others were radio sensations. They brought their audiences into the studios, used their theater techniques and their old vaudeville jokes, and laughter, rehearsed or spontaneous, started exploding between the commercials..."

Allen was one of the growing number of comedians who sensed that radio comedy programs should be more than a host comedian reciting a long string of unrelated jokes. Like Jack Benny, he began developing ideas that were more situational. Without mentioning Ed Wynn and other comedians of that ilk by name, Allen said, "It seemed to me that the bizarre-garbed, joke-telling funster was ogling extinction. The monotony of his weekly recital of unrelated jokes would soon drive listeners to other diversions...Hoping for longevity in the new medium, I planned a series of programs using a different business background each week—a newspaper office, a department store, a bank, a detective agency, etc. The comedy would involve the characters employed in, or indigenous to, the assorted locales." He further reasoned that such a format would encourage the listener to flex his or her imagination more, and take a real interest in the characters and their experiences. "This, if it worked, would insure the radio comedian a longer life." He also enlisted the on-air support of his wife, Portland Hoffa, who had been his partner in vaudeville, and whose ditsy character resembled a somewhat younger, higher-pitched Gracie Allen.

Fred Allen and Portland Hoffa. Author's collection.

1932

As was the case with other programs hosted by the comedians of the day, Allen's comedy often had to stop in its tracks in order to present a singing performance (aside from the commercial messages, of course). Nevertheless, Allen's peers often expressed their admiration for his clever scripts, which always reflected his love of puns and other playful ways of using the English language. His legendary "feud" with Jack Benny would not heat up for another four years, and his famous "Allen's Alley" segment wouldn't first endear itself to listeners for another *ten* years. Nonetheless, he got off to a fine start in 1932, as expressed in *Variety*'s review.

> "Fred Allen seems destined for the next ether comedy sensation honors. He has a refreshingly humorous style and already they're talking about him...Allen's comedy, fresh and crisp as it is, seems patently of his own authorship but at the same time it creates the concern as to how long he can keep it up? The lines, sure-fire, were a succession of laughs. Coming on at 9 p.m. EST on WABC, just after Eddie Cantor's mike return to Chase & Sanborn at 8-9 p.m. on WEAF had concluded, an odious comparison arose. For Allen's funning eclipsed Cantor's...Portland Hoffa (Mrs. Allen) is a corking foil throughout. They'll be hurrying home at 9 p.m. Sunday nights for Allen if the pace keeps up."

It's worth noting that by the end of that year, there were no fewer than five real-life husband & wife couples performing regularly on network comedy programs: Goodman and Jane Ace, George Burns and Gracie Allen, Jesse Block and Eve Sully (whose act was quite similar in nature to that of Burns & Allen), Jack Benny and Mary Livingstone, and Fred Allen and Portland Hoffa. Yet another couple, Jim and Marion Jordan, would join their ranks in *Fibber McGee and Molly* in 1935.

Some of the wives felt more comfortable as performers than others (Mary

Livingstone famously suffered from stage fright, as did Gracie Allen). These radio stars, who arrived by way of vaudeville, were among many married teams—comedians, singers, dancers—who performed together for financial as well as creative reasons. "In vaudeville," Allen explained, "when a comedian married he immediately put his wife in the act. The wife didn't have to have any talent. It was economic strategy. With a double act a comedian could get a salary increase from the booking office. The additional money would pay for his wife's wardrobe, her railroad fares and the extra hotel expenses."

As Jack Benny pointed out, "We all remained married to our original mates. I know that people assume actors and actresses are bad marriage risks, yet not one couple in that group was ever divorced."

George Burns credited the very nature of radio work, as opposed to that of films, for the healthy marriages among so many real-life radio couples. Radio was treated more as a business, without the glamour of movies.

> "We're not being constantly reminded of love and sex and beauty and glamour in a radio studio. The movie studios, on the other hand, run over with powder-puffs and seductive costumes and soft music and couples who are not married to each other. In a radio station all you get is a gruff voice front the control-room shouting: 'Stand over there another inch!' Or 'We're eighteen seconds late!'

While performing on radio was not, to Burns' thinking, inherently glamorous, he and his creative team had at one point discovered why Gracie's first laugh line of each broadcast never seemed to get the laugh the writers had anticipated. George's brother Bill noticed how the women in the audience always seemed to take a moment to give Gracie's wardrobe a thorough once-over, without paying attention to her opening remarks. The problem was solved by having Gracie take a brief bow without a punch line, giving the women time to gaze at her outfit before getting involved in the comedy dialogue as Gracie approached the mike.

As comforting as it may have been for the early comedy stars to have had a fairly easy and lucrative job performing weekly on radio, they were constantly under the gun to provide their listening audiences with something new and fresh each time the public tuned in. This was the toughest aspect of starring on radio that every vaudevillian-turned-radio comedian now had to deal with. Their biggest headaches, of the truly migraine variety, came courtesy of the voracious appetite radio had for new comedy material every week. As vaudevillians, they were accustomed to performing roughly the same proven act to local audiences at each stop on any given circuit, and enjoyed the comfort of knowing they were facing a totally different audience each time they stepped onto the stage. They could use the same material almost indefinitely as they crisscrossed the country.

With the expansion of network radio, that all changed. Millions of people across the nation could now hear a comedian's best material on a single night—material that may have taken months or years to perfect. And those same millions of listeners certainly didn't want to hear the same material the following week. George Burns summed it up best: "I guess the biggest adjustment we all had to make between vaudeville and radio was that in vaudeville seventeen minutes of good material could last for years, while on radio seventeen minutes of good material would last seventeen minutes."

Consequently, even successful vaudevillians who hoped to make a successful transition to radio soon found their creative wells running dry. With the explosion of comedy on radio in 1932, the top comedians discovered the strain involved in writing and sustaining a weekly comedy program—be it fifteen, thirty, or sixty minutes in length. A big-time comedian signing a hefty contract to star in his own weekly program would inevitably feel his self-satisfaction dissolve into near-panic, born out of a need to create, adapt, borrow, and steal *a lot* of comedy material every few days, and still try to keep it sounding fresh. "When we all went into radio I don't think any of us realized how much material we would need," Burns said. "Even with all back issues of *College Humor* and *Whiz Bang*, by the end of the third or fourth week we were out of new material. So we began hiring writers to work for us full-time."

Thus, the creature to become known as the modern-day comedy writer was born. This first generation of radio comedy writers had not grown up with radio, which had only been in existence for little more than a decade; the first commercial station in the country, KDKA in Pittsburgh, went on the air in November of 1920. Rather, the older, more experienced writers in 1932 knew their way around writing for stage productions, either as monologue or sketch writers for vaudevillians, or as librettists for Broadway revues. The younger crop consisted of new college graduates who had gotten the bug writing for their campus humor magazines. "When they entered the university gates," *The New York Times* reported, "they may have had visions of being doctors or lawyers, but fate decreed otherwise and gave them a place in radio as authors of comedy. Today they are found working for comedians. They are in the broadcasting station's continuity division, and on the radio staffs of advertising agencies that prepare ethereal scenarios for their clients. Theirs is a new profession, despite the fact that they may have majored in chemistry or economics at college."

Both the stage veterans and fresh-faced graduate rookies were just as new at writing for the airwaves as the comedians themselves were at delivering the material. Instead of the more familiar work of creating characters and gags that audiences could see on a stage, this first generation of radio writers had to create a world consisting solely of voices and sounds that could tap into the listener's imagination to elicit laughter. The one consolation for a radio comedian was knowing that the task of creating each week's program could be shared among himself and one or two writers.

However, there were still some who stubbornly felt compelled to hammer out each program more or less single-handedly, accepting only peripheral help from assistants. Fred Allen's desire to write each of his own broadcasts himself, like Ed Wynn, proved to be impractical due to the back-breaking workload. Allen confessed that "after the first few programs, I realized that a person who attempted to write a half-hour comedy show week after week had to end up talking to himself. I was not only writing the entire program, I was eternally re-writing it, rehearsing it and appearing on it. The day after each show I had to attend a meeting at which a transcription of the program was played. [The sponsor executives] regaled me with the post-mortems. They commented on the comedy, the singing, the music and the sound effects. The show had been done. It was like trying to breathe yesterday's air."

Barely a month into his Texaco program, Wynn confessed, "I have never worked so hard on any job in my life as at this job of broadcasting. I've been up until the wee hours of the morning working up new gags for future broadcasts. This business of being funny is no joke. In four programs, I have written dialogue that runs an hour and five minutes. Why, by the time the thirteen engagements are filled I will have written enough material for three [Broadway] shows."

"Radio was new," Allen explained. "It hadn't developed any comedy writers. David Freedman, who was writing the Eddie Cantor program, Billy Wells, writing Jack Pearl's Baron Munchausen routines, Harry Conn, Jack Benny's first writer, and a few others were really high-priced revue and vaudeville writers. They were enticed into radio with bonanza salaries and I suspect that each of them was earning more than the $1,000 we had available for our entire show."

The New York Times further assessed of the situation: "Indeed, with the accelerated pace at which the entire entertainment world has come to speed of late, the coiner of gags has become a mogul of mass production. With stage, motion picture and radio entertainers clamoring for new material with which to be louder and funnier, he is the man to whom they turn for grist to feel their mills. They take it as he gives it out. Hark to the lay of the gagster!"

Allen learned of a young critic, Harry Tugend, who worked at the Motion Picture Herald and had expressed in an interest in writing for radio. The two met and talked, and soon Tugend was writing for the comedian. "For four years Harry and I wrote the programs and coped with the forces that attempted to impede our weekly trek from the writing session to the microphone."

A few years down the road, future novelist Herman Wouk (*The Caine Mutiny, The Winds of War*) would become another young writer hired by Allen to share the load. Wouk said of his boss, "He was a role model and still is. Fred was one of the most honorable men I've ever met. He was the best comic writer radio ever developed, and here we were handing him what must have seemed like mediocre material. I was twenty-one years old and making two hundred dollars a week, a remarkable salary for the Depression. Not once did he tell us our contribution wasn't good enough."

George Burns admitted that it wasn't easy for comedians to rely on others, after creating material on their own during the vaudeville years. "We were all tough on our writers. I think a lot of that came from fear. Most of us had become successful by writing our own material, and it was hard for us to trust our careers to other people."

Comedy writer Dave Freedman sympathized with the dilemma comedians faced. "In fifteen short minutes," he said, "you play to forty million people. Once used, the material is gone forever. The next program has got to be just as good, or even better, or people will say the comedian is slipping. That's why comedians can't afford to take chances. They buy from a comparatively small group of known, successful writers because they don't dare to do anything else. Comedians, even the best ones, are often poor judges of material. They buy their comedy from known writers to make sure they aren't buying tragedy instead!"

Ed Wynn echoed Freedman's sentiment. "The critics who belabor comedians for using old and stale material can't know much about comedy," he said. "They would already understand that all humor is old, that interpretation refreshes it. Aside from that, a comedian from years of experience with audiences knows experiments are dangerous. He has learned from visible and audible audiences what types of jokes can be depended upon for laughs. If I tried uncertain types over the radio, how would I know they were going over?

1932

If I tried experiments I would be scared to death, nervous, apprehensive. I couldn't be myself. I'd lose my appeal."

Comedy writers for all available entertainment venues became much sought-after, and, due to the degree to which the stars needed them, very well paid, especially on radio. But the biggest stars, at this point, trusted only those who had already earned solid reputations as writers for vaudeville and revues. Of these, only a handful were responsible for the majority of the radio comedy listeners enjoyed in the early 1930s, with some writers working for two or three different programs simultaneously. Some even achieved a modicum of celebrity themselves, appearing on the feature pages of various radio-centric magazines of the time.

As for Dave Freedman himself, he had written material for Fannie Brice (*Sweet and Low*), Eddie Cantor, and others. He would soon find himself writing for Cantor, dialect comedian George Givot, and the *Block and Sully* program simultaneously, every week. It was a mind-numbing workload, but Freedman was so well compensated that he and his family lived in a 14-room penthouse apartment in New York, which also housed file cabinets containing as many as three million jokes. He also had a staff of three assistants, who hunted for old gags to adapt for their current employers, in addition to writing new ones. Working on the tightest of deadlines became the norm. Often a freshly-written script would arrive at the broadcast studio with barely an hour to spare before being read live on the air.

The other top writers were living quite well, too, such as Billy Wells. Unlike Freedman's tendency to spread himself among several radio programs as thinly as possible, Wells served as exclusive writer to Jack Pearl. He had previously written for George White's *Scandals*, and authored *Manhattan Mary*, starring Ed Wynn, as well as shows starring Clark & McCullough.

As we previously mentioned, Burns & Allen at the time had John P. Medbury as their head writer, who had been supplying material for them since they first took to the airwaves. Eugene Conrad also signed to write for the team on radio, and would accompany them to Hollywood the following year for their scenes in *International House*.

Jack Benny, who by all accounts was a genuinely humble and generous individual, deflected much of the praise he received onto his writers. In his early years on the air, he especially relied on Harry Conn to help produce quality jokes, and for a hefty $1,200 a week paycheck. "His is a tough job," Benny said at the time, "because he has to adapt himself to my mental processes, if any. A script writer, to deliver the goods, must, to all intents and purposes become the mental double of the comic - and believe me that's some chore."

And then there was Al Boasberg, whose shadow loomed large, both figuratively and literally, in that still-small community of comedy writers. Boasberg's reputation as a gag writer grew steadily throughout the 1920s. Benny first called upon him to hone his stand-up act, which Boasberg helped shape from a basically violin-playing shtick to more of a monologue style. Benny then began to cultivate his on-stage character, one who would eventually develop into his vain, self-delusional ladies' man persona (the image of him as a cheapskate would come later). Boasberg is also credited with giving the struggling young comedian Bob Hope a boost with snappier one-liners, as well as writing Burns & Allen's "Lamb Chops" sketch, which solidified the team's switch from George as the comic to the straight man, reacting to Gracie's flights of fancy.

"All the comedians knew him," Benny said of Boasberg. "When I was in vaudeville, I would send him fifty dollars and he would send me two jokes or something to do onstage. You see, he wasn't a script writer but rather a doctor of scripts. He took care of a lot of stars. Burns and Allen used him, but he didn't really work steady until radio. By then I was making so much money that it didn't make any difference to me what I paid him."

Benny found Boasberg's real talent to be that of polishing existing scripts Benny and his two writers had completed. To the comedian, this skill was especially valuable.

"All he'd have to do was to look at what we had written and if he thought it was fine he didn't have to write a word. But if he could add something to it, perhaps there might be a weak spot here or there, then he was to do so. But either way, I paid him a thousand dollars each week. Now, I wouldn't have given him ten cents to sit down and write me a script. Even if I had told him what I wanted. He just wasn't the man for that. But he could sit down and go over a script and fill in the weak spots and that was worth a thousand dollars."

After moving to Beverly Hills in 1936, Benny established a work routine in which he would meet with his writers in the library of his home to work on each week's script. His young daughter Joanie was always welcome to sit in and watch them work after she returned home from school. "There they would be; one of the writers stretched out on the sofa, the others in various chairs, Jeanette, the secretary, furiously writing at the round table, and Daddy in, of course, the winged chair. I loved to hear them going over each sentence, each line; discussing whether it was funnier to emphasize this word or that word, whether a line should read 'the' something or 'that' something. The attention to detail, to fine points, was amazing. They all laughed a lot, but they were serious, too."

For all of the energy and money spent by the top comedians to ensure acquiring the best writers for their shows, there was one team who dared to face the microphone twice a week without a script in sight. Tom Howard and George Shelton had performed onstage individually, with Howard making his mark in 1928 with a sketch called "The Spy." It won a New York critics' award as the best comedy sketch of that year. Beginning the following year, he starred in a handful of shorts for Paramount, and played supporting roles in a few features.

Howard, lanky and droll in his delivery, teamed with Shelton (who would feign impatience at Howard's endless pontifications) for a stage act, which reportedly earned them consideration to star in the production *Of Thee I Sing* and other top shows. Their new radio venture began on January 3, as a twice-weekly gig on the *Chesterfield Show*, in which they alternated with other hosts, such as new star Bing Crosby.

As the first truly improvisational comedy team on radio, Howard and Shelton's derring-do in front of a live microphone twice a week had showbiz journalists shaking their heads in befuddlement, and the CBS control room men shaking with anxiety. A typical "rehearsal" would consist of the team going off in a corner at the Columbia studios, and feeding each other lines while their manager, Rush Jermon, would time them with his watch, making occasional suggestions. Their opening and closing cues would be given to conductor Leonard Hayton and announcer Norman Brokenshire, neither of whom had any idea of what to expect from the show.

The *Radio Mirror* detailed the team's technique, or lack thereof:

"Howard and Shelton depend primarily upon ridiculous
characterization and outlandish situations, far removed
from the straight gag type common to the funnymen today.
They are turned loose among the microphones without
even so much as a dress rehearsal and, with the uncanny
sixth sense of the veteran trouper, and their turns 'on the nose.'"

The team would score an even bigger radio success several years down the road, in 1942, with *It Pays to Be Ignorant*, a satirical quiz show starring Shelton as host, and Howard, Lulu McConnell, and British comic Harry McNaughton as the panelists. Even ridiculously simple questions such as "What hot drink is made out of tea leaves?" would never get direct answers, but instead lead to rambling anecdotes and one-liners from the panelists, with Shelton interrupting them with a variety of putdowns as they fumbled their way to their (wrong) answers. The program, airing mostly as an annual summer replacement, ran for nearly a decade.

1932

November 28 - Groucho and Chico Marx debut the radio program *Flywheel, Shyster, Flywheel*.

In this year when so many popular vaudevillians and/or film rookies were also trying their hand at starring on their own radio programs, the Marx Brothers, who were arguably the most popular film comedy team at the time, were asked to do the same, for a program sponsored by Standard Oil and Esso gasoline. Groucho in particular hoped to find the same kind of success on radio as he had enjoyed on stage and film. The brothers' first opportunity came with this show (originally titled *Beagle, Shyster, Beagle*) starring Groucho as an attorney and Chico as his assistant, and was broadcast as the Monday evening installment of *Five-Star Theatre* on the CBS network. Groucho and Chico shared a $6,500 weekly salary for the gig.

A good deal of the dialogue, written by Arthur Sheekman and Nat Perrin (co-writers of *Monkey Business* and *Horsefeathers*) was cherry-picked from the Marx Brothers' stage and film successes to that point, but also contained material that would later turn up in their next film, *Duck Soup*.

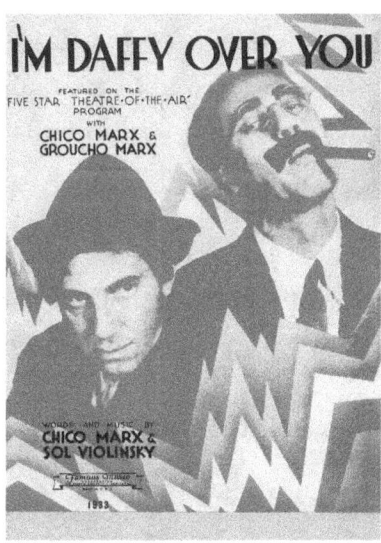

As with virtually all radio comedy programs, music played a big part in the Marx Brothers' show. Author's collection.

The program was aired from the WJZ studios for the first two months, necessitating quite a bit of cross-country commuting from Los Angeles for Groucho, Chico, and staff. It finally moved to L.A., where the lack of radio studios at the time required the show to use an RKO soundstage. A small audience was invited to attend each episode. After thirteen more episodes, it was back to New York for the final four shows of the season. Once the twenty-six episodes were complete, lackluster ratings discouraged CBS from renewing the program.

As *Radio Digest* summed up 1932 in its year-end issue, "Comedians certainly have had the spot during the past year. Ed Wynn leaped to the top at one bound. Baron Munchausen also made a quick climb, then Eddie Cantor came rushing back to New York from Hollywood to reclaim the very popular place he had made for himself before deserting the mike for pictures last Spring. There have been other comedians but none that could really compare with the popularity achieved by these three."

November 12 - Roscoe Arbuckle's first sound film, *Hey Pop!* premieres.

Hey Pop! was the first and best received of Arbuckle's shorts for Warner Brothers. In the story, his character takes care of an abandoned boy, dodging the police and the "man from the orphan asylum" (curiously, these other male characters come off as if they're hardened gangsters).

The very first two minutes or so of *Hey, Pop!* are chock full of memorable sight gags, with Arbuckle cooking up a meal in a restaurant kitchen, showing off his still sharp timing and dexterity. As a talkie, it also reveals his pleasant speaking voice and agreeable demeanor, negating any doubt that he could do well in sound films.

Unfortunately, his staunchest advocate in the show business press, James Quirk, would never get to see the comedian's return to the screen. Quirk died of a heart attack on August 1, at the age of 48, about three weeks before Arbuckle began production on *Hey, Pop!*.

Arbuckle himself had been battling health issues at the time. He was drinking often, and was slowed by an irregular heartbeat.

November 16 - The Palace Theatre discontinues its all-vaudeville policy.

As robust a year 1932 was for radio comedy, the entertainment world on the stage continued to watch vaudeville die a slow but steady death. The Palace theatre, that Taj Mahal of vaudeville, was losing $2,000 -$3,000 a week, and had decided a few months earlier that movies, not stage shows, were now the most popular and financially rewarding form of mass entertainment. The Palace had slipped from the high echelon of two-a-day presentations to that of three-a-day programs, with films becoming part of each bill. Vaudeville alone just couldn't pay the bills anymore, and, after adding films in May, it became plain to see that audiences had a heightened interest in the action on the screen over that which played out before them in the flesh. The addition of films to the Palace's bill served as the loudest death knell yet for vaudeville. Ironically, the first film to be shown in the theatre was *The Kid from Spain*, starring Eddie Cantor, who entered the 1930s as a smash return emcee at the Palace, for several long runs.

Columns in both mainstream and show business papers began to take on the feeling and wording of obituaries for the Palace, and by extension, for vaudeville itself. A few days before the theatre's total conversion into an all-picture venue, *The New York Times* mourned, "Vaudeville is singing its swansong at the Palace this week, prior to the deflection of that time-honored variety house to the ranks of the two-a-day motion picture theatres on Thursday night. In honor of its passing, perhaps, the program this week approaches more closely than it has in several weeks gone by the honored tradition of the house and presents nothing if not typical old-time variety acts."

In January of 1932, Milton Berle, at the age of 24, became the youngest emcee in the history of the Palace. He wistfully recalled how it felt to later see the Palace give up its standing as the last major theatre to present strictly stage acts, after fending off movies as long as possible. "Vaudeville as we knew it was dead," he wrote, "You only had to walk down Broadway to 47th Street and look at the once great Palace, turned into a grind picture house. What we called vaudeville was just a stage show between pictures at those houses that could still afford the luxury of live entertainment. The movies, which once were the 'chasers' between vaudeville shows, were now the main attraction, and we were the "extra added,' and even that was fading out."

As a stark example of how the entertainment world was changing, on the same day as the Palace announcement, the first broadcast from Radio City was sent out on NBC. S.L. Rothafel (a.k.a. Roxy) presided and presented various singers and musicians. The program was heard around the world on a shortwave pickup. The 1,400-seat radio broadcasting auditorium would become the home of countless programs, such as Fred Allen's.

Postcard of Radio City's new broadcasting auditorium. Author's collection.

Other big time vaudeville houses also saw the future in movies, and converted themselves accordingly. Vaudeville did not evaporate instantly, however, and even burlesque was able to carry on for several more years. Up-and-coming entertainers continued to make their names known to vaudeville audiences on their way to radio and films. Still, with the most prestigious and renown theatre in America making such a sweeping change in policy, vaudeville as it had existed for the previous half century, effectively died. "Vaudeville didn't just drop dead," George Burns noted, "it faded slowly, like applause after a second encore."

However, more of vaudeville and burlesque comedy has survived than is obvious at first glance. For instance, anyone who would like to experience a classic routine by early 20th century stars Weber & Fields, in which they scheme to pay for a single meal and then share it between them, can find Abbott & Costello performing a marvelous rendition of it in their 1941 film *Keep 'Em Flying*. For that matter, we have Abbott & Costello to thank for preserving dozens of vaudeville and burlesque routines virtually intact in their films, which are easily accessible today.

Remnants of vaudeville have stayed with us far beyond the works of the original stars. The vaudeville form itself survived on television for twenty-three years, under our very noses, as the *Ed Sullivan Show*. Unlike a typical master of ceremonies on the stage, however, Sullivan told no jokes, but simply presented an array of acts, be they novelty, singing, comedy, acrobatic, ranging from world-famous to obscure, in a manner not very different from what we may have seen seated in the audience at the Palace during its heyday. Echoes of vaudeville also still reverberate on TV today, albeit in a flashier presentation, with *America's Got Talent* and other competitions.

Finally, if you've ever seen a movie at an Orpheum, Pantages, Loews, or Paramount megaplex, you've patronized a theatre named after one of the original vaudeville circuits that date back nearly a century. So, while vaudeville in its purist form effectively died on that November day in 1932, its friendly ghost occasionally still haunts modern-day show business.

December 7 - *Walk a Little Faster* opens on Broadway.
As traditional vaudeville continued to fade as an institution, revues continued to flourish. Many were the result of collaborations among the most talented names in the business. Sometimes, however, even a show assembled by a Who's Who in entertainment wasn't guaranteed to be an unqualified success. While

Walk a Little Faster ran for a fairly modest 119 performances, it's notable for having boasted headliners Beatrice Lillie and Clark & McCullough, with sketches written by S.J. Perelman, the tune "April in Paris" by Vernon Duke and E.Y. Harburg (and future Count Basie standard), and overall direction by Monty Wooley. Despite such an abundance of talent, the revue was given a mediocre notice in *Variety*, although Lillie, as usual, was singled out for "her own style of breathtaking stuff."

December 9 - W.C. Fields stars in *The Dentist*, produced by Mack Sennett.

W. C. Fields' collaboration with Mack Sennett came to fruition almost a decade after they first talked about working together, and would result in four two-reelers: *The Dentist*, *The Pharmacist*, *The Fatal Glass of Beer* and *The Barber Shop*. Fields collected a salary of $5,000 a week, and wrote all four shorts, adapting many of the routines he had performed onstage to re-create for the films. Most of *The Dentist*, for instance, is basically a version of a sketch Fields devised for the 1928 edition of Earl Carroll's *Vanities*.

The second of the four films, *The Fatal Glass of Beer*, was released in March of 1933, but the collaboration between the two men had already begun to show signs of strain. Fields' insistence on having complete control over his material clashed with Sennett's established way of overseeing his comedy product. Upon viewing *The Fatal Glass of Beer*, Sennett hated it, and wanted several changes made, which did not sit well with Fields.

In a letter he wrote to Sennett in December, Fields firmly but diplomatically aired his grievances to his boss, not the least of which was the objection to Sennett making changes to the film, and adding a scene that Fields found inappropriate. Sennett then hinted he might re-shoot the film with comedian Lloyd Hamilton instead, to which Fields replied:

"Mack, I do not wish to run your studio or change one idea you have. You have been a tremendous success with your formula, but it is new to me and I can't change my way of working at this late stage of the game. When I have the stage all set for a Fields picture and you come in and have everything changed for a Sennett picture, you can see how you have rendered me helpless. You told me I would get screen credit for the stories I wrote and that I could do as I wished until I went wrong. If the pictures made are not what you want, tear up the contract. You know I would never hold you to a piece of paper. We are friends."

Fields in *The Pharmacist* (1933). Author's collection.

Sennett appears to have remembered working with Fields a little differently, when he spoke about it over twenty-five years later. "It's all well and good to try for gag lines," he said in an interview. "But you have to know when not to talk. Now Bill Fields when he worked for me, he knew about that. Our writers would work out a situation. Bill would do the lines and then when he came to the topper he would go into pantomime and hit them right in the belly."

There were still two more films to make under the contract, *The Pharmacist*, released in April of 1933, and *The Barber Shop*, released in July.

1933

As 1933 began, the Great Depression continued to deepen, Franklin Roosevelt became President in March (before the official inauguration date was changed to January), and Adolf Hitler came to power in Germany. There was plenty of cause for anxiety throughout America, although Roosevelt's first radio "Fireside Chat" in March was to set the tone for a series of such broadcasts, designed to allow the country to take a breath during its struggles, and hear the confident words of reassurance from its leader.

In the entertainment business, and for vaudeville in particular, the economic circumstances of the time continued to crush the hope that vaudeville might survive. The odds were stacked against it. Going to the movies was cheaper, and listening to the radio at home was cheaper still. "These media had hardened the theatregoers to the corn which was too often the stock in trade of vaudeville," wrote longtime *Variety* writer Abel Green. "Some circuit theatres still offered vaude [sic] acts, but only—as usual—to bolster bad films, or because competition made a plus value necessary. Most stage shows were dropped to cut expenses."

Whereas vaudeville continued to suffer, comedy on radio continued to thrive, providing invaluable emotional relief from the stress of the times. A *Radio Digest* editorial perfectly reflected the mood of the nation in 1933, as it lauded the onslaught of laughter coming out of radio speakers during the depths of the ongoing Depression. It deserves to be reproduced in full:

> "Have you noticed the frequent use of the expression 'a couple of laughs' during the past few months? It is Broadway born. It is the answer to the empty pocket and the run-down heel. Somebody says, 'let's listen to the radio and get a couple of laughs.' No dime for a cup of coffee and roll, but there's always a chance to stop in somewhere and get a couple of laughs from the radio. Perhaps that is the reason for the success of comedy on the air during the past year. It is one way to put worries by for a quarter-hour, half-hour or an hour. Who can estimate the good provided by Ed Wynn, Eddie Cantor, Baron Munchausen, Burns and Allen? The same goes for all those other humorous souls who find in radio a way to purvey a couple of laughs to a world so harassed it knows not which way to turn! If it is a good laugh with encores you may even hear it called 'terrific.'
>
> Of course we can't be too particular when the demand has been so heavy. Even the laugh market has its limitations. If they will just give us a couple of new laughs now and then, we'll try to laugh at the old ones as they come. What a mercy that we find radio so conveniently at hand!
>
> It is available for rich and poor like a glass of refreshing water. There may be music, feasting, bedlam, wise-cracking—then a lone voice singing, 'Brother, Can You Spare a Dime?' But you can tune out if you 'can't take it' and need more laughs for your daily tonic."

Jan. 27 - *She Done Him Wrong*, starring Mae West, is released.

She Done Him Wrong, based on her 1928 Broadway hit *Diamond Lil*, was

1933

West's second film role since signing with Paramount in 1932, but her first as the unmistakable star.

West had been singing and dancing since childhood. She performed as a singer, often of risqué songs, and dancer in vaudeville and in various revues since her teens. She landed a key role, at twenty-five, in the 1918 production *Sometime*, with Ed Wynn. However, her character's storyline inevitably took a back seat to Wynn's antics, which won him enthusiastic reviews, but the experience still proved educational to her. West watched and studied as Wynn commanded most of the attention and praise in the early weeks of the show's run. As much as she admired his talents, she began to feel frustrated by her failing efforts to capture some attention for herself. "I found I was throwing away all my lines," she said. "So I learned to catch the eye of the audience first—usually with some movement. Everything I do and say is based on rhythm…All I had to do, I discovered, was to wander around the stage like so much bait while the boys kept the audience happy with laughs." One matinee, during a scene in which she needed to cross the stage behind Wynn, she added a bit of slowly gyrating hip action to her stride, which would become her famous walk. The deliberate pace of her swagger distracted Wynn as well as the audience. "The audience forgot the comedians," she said. "They forgot the patter…They just looked." She had made her point that she was fast becoming a force to be reckoned with.

Although she never graduated high school, West had the natural creative talent to write her own plays; she wrote, produced, and directed *Sex* in 1926, which created the kind of scandal she would encounter, and exploit, in reaction to many of her works yet to come. *Sex*, in which she played a prostitute, opened to poor reviews, especially by squeamish critics, but still ran for nearly a year before a performance was raided by order of the district attorney. Twenty-two cast members, plus the producers, were arrested on charges of performing an obscene play. After a stormy trial, all were found guilty, but only West and the two other producers were given ten-day jail terms, plus fines. The incident secured her notorious image as a seductress who maintained a firm control of her intimate relationships, allowing men to believe they had the upper hand, even when they didn't. She wasn't about to back down with either the content, or performance style of her subsequent plays, whose titles alone (*The Drag, The Wicked Age, Pleasure Man, The Constant Sinner*) hinted at the provocative nature of their themes.

A young Mae West, already familiar with controversy.
Courtesy of Steve Cox.

"Audiences have always been pleased by what I do," she said, "and I have always been doing the same basic thing, with different trimmings. I didn't recognize what I did myself at that time. I didn't know what it was I had. It wasn't until much later that anyone, including myself, realized that it was the force of an extraordinary sex-personality that made quite harmless lines and mannerisms seem suggestive. It wasn't what I did, but how I did it. It wasn't what I said, but how I said it; and how I looked when I did it and said it. I had evolved into a symbol and didn't know it."

1933

Her film debut was in a supporting, comedy relief role in the drama *Night After Night*, starring George Raft, from whom she nearly stole the movie. *Picture Play* announced that her film debut "proves her to be a real find. She is flagrantly hard-boiled and yet manages curiously to be likable and even sympathetic as well as handsome. There isn't any one quite like her and she leaves the vast wisecracking sisterhood far behind."

She Done Him Wrong, being the film version of *Diamond Lil*, soon fell victim to Hays office censorship, even before the Production Code had become fully enforced. West reportedly complained that the resulting script edits "spoiled *Diamond Lil* by making it cheap and tawdry."

She was just shy of forty when *She Done Him Wrong* premiered, which, at that time, may have been considered a tad mature for the screen image she was about to unleash on the world, but that didn't seem to matter. The plot has West as a performer in an 1890s Bowery saloon who crosses paths with various criminals and ne'er-do-wells, including her imprisoned lover. He escapes and discovers she hasn't exactly been biding her time waiting for him, but has instead set her eyes on a mission worker (film newbie Cary Grant) next door to the saloon. She later discovers Grant is, in fact, a detective doing undercover work, and, once the bad guys are snagged, the two embark on their unlikely whirlwind romance as the film fades out.

The New Movie Magazine chose its words carefully in its review:

> "In *She Done Him Wrong* Mae sets about the life work of collecting as many diamonds as possible from as many men who will show interest. You may take your reviewer's word for it that the results are staggering.
> …You can be very sure that this picture is something quite new for your movie experiences. a trifle strong for the weak sisters … but rare stuff for any who like brisk entertainment with a kick."

Picture Play magazine took an even greater delight in the spicy nature of the film.

"Ribald, rowdy, and unashamed…It is extraordinarily funny. Miss West recaptures the spirit of the time more surely than any of her predecessors in films of the gay '90s. She swaggers with brazen assurance uttering speeches that should make one's hair curl by their implications, but they don't. Instead, you laugh at her crudity and applaud her lack of hypocrisy."

The same reviewer provided some reassurance, however, for those who may have had misgivings about West's reputation:

"There isn't an unseemly word in the piece nor even the sort of kissing found in ninety-nine out of a hundred films which haven't the courage to say what Miss West does without subterfuge or subtlety.
Another virtue is that Mae…remains likable and humorous in all her outrageousness. She makes you feel that she doesn't take herself seriously and that she won't make a bid for your tears by attempting repentance and refinement in the end…The entire cast is admirable as one discovers when his eyes reluctantly leave Mae."

The film was added to the National Film Registry in 1996.

West's indelible character proved to be a double-edged sword. While her talents were undeniable, and felt like a breath of fresh air for most moviegoers, she played her character almost too well, and without deviation, keeping it up for her public appearances and newsreel interviews. In the public's mind, her image as the "Queen of Sex," blended inextricably with her real-life personality. And that wasn't necessarily a good thing.

1933

Her sister Beverly, troubled by Mae's image, expressed her concerns in a print interview that year. She saw the press as uninterested in learning about the real Mae West, which was far from the character she portrayed. "They write about what they think must be her real life, based on what they know of her stage life. And they are far from the truth. Why don't they write about how Mae is up every morning at nine, working like a slave all day? Why don't they write about how she works until long past midnight studying her characters and writing plays and books with authentic backgrounds?" Beverly added that her famous sister avoided indulging in the night life of clubs, and didn't smoke or drink (while Beverly herself battled alcoholism).

Mae spoke of the type of woman she had been portraying in dialogue and song since her early teens; teasing and/or promiscuous, complete with provocative clothing, designed by her French mother, who loved European fashions. Many concluded that she couldn't be so convincing as "bad woman" unless that was her true nature. "People have come right up to me and said I couldn't play bad women without being bad myself, or knowing and liking that kind of women," she said. "I'm going to be honest with you now! In all my life I've never met a really bad woman—and the reason I can make them so glamourous on the stage is because they're not real."

West with friend in *I'm No Angel*. Courtesy of Steve Cox.

Her second film of the year, *I'm No Angel*, premiered on October 6, and again co-starred Cary Grant. It would become an even bigger box office hit than *She Done Him Wrong*. However, even at this early stage of her screen career, there were those show business observers who, noting the single-themed nature of her work as both writer and performer, warned of its repetitious nature. West was daring, of course, but also quickly in danger of becoming one-note. *The New Movie Magazine* represented the "don't-say-I-didn't-warn-you" school on the matter:

> "This month may also mark the beginning of Mae West's slide down from her current peak of popularity—unless she does something different. In *I'm No Angel*, she repeats the formula that brought her such immense original success. No trick is quite so good the second time it's played, and Miss West's formula has been simple…The trouble with novelty is that it doesn't bear repetition and Miss West, this time, has merely recited her formula again…"

Despite her detractors, both of her films in 1933 combined to create a sensation throughout show business, serving as a double jolt of publicity for the star.

By the end of the year, West would be the talk of Hollywood, as well as the top box office attraction—and the highest paid woman—in the country. A new $100,000 contract added half that sum for her to write her own screenplays, which she intended to do anyway. *Variety* reported, "The past year brought three overnight stars (Mae West, Katherine Hepburn, Bing Crosby) who hit the public favor with a solid sock. Most sensational of the trio was Mae West, the biggest sensation the Paramount organization has had in more than 10 years. Miss West leads the star group, as far as box office prestige is concerned, by a mile. Her two pictures, *She Done Him Wrong* and *I'm No Angel*, besides setting records on initial runs, were repeaters with 'Wrong' playing as many as 12 return dates in one theatre."

1933

While her films boasted their share of shock value in dialogue, they are not exactly laugh riots. Her talent at writing clever dialogue was praise-worthy to be sure, and not all of that cleverness was immersed in sexual innuendo. For instance, while resisting a marriage proposal in *Goin' To Town* (1935), she explains to her suitor, "We're intellectual opposites. I'm intellectual, and you're opposite." She wasn't one to indulge in broad slapstick, or much of anything in the way of sight gags or physical action, beyond setting her undulating hips in motion. In hindsight, the attention lavished upon her was more a reaction to her brazen characterization and double entendres, rather than for generating any real, sustained belly laughs.

Nevertheless, Paramount's financial troubles to that time, due to a combination of the Depression and various economic setbacks within the studio itself, were in no small part alleviated by the success of West's films. Once the studio's recovery seemed assured, *Variety* noted, "The two Mae West releases are credited as an important factor here. It was one of the major surprises of the year, Paramount by December having rolled up $6,000,000 and reorganized its structure under bankruptcy so competently that fears are no longer felt for it."

West didn't have time to bask in such glory before her well-cultivated, comically sexy image would be severely challenged a little more than a year later, when the more heavily enforced moral code would further stifle nearly all of Hollywood's new film product.

The New Movie Magazine reflected on her whirlwind year thusly:

> "Well, it's quite an achievement, and you must hand it to Mae. Not so long ago, she came to Hollywood with ominous prophecies echoing in her ears. The smart fellows on Broadway opined that she could never get into a studio, let alone get herself a lucrative contract. They figured that, because of those ultra-sexy things she did on the stage, Will Hays would frown upon her cinema ambitions sufficiently to wilt them. Instead, Mae started a vogue that

will net her a fortune before they get tired of her so-called 'restricted' talents."

The fortune was there for her, certainly, but in fact further warnings of how her shtick could quickly grow stale began growing in number. Within a mere three years after her initial movie successes, *Picture Play* was describing her as "another whose success has been built around one very definite type of character. It is unfortunate for her that her famous creation is so limited in scope. The role is not adaptable to interesting variations, such as are possible with many other screen types, and Mae's future is problematical."

It may come as a surprise that West starred in only eight films throughout the Golden Decade of the 1930s (and that's counting *My Little Chickadee* with W.C. Fields, which was filmed in 1939 and released in 1940). Her screen character became so deeply entrenched with her first few screen efforts that there wasn't really anywhere for her to go from that point onward, unless she were to decide to initiate a nearly-total metamorphosis. With the Hays Office putting such a tight-fitting muzzle on most of her trademark style, her fire burned brightly, but, in hindsight, relatively briefly.

April 29 - *Diplomaniacs*, starring Wheeler & Woolsey, premieres.

The team's output to this point included features ranging from middling to quite entertaining. Among their best efforts to date include *Caught Plastered, Peach O'Reno, Hips, Hips, Hooray!,* and *Cockeyed Cavaliers*.

Diplomaniacs was one of a few comedy features of the time to use political issues (mostly fictional) as a backdrop. W.C. Fields did so as the eccentric leader of Klopstokia in *Million Dollar Legs*, the Marx Brothers would soon release *Duck Soup* with Groucho as leader of Fredonia, and here Wheeler & Woolsey pose as ambassadors at a Geneva meeting of world representatives. The script was co-written by Joseph Mankewitz, and William Seiter directed, as he had for most of the above-mentioned W&W features (and would helm Laurel & Hardy's classic *Sons of the Desert* in another year's time).

Diplomaniacs poster. Courtesy of Steve Cox.

New Movie Magazine had a generally positive view of the film:

"This time the double W's end up at a peace conference in Geneva and there is one sequence that is genuinely funny. The gags are fast and sappy and there are a couple of scenes that you'll have to see twice because of audience laughs, unless we miss our guess. Anyone who could use a laugh should make a note of this one."

* * *

On radio, some comedians, even those who had only completed their first season on the air, were already feeling the pressures of producing new material each week for broadcast. Ed Wynn began to hear grumbling from both the public and show biz journalists about how a number of his jokes were beginning to sound familiar (he estimated receiving 300,000 letters during his first year on the air). *Radio Digest* griped, "No one has enjoyed Ed on stage and radio more than we have, and occasionally he still seems to have some of the old sparkle. But most of his jokes are getting older and older, and it is obvious that he and Graham McNamee are having to work harder than ever for the laughs."

Wynn defended himself by noting that he told an average of fifty-nine jokes per program, totaling about 3,000 gags in a single year of his *Fire Chief* broadcasts. Out of his personal file of more than 200,000 jokes, he said, "approximately 200 possibilities are discarded for every one that is included on a program. Most of them are new; a few may be old. And still a listener will write to say, 'Last week I was surprised to hear you tell two old jokes.' They will not put it this way: 'Last week you told fifty-seven new ones.' And yet that is the average I have maintained each week."

Burns & Allen received a few harrumphs from *Radio Digest*, despite the team's tremendous popularity:

1933

"We've been told that Gracie Allen's Dumb Dora character is a perfect humorous type, because she reminds every male listener of his sister-in-law, and every female listener of her husband's folks. It certainly is true that we all like to laugh at other people's dumbness, but not forever. Perhaps Gracie and George could vary their routine if they relied less on gags and more on humorous situations which they, and other players, acted out... As it is, these comics never do anything but *tell* each other what happens. This form of humor is not so convincing as it would be if they took the parts of characters in a situation..."

Some people are never satisfied.

June 29 - Roscoe Arbuckle dies.

The comic genius, who had risen to the upper echelon of silent film comedy, and who mentored Buster Keaton on the finer points of filmmaking and editing, died in his sleep of heart disease, after an evening of celebrating the one-year anniversary of his marriage to Addie McPhail. Arbuckle was only forty-six years old, and still struggling to reassert himself as a film comedian.

Earlier in the day, he completed filming of the last short in his contract with Warner Brothers, *Tomalio*, and at one point asked for a break in filming due to shortness of breath. However, he later felt good enough to attend the party in honor of his anniversary. His manager and friend, Joe Rivkin, reported that Arbuckle told him, "This is the happiest day of my life, Joe; it's a second honeymoon." He didn't awake the next morning.

It was reported that as many as 1,000 fans visited his casket at the Campbell Funeral Church in Manhattan. Honorary pallbearers included Rivkin, Bert Lahr, Bert Wheeler, and Gus Edwards.

While his name will forever be connected with the events that brought down his career, to point of nearly overshadowing his tremendous success in comedy, few among us can identify with, let alone imagine, the tribulations that turned Arbuckle's life upside down.

October/November - Jack Pearl stars in *Meet the Baron*, Ed Wynn stars in *The Chief*.

Both Jack Pearl and Ed Wynn proved to be two enormously popular stars on the air who attempted to translate the public's good will to their film efforts. With a number of vaudeville comedy veterans having reached nationwide popularity on radio in the span on just over a year, it was no surprise to see them acquiesce to the temptation of extending their popularity into film, and accepting hefty paychecks from film studios eager to cash in on the comedians' broadcasting successes.

Cantor's success onscreen, including *Roman Scandals*, proved a rare feat among his fellow radio comedians in the early 1930s. Author's collection.

1933

Eddie Cantor and Burns & Allen had already made successful early forays into films, prompting most of their comedy peers to follow suit, albeit with varying results.

Cantor had the luxury of starring in a pair of silent feature hits, *Kid Boots* (1926) and *Special Delivery* (1927) before he embarked on his radio career. His first talkie, *Whoopie!*, filmed in two-color Technicolor, was a smash hit in 1930, followed by successes including *Palmy Days* the following year, *The Kid from Spain* (1932), and *Roman Scandals* (1933).

Paramount studios gave Burns & Allen, in addition to their short films, prime spots in three incarnations of *The Big Broadcast* series (1932, 1936, and 1937). They also would star alongside W.C. Fields in both *International House* (1933) and *Six of a Kind* (1934), and in the Carole Lombard/Bing Crosby stranded-on-an-island comedy *We're Not Dressing* (1934), with George and Gracie ultimately appearing in twelve Paramount features in all.

However, Wynn and Pearl, both of whom became ratings smashes in 1932, came up with disappointing results when each attempted to parlay that success to film—both at MGM—in 1933.

Pearl, in his screen debut *Meet the Baron* (released on October 20) had an impressive line-up working with him. The screenplay is credited to prolific script writers Norman Krasna and Herman Mankiewicz; Pearl's co-stars included Jimmy Durante, Edna May Oliver, Zasu Pitts as a chambermaid, and even Ted Healy and his Stooges, (Moe Howard, Larry Fine, and Curly Howard) as janitors, not long before the Stooges left Healy to begin their own series of shorts for Columbia.

The plot has Pearl and Durante rescued from an African jungle after being abandoned by the "real" Baron Munchausen, but the rescuers mistake Pearl for the Baron, necessitating him to maintain the phony act throughout his hero's welcome in New York, and as a guest speaker at a girls' college. In between random interruptions by Healy and the Stooges, Pearl and ZaSu find themselves smitten with each other.

One extended scene, an obligatory bit in front of a radio microphone with straight man in tow, gives Pearl's radio fans a good dose of what had propelled him to stardom in the first place, with the Baron telling tall tales, complete with groan-worthy puns delivered in his famous German accent (which, ironically, actually makes Durante sound the more articulate of the two). The wildly varying comedy styles of his co-stars, however, simply don't mesh well with each other (plus, there are also several doses of unfortunate racist humor), although Pearl and Pitts do demonstrate, with their flirtatious exchanges, some promising comedy chemistry together.

Wynn's *The Chief*, premiered on November 3, and takes place in New York's Bowery in the 1890s. Wynn, as Henry Summers, is the son of a deceased fire-fighting hero who becomes a hero himself by somewhat clumsily rescuing a woman from a burning building. This leads to his run for city alderman, but he is unaware that his incumbent opponent, named Clayton, is a corrupt and sinister rival. After failing to bully Henry into dropping out of the race, Clayton has Henry's mother kidnapped to get him to quit (the funniest scene in the film shows Ma cooking breakfast and fussing over her captors at their hideout). Henry, panic-stricken over Ma's abduction, decides to act as if he has gone crazy, hoping this would discourage his potential voters from electing him. Of course, Clayton gets his comeuppance in the end, and Ma returns unharmed.

Once that plot is resolved, the film abruptly and inexplicably switches to a radio studio for a *Fire Chief* broadcast, with Wynn, his announcer Graham McNamee, the orchestra, and audience having a great time. Wynn provides an epilogue to the Ed Summers story movie-goers had just seen, and then answers a few write-in questions from listeners, which had become a regular part of his radio program. If nothing else, the sequence gives us a look at Wynn in action as a radio comedian.

Despite both Wynn's and Pearl's radio popularity at the time, their respective films generated somewhat guarded anticipation. Upon their release, *Radioland* magazine cautioned, "Neither of these promises to be the box office hit that might have been expected from their radio ratings, though *Meet the Baron* has a bit of an edge on *The Chief*. Perhaps that is just the law of compensation balancing things up, for Wynn continues to hold his own with radio fans, though he, too, is beginning to suffer a bit from mannerisms that may react to his detriment as they did with Pearl."

The New York Times' review of *The Chief* called this final add-on scene "a somewhat desperate effort to corral the comedian's radio public," but went easier on Wynn himself. "It is the finest tribute to Mr. Wynn's comic ingenuity that he persuades his audiences at the Mayfair [theatre] to laugh at such antique side-ticklers as the release of a water hose into a holiday crowd, the ferocious struggle with a pet bear and the destruction of a valuable vase." The review concluded, "What it all comes down to is that Mr. Wynn is genuinely funny and *The Chief* is not."

MGM did not offer Wynn a contract for another film.

Seeing both *The Chief* and *Meet the Baron* disappoint both commercially and critically (between the two, *Meet the Baron* received somewhat kinder reviews and better box office returns), Wynn claimed that the movie industry was luring top radio comedians to Hollywood to deliberately put them in bad films. The scheme, he believed, was "to get people to go out, not sit home" listening to the radio, thereby putting a significant dent in radio's popularity. Thirty years later, he was still holding fast, saying, "This has been my contention all these years, and I haven't changed a bit from it."

Pearl took it all more in stride, resisting Wynn's bitterness and suspicions. "Well, you know how those things go," Pearl said. "The boys out on the [west] coast like to take anyone down a little who has made a reputation in the east on the stage or on the air. So many of the Broadway boys and girls have gone out and high-hatted them that they are on the defensive. But I'm not complaining. *Meet the Baron* has made money at the box office. And I'm going to make another picture in September [*Hollywood Party*], so that's your answer."

While Wynn may have had an interesting contention (or, conspiracy theory, in modern parlance), the facts bear him out only partially. It's true that several radio favorites were unable to make a successful transition to the screen, as nearly every radio comedian took a shot at films in the 1930s. Amos

& Andy, Jack Benny, Fred Allen, Goodman and Jane Ace, and others all tried their hand at film work, but movies simply weren't a great fit for each and every radio comedy star.

George Burns reasoned that one driving force behind the trend of radio comedians taking their shot at success on the screen was simply to satisfy the public's sheer curiosity, rather than aspiring to produce great cinematic art. "Probably the thing that almost all of the films we made had in common," he said, "was that the plot wasn't important. Important? Sometimes it didn't even exist. The whole purpose of these films was to give audiences a chance to see vaudeville and radio stars they'd seen or heard playing the characters they were known for."

As for Wynn's assertion that conspiratorial forces were at work, it could be argued more convincingly that the popularity of motion pictures caused *vaudeville* to suffer more in the 1930s than radio. It's also important to remember that just about every radio favorite who did find some success on the screen gladly returned to the more familiar confines of the broadcast studio, with its less strenuous work week than that of motion pictures.

As usual, Fred Allen could be relied upon to provide an intelligent and articulate take on how radio comedy stars were wise not to consider film success a guarantee.

> "Hollywood offers a radio star the biggest gamble he'll ever be expected to take but, in turn, it gives him the largest salary he'll ever make. So most of us are taking the chance and praying for the best…Everybody knows the first appearances of Rudy Vallee, Amos and Andy, Ed Wynn and several others hurt them. They're excellent entertainers. The trouble was due to the fact that they were rushed into a medium about which they knew nothing, forced to do things new to them and out of keeping with their own sense of showmanship. Well, I've tried to profit by these mistakes. And so when you see me it

won't be as a screen lover but as the sour-voiced, sarcastic wisecracker which is my trademark on the air."

Almost predictably, Allen's vast popularity in radio didn't translate to the screen for him, either. Most of his film appearances were in supporting roles, and the few in which he received top billing were both critical and commercial disappointments. Besides, his work writing each of his radio scripts kept him too busy for most of each year to pursue films seriously.

His friend Jack Benny felt that radio comedians had little choice but to expand into films, even if the results weren't necessarily comedy masterpieces.

> "We really have to make pictures, because the money they offer is our salvation. Show business isn't what it used to be. Either you're on top today or you're practically nothing. There's little middle ground. And you have only a short road up very often and always a very, very short road down. Once upon a time when you passed your peak you could count on a few years in vaudeville on the strength of your name. Vaudeville today amounts to practically nothing. …We need at least ten years of a high income, especially now that different taxes take so much of all we earn away from us. And to insure ourselves these ten years we've got to do different kinds of things, not let the public get tired of us in any one medium.…We can't afford to keep all our eggs in one basket. There's too much at stake!"

Benny, however, would soon surprise the public, and perhaps even himself, with his much-lauded performance in the 1934 comedy-drama *To Be Or Not To Be* (co-starring Carole Lombard), the most noteworthy of nearly twenty films in which he would star as a result of his radio success.

After Jack Pearl's *The Baron* met with disappointing results, his participation in MGM's *Hollywood Party*, despite his display of confidence ahead of its premiere, sealed his cinematic fate. The episodic film, with each segment written and directed by a different team, boasted an all-star cast, including Laurel & Hardy (conversing with "Mexican Spitfire" Lupe Velez), Jimmy Durante, Ted Healy & the Three Stooges, and others, but it was a mish-mash of unrelated scenes that didn't add up to much. Despite Pearl's own talents, it had become clear that he was not destined to become a comedy film star (to be fair, *Hollywood Party* didn't do much to boost the careers of *any* of its stars). So, he returned to radio, but there were hints that Baron Munchausen, riding high only six months earlier, was already beginning to wear out his welcome.

Radio Digest attempted to put an optimistic, if not entirely forthright, spin on the situation:

> "Jack Pearl has gradually built up an acceptance for Baron Munchausen that is now, deservedly, almost universal. The mistake has not been made of giving the listeners too much of the Baron at a time. He leaves 'em when they're laughing hardest (other stars and sponsors might well study the Pearl technique.) Also, Jack changes his routine just enough on each program so that the Baron, with good jokes or bad, is never quite the same fellow. In other words, the fans can't always tell what to expect. (Nothing will kill a popular program so quickly as taking every surprise out of it, as has been done in radio so often.)…"

This rosy assessment concluded with a caveat that popularity, even of a beloved character, could still fade swiftly, especially if the jokes begin to sound a bit too familiar and shopworn. "There are limits to affection," continued *Radio Digest*, "and the slogan of the American people seems to be, 'You can do anything but bore us.' Even the swell Lucky Strike music wouldn't save the program if the Baron got *really* insulting about our memory for jokes." Pearl's tremendous success in 1933 proved unable to sustain itself, as listeners became increasingly weary of the character and his catchphrase "Vas you dere, Sharlie?"

"When listeners finally began getting tired of the line," George Burns said, "Jack Pearl had no insurance. After two successful seasons the show lost its popularity. Jack told me once that "Vas you dere, Sharlie" became 'The Frankenstein of lines.' The Baron had become bigger than his creator. Jack couldn't get away from him; he was so well known as the Baron that no one would hire him to do anything else."

The February issue of *Radioland* printed was was essentially the Baron's obituary, albeit somewhat prematurely, claiming that the character was "definitely through," and then offered an explanation. "It can't be because he used old gags: Cantor and Wynn and The Two Black Crows do that, with uniform success. To our mind the Baron failed because he was too much Baron. In the nature of things he couldn't be much else, but his dialect aberrations gave every program a semblance of monotony. Jack Pearl understands the value of variety. A good program doctor could bring Jack Pearl back to the top of the heap."

The Baron survived until that September, but by then Pearl knew when it was time to say goodbye to the character and look for a fresh approach. While he seemed to be among the last to come to that realization, perhaps he was too fond of the Baron to let go easily. "Baron Munchausen is one of the grandest characters I ever played in my twenty-three years in show business," he said. "He was a real creation, but he had what you might call a single track mind…No matter what the Baron was doing—hunting, fishing, exploring, or what—you knew he was going to lie about it. Whatever the situation, the humor arose from the whoppers the Baron would tell about it. That was a swell comedy situation, but it has its limits. After such a long time, anyone will eventually get tired of it."

Pearl would return in the spring of 1935 with a new character, a German hotel and tavern owner named Peter Pfeiffer. The response ran along the lines of this review: "Jack Pearl is getting some stiff competition not only from the other comedians, but from the ghost of his old character, and even against the beloved Baron, Peter Pfeiffer comes off a bad second. Maybe we'll like Peter when we know him better. Maybe when Jack Pearl knows him better." Listeners, however, weren't interested in getting to know Peter Pfeiffer, and the program was off the air quickly.

Another effort, *The Jack Pearl Show*, premiered late the following year, reuniting Pearl with Cliff "Sharlie" Hall, and with the writing help of Eugene Conrad. *Variety* noted, "There is a vaudeville background to this framework which, even if it does resurrect a couple of familiars, is sturdy stuff." This program was also short-lived, and pretty much sealed Pearl's career as a major radio star.

October 8 - Joe Penner's *The Baker's Broadcast* debuts.

A seasoned burlesque and vaudeville comedian, Penner joined an increasingly crowded comedy field on the air when he appeared on Rudy Vallee's Fleischmann-sponsored show. Armed with his cartoonish voice and giggle, and goofy catchphrases like "Wanna buy a duck?" and "Ooh, you nasty man!" he made a hit with Vallee's audience, and, as was the case with so many Vallee guests, landed his own program shortly thereafter, also sponsored by Fleischmann.

There wasn't much to Penner's character. He was amiable and goofy, recognized for his ever-present and somewhat askew porkpie hat, but one would be hard pressed to describe him as hilarious. Still, he was an undeniable smash throughout 1934, and voted radio's top comedian. The novelty of his paper-thin act and catchphrases, combined with radio's famous demands for new material each week, did not bode well for him by the following year.

George Burns said of Penner, "The problem with relying on catchphrases is that they get very old while they're still new. A year after Penner had been named the most popular comedian on radio his show was canceled because of poor ratings. Gracie and Jack [Benny] were smart enough to stop using a catchphrase very soon after it caught on, then they'd use it once in a while, so that every time they did the audience was surprised and the line got a good reaction."

Burns got most of it right, except that Penner's program was *not* canceled. He quit the show in June of 1935, due to a dispute with sponsor Fleishmann. He wanted to try new things for the program, such as bringing on guest stars for him to interact with on the air, but was met with a "If it ain't broke, don't fix it" response from the head honchos.

"I wasn't happy," he told an interviewer. "I wasn't satisfied with the sort of comedy I did, and I wasn't even making very much money. At one time, just before I quit, I had five gagmen.

It seemed as if I was always hiring a new writer, only to find that everything he wrote sounded like the jokes the others had been writing…But I had to go on paying them all out of the salary my sponsors paid me."

To his credit, Penner aspired to a higher form of radio comedy, like that of Jack Benny.

"I got so sick of the mechanical kind of comedy I worked with, too. I used to listen to Jack Benny and think, 'Gee, I wish I could be like that—breezy and flip and smart!' Ever since I went into vaudeville I'd worked from a script, memorizing a lot of sure-fire gags and reeling them off like a parrot. In radio it was just the same, except that I didn't bother to memorize them but read them instead. I got to feeling that I was nothing but a mouthpiece, without any real ability of my own."

On the other hand, Penner was also reticent to try something *too* different, especially ad-libbing on the air, for fear of throwing off the flow and timing of the program. Having fallen into a rut, he couldn't bear to continue, and quit the program at the end of June. It would be some time before making his next attempt at starring in a radio show he could live with.

November 17 - Paramount releases the Marx Brothers in *Duck Soup*.

This was the brothers' final and most polished film for Paramount, and arguably the best film they made, period. Beginning with Groucho's grand entrance as Freedonia's new president, Rufus T. Firefly, *Duck Soup* maintains an impressively consistent quality of both verbal and visual hilarity from start to finish, and without a tedious romantic subplot, or even solo musical numbers by Harpo and Chico. The script was written by Bert Kalmar and Harry Ruby, who had co-written the brothers' previous film, *Horsefeathers*, as well as the songs performed in the Marx films to date. The director of *Duck Soup*, Leo McCarey, had already demonstrated his tremendous creative influence at Roach Studios, having a hand in creating some of the best comedies *anywhere* to date. Groucho later referred to McCarey as "the only first class director we ever had."

Duck Soup lobby card. Author's collection.

The plot of the film centers on the personal clash between Firefly and neighboring Sylvania's ambassador, Trentino. Highlights include Harpo and Chico (whom Trentino has hired to spy on Firefly) harassing lemonade vendor Edgar Kennedy, and an astounding sequence with both Harpo and

1933

Chico disguised as Groucho, befuddling the team's foil, Margaret Dumont, before culminating in the celebrated "mirror scene" (suggested by McCarey, based on similar scenes from the silent movie days). Chico's pun-filled trial for treason leads into a deliberately campy musical number, declaring war on Sylvania, followed the climactic battle sequence.

While film is noticeably devoid of individual musical pieces by Harpo and Chico, one song Kalmar and Ruby wrote for the film, "Keep Doing What You're Doing" ended up in the Wheeler & Woolsey film *Hips, Hips, Hooray* the following year, for which Kalmar and Ruby also wrote the script (that particular musical number, featuring Thelma Todd and Dorothy Lee, is one of the Golden Decade's most wonderfully silly musical sequences).

It has often been written that *Duck Soup* received negative reviews and poor box office, causing Paramount to decide against offering a new contract to the team. This is contradicted not only by simply reading the reviews themselves, but also by the fact that the film was the sixth-highest grossing film of 1933—not a shabby accomplishment at all.

Photoplay raved, "Again the four Marx Brothers crash through with a package of hilarious nonsense that is rib-tickling fun for all who don't care whether their fun has reason to it. They're all mixed up this time in a revolution and other troubles in mythical Fredonia—and what a land it must be, judging from what happens! But the action is fast, the dialogue is faster, and the Marxes fastest of all. It's a riot!"

Variety was also quite taken with the film:

> "Practically everybody wants a good laugh right now and *Duck Soup* should make practically everybody laugh. The picture should draw and please all over. The laughs come often…although in this instance more care appears to have been taken with the timing, since the step-on gags don't occur as frequently as in the past. But a picture that contains enough howls to lose some of them without the losses being noticed needn't fret.

...In place of the constant punning and dame chasing, *Duck Soup* has the Marxes madcapping through such bits as the old Schwartz Bros. mirror routine, so well done in the hands of Groucho, Harpo and Chico that it gathers a new and hilarious comedy momentum all over again. Everything's in keeping with the tempo of the production, the Marxes personally staying on top of the story at all times and on top of the music as well."

The New Movie Magazine also offered praise:

"With each fresh appearance of the Four Marx Brothers in films, the plot of the production grows thinner, the puns become more atrocious and the whole affair, for some mysterious reason, seems funnier than any of its forerunners. *Duck Soup* is no exception. Groucho, Harpo, Chico, with Zeppo playing straight, can take ancient gags and the most venerable situations and by some sort of goofy hocus-pocus, turn these shopworn matters into enduring hilarity…the trio are goofier than ever with Groucho rising above the others. …*Duck Soup* should come like a reviving breath of air, straight from the insane asylum."

As the movie-going public attended *Duck Soup* and all of its near-perfect madness, one Marx Brother in particular was about to make real history. Harpo, much to his own surprise, was to become the first American entertainer to perform in the U.S.S.R. after the U.S. formally recognized the Soviet Union on November 16. The trip was conceived and arranged by his close friend Alexander Wollcott, writer and theatre critic for *The New York Times*.

"Wollcott was a particularly good friend of Mrs. Roosevelt," Harpo explained in his autobiography, "and he flounced in and out of the White House like he owned a piece of the joint…Early that fall he called me from New York. He'd just learned, he said, that President Roosevelt was about to carry out his campaign promise of recognizing the Soviet Union. That was nice, I said, and what else was new? Nothing, said Aleck, except that I was going to Russia. I told him he was crazy I didn't want to go to Winnipeg, Manitoba, let alone Russia." Despite Harpo's protestations, Wollcott started pulling strings to arrange for his friend's visa. Once in Moscow, Harpo rehearsed for ten days with performers from the Moscow Art Theatre.

"It sure as hell hadn't been easy to put my act together in Moscow," he said. "I had never in my life worked harder for an opening. The Russian sense of humor was a wonderful thing once you got it going for you. But how to get it going? That was the catch."

As part of a revue-style program, Harpo was assigned four spots in the show. His first consisted of a harp solo, a brief introduction, and a bit with a clarinet that blew bubbles. He later replicated his *Animal Crackers* scene in which a seemingly endless stream of stolen knives and other silverware drop out of his coat sleeve. He returned to the harp for his final spot, playing "as long as the crowd wanted more."

The New York Times reported:

"Harpo Marx received an ovation here tonight. Making his first appearance before a Russian audience in his celebrated knife-dropping act, the American comedian brought down the house in the Music Hall as a capacity audience of usually phlegmatic Soviet theatregoers applauded, stamped and cheered for twenty-five minutes during and after his six-minute act. He wore a wig, played a harp and preserved his usual waggish silence, and was assisted by two members of the cast of the Moscow Art Theatre…"

Harpo later received a phone call from American Ambassador William C. Bullitt, who congratulated him on his success. Before returning to the U.S.,

Harpo also played a very real role of a spy, agreeing to smuggle secret documents out of the country, taped to his leg.

While Harpo was in Russia, the Marx Brothers' future plans became the source of speculation in the trade papers, via erroneous reports that ultimately lead up several blind alleys. *Variety* reported on December 12 that the team had made a deal to continue making films with Paramount. "Re-signing of the Marx Brothers at Paramount kills plans of the quartet and Sam Harris for a Broadway musical in January. Plans had been completed when the Paramount deal washed them out. Chico and Groucho, who left for New York Friday (Dec. 8) will remain in the east for three weeks. Arrival of Harpo from Russia around Christmas will be their signal to return to the coast and start working on their first picture yarn. Production will get started around March 15."

Of course, the Marx Brothers: a) were never to return to Broadway as a team, b) did not remain a quartet beyond *Duck Soup*'s release, and c) did not sign a new contract with Paramount. The studio passed on renewing their contract. While *Duck Soup* made a respectable showing at the box office, the studio's new favorite of that year was the woman who had saved it from financial disaster, Mae West.

The brothers were indeed without a studio for the following year (leaving *Variety* with a bit of egg on its face). On the bright side, they did maintain their standing among the top five Paramount stars of 1933, along with West, Bing Crosby, Harold Lloyd, and Frederic March. Others claiming top honors at the studio included Carol Lombard, Burns & Allen, Jack Oakie, and W.C. Fields.

December 7 - Hal Roach Studios celebrates its 20th anniversary.

The studio at the time was at a peak, cranking out high-quality comedies at an impressive rate, by the most creative minds in the business. Roach threw a party, part of which was broadcast on radio, for his stars and behind-the-scenes employees. Those who stepped before the microphone included Charley

Chase, Will Rogers, MGM chief Louis B. Mayer, Jean Harlow, Thelma Todd and Patsy Kelly, and Laurel & Hardy. Despite such a line-up paying tribute to their boss, *Variety* was less than impressed by their radio presence: "Hollywood ought to do better than this when going on the air. And a studio identified with comedies should be a lot funnier in its air presentation. Roach himself was in good taste and simple dignity when responding."

Hal Roach celebrates with Laurel & Hardy and Thelma Todd.
Author's collection.

December 29 - Laurel & Hardy's *Sons of the Desert* premieres.

This feature has been widely regarded, along with their later *Way out West*, as the best of Laurel & Hardy's feature films, one that actually relies more on plot than broad slapstick for most of its laughs.

The story involves Stan and Ollie and their fraternal lodge, the Sons of the Desert. They attempt to explain to their wives that the upcoming convention in Chicago is for the lodge brothers only, and that the wives will have to stay home. However, the wives (Mae Busch as Ollie's wife Lolly, Dorothy Christie as Stan's wife Betty) forbid them to go. When Ollie feigns illness, a doctor (actually a veterinarian Stan called by mistake) recommends a recuperative vacation. Ollie asks Stan to accompany him on an ocean voyage, and their spouses agree to let them go. Instead, of course, the boys make a bee line to Chicago, where they take part in a parade, and meet their fellow lodge brothers, including practical joker Charley Chase.

On the day they are to return from their supposed stay in Hawaii, word arrives that their ship has encountered a typhoon and is sinking. While the wives anxiously await word of the rescue, the boys arrive home (complete with leis on their necks and a ukulele), and, confused that no one is home to greet them, see the newspaper headlines about the shipwreck. When the wives return, Stan and Ollie seek refuge in the attic, but the women are too upset to stay home, and try to distract themselves by going to the movies, where the newsreel they see has captured Stan and Ollie frolicking in Chicago.

The furious wives return home, only to listen to Stan and Ollie fabricate the story of their rescue. Of course, Stan quickly breaks down and confesses their ruse. He is rewarded for his honesty by his sympathetic wife, while a less fortunate Ollie gets a kitchen full of pots and pans hurled his way by his furious spouse.

Sons of the Desert was selected for addition to the National Film Registry in 2012. The film title was also adopted as the more common name of the Laurel & Hardy Appreciation Society, which was founded in 1964 by the team's biographer John McCabe (with Stan's encouragement and support), shortly before Stan's death the following year. Sons of the Desert boasts over 100 chapters, or "tents," across the U.S., and twenty more in a half-dozen European countries, Canada, and Australia. Each tent is named after a Laurel & Hardy film.

Promotional art for *Sons of the Desert*. Author's collection.

1934

Radio comedy matured and evolved at a rapid pace within the first few years of the Golden Decade alone. In 1931 and 1932, for instance, most comedians and their audiences were happy with rapid-fire one-liners and unrelated gags to sustain the bulk of each program, in between musical numbers and lengthy commercial messages from their sponsors. Soon, though, a change of attitude, in favor of more situational comedy, began to take a firmer hold.

In January, Eddie Cantor wrote in *Variety* how his prediction the previous year concerning radio comedy had come true, claiming that "out and out gag comedy on the air was due to flop; that radio audiences were becoming smarter with each program, and rather than be gagged to death they would just stop dialing in to the people who recited a series of jokes...The radio public is giving the gag the go-by for the situation-laugh guy."

Burns & Allen's chief writer, Eugene Conrad, had already expressed the same sentiment. "Delivering a mere string of jokes is already a thing of the past in radio," he said. "Comedy passages are now definite scenes, definite episodes. They require their own radio technique, a more difficult technique than the stage." Even Ed Wynn, who thrived on stringing unrelated jokes and anecdotes together while constructing his weekly scripts, began efforts to adapt to the new trend.

The new year of 1934 looked every bit as promising for radio comedy as had the previous few seasons. There would be a number of failures, of course, but comedy as a genre was proving to be a reliable mainstay of the medium. Continuing his thoughts about the state of comedy on radio at the time, Eddie Cantor wrote, "I want to go on the record with the statement that comedy—good comedy—will always be top in radio. If there are no laughs coming into the homes of the millions of radio owners, radio manufacturers will soon find themselves in a new business."

February 9 - W.C. Fields stars in *Six of a Kind*.

Fields' upward trajectory as a true film comedy star received another boost with his four Mack Sennett shorts, which provided him with some creative satisfaction, as did the features *Million Dollar Legs* in 1932, and *Tillie and Gus* the following year. It could be argued, though, that 1934 would be his most successful year in films. It was certainly his busiest. In this year alone, he was either the star or featured player in no fewer than five features, beginning with *Six of a Kind*. Directed by Leo McCarey, fresh from his triumphant work directing *Duck Soup*, Fields' fellow ensemble players here include Burns & Allen, Charlie Ruggles, Mary Boland, and Alison Skipworth.

As for Fields himself, McCarey once conceded, "The hell of it was he was basically so funny that I'd start to wail to the front office about how difficult he was, and I got no sympathy."

Burns was allowed to work material for himself and Gracie into the script. "Mr. Burns writes all the dialogue for the team," it was reported, "both radio and screen, as he did in the old days when Burns and Allen limited their activities to the vaudeville stages. When they are working in a film, Mr. Burns receives a dummy script, and he writes in the Burns and Allen part himself, gags and all. Their next film, *Many Happy Returns*, which will be released in about four weeks, was an exception. Mr. Burns said it was a strain not writing gags for the picture."

February 22 - *It Happened One Night* premieres.

This comedy is credited for leading a new style that produced several truly hilarious films throughout the 1930s. Its special significance might be lost on

1934

most modern-day viewers, so a bit of context would be helpful, requiring us to hearken back quite a long time.

Stage comedians, from the day the very first stage was built, presented themselves as characters who stood apart from the crowd, even if by appearance alone. Whether it was a distinctive or silly hat, cane, bushy moustache, exaggerated facial features (sometimes drawn on with greasepaint), ill-fitting or otherwise unique clothing and shoes, it wasn't difficult to identify the comic character when he entered a scene. He was, simply put, a clown, standing out like a sore thumb, perhaps awkwardly moving through the room, and often surrounded by those of a higher social stature. Traditions proved tough to break, and most vaudevillians saw little need to change their stripes after drifting into film. Not every comedian resorted to such measures, but even a humble bowler hat, for instance, when spotted in a sea of top hats, or a bowtie among a crowd of ascots, would be enough to identify the "funny" guy that an audience would be wise to keep an eye on.

In the mid-1930s, however, a different approach to comedy, as exemplified by *It Happened One Night*, landed on theatre screens. This film in particular sparked the true rise of a new sub-genre—the "screwball" comedy—which usually played as a romantic farce, and with stars who were not strictly comedians per se, but rather actors who had talent (to varying degrees) for playing light comedy.

As Capra explained on Dick Cavett's talk show in 1972, "I came along with *It Happened One Night* and tried something. I tried to combine the leading man and the comedian in one, rather than the comic relief. It was the first time it was done. The leading man was getting the laughs. It was a very felicitous combination."

In the film's story, Colbert, as young heiress Ellie, with an overprotective father, elopes with a pilot named King Westly, whom her father distrusts, and who demands an annulment. Angered by his domineering, Ellie jumps off their yacht in Florida and boards a Greyhound bus on the way to New York, and her new husband. Gable, as newspaperman Peter Warne, meets her on the bus and recognizes her. He offers to help her reunite with Westly if she gives him her exclusive story. Most of the story centers on their adventures en route to New York, during which they bicker but eventually fall in love. Complications ensue, but Ellie's father, upon seeing Peter as an honest man who loves her, and who doesn't care about the family's wealth (or the reward money for returning her safely), sees that Peter's the better man for her, and encourages Ellie to cancel the formal wedding and annul the marriage—with a financial incentive for Westly if he agrees, which he does.

While it remains a classic, and was the first film ever to win in the top five Academy Award categories for Best Picture, direction (Frank Capra), screenplay (Robert Riskin), lead actor (Clark Gable), and lead actress (Claudette Colbert), *It Happened One Night* holds up well as an amusing romantic comedy, while it isn't especially side-splitting when compared to the screwball films to come, such as *My Man Godfrey* and *Nothing Sacred* (both of which benefitted from the superb comic skills of Carole Lombard). Of course, *It Happened One Night* does have a number of celebrated moments which have long since become popular clips shown at the Academy Awards and other celebrations of film: Colbert, hitchhiking, exposing quite a bit of her leg to stop a passing motorist; she and Gable sleeping in the same room with blankets strung on a line between them for privacy.

Capra said of the film, "Really, that's the only picture that Gable ever played himself. He was that character and he loved doing those scenes. We didn't write the film for Gable. We wrote it for Robert Montgomery, who turned it down. Nobody would play it. No women would play it. Comedies don't read very well in script form, especially light comedies. They're too fluffy. Nobody gets killed, there are no wars, no whores. Five girls turned it down, and finally Claudette Colbert took it because we paid her a lot of money."

A little over two months after *It Happened One Night* premiered, *Twentieth Century*, directed by Howard Hawks and starring John Barrymore and Carole Lombard, opened on May 3.

Lombard had been a contract player with Paramount since her signing with the studio in 1930, as was noted in the press. A brief blurb in *The New York Times* reported: "Risen from the Mack Sennett ranks of comediennes,

1934

Carol Lombard ascends the proverbial ladder into the higher reaches with a new contractual arrangement with Paramount, whereby she becomes a featured player...Miss Lombard, a tall, classic blonde, appeared in *Me, Gangster, Show Folkers*, and other films."

Four years later, the newspaper called her performance in *Twentieth Century* "the outstanding portrayal of her Hollywood career." That is, of course, until her skills as a screwball comedian over the subsequent few years would produce even funnier results.

Interestingly, Hawks' reflections on *Twentieth Century* mirror Capra's own boast about *It Happened One Night* almost word for word. As Hawks claimed, *Twentieth Century* "was the first time the dramatic leads, instead of secondary comics, played for laughs. I mean we got the fun out of John Barrymore and Carole Lombard. It was two or three years ahead of its time... the laughs are born out of the inhibitions that restrict each of us and are here abruptly removed by rejuvenation. It was a good story. Perhaps we pushed the point a bit too far for the public."

It Happened One Night was added to the National Film Registry in 1993, while *Twentieth Century* was selected in 2011.

It can be debated that earlier films could qualify as the first screwball comedies, such as *Bombshell* (1933) starring Jean Harlow, or even *The Front Page* (1931), which perhaps could also be considered the talkies' first "bromance."

March 4 - Groucho and Chico Marx star in *The Marx of Time* on radio.

Without a film to work on throughout all of 1934 (or even a studio, for that matter), Groucho and Chico attempted a second radio program, this time for American Oil. For *The Marx of Time*, Groucho played "Ulysses H. Drivel" and Chico "Penelli". The goal was to satirize the news of the world, with the timeslot of Sundays at 7 p.m. It's been speculated that this was perhaps too early in the evening for the Marx brand of humor, and, as a consequence of poor ratings, it lasted only six episodes (of course, that same 7 o'clock slot on Sundays didn't do Jack Benny any harm in his two decades on the air).

"There was just no way of figuring out who would be good on the radio," George Burns said. "Some people who should have been big stars just never made it." He cited the likes of George Jessel and other popular vaudevillians such as Lou Holtz, Frank Fay, Milton Berle, and, yes, Groucho and Chico. "Harpo I could understand." Burns conceded. However, even Harpo popped up on radio occasionally, answering questions from program hosts by communicating through whistles and honking his horn.

An issue of considerable debate in the world of radio gained increasing attention throughout 1934, as grumbling became louder among some comedians and a number of their listeners, over the presence of studio audiences on comedy programs. The question whether audience laughter enhanced or impeded the proceedings of any comedy show became a hot topic.

It's understandable to assume that all radio comedians enjoyed performing their programs in front of live audiences. Surely, a radio performer, having paid his (or her) dues in vaudeville, would want to see and hear the spontaneous laughter of an audience to infuse added energy into a radio broadcast. It would also provide some indication of how home listeners across the country were likely reacting to the same material. Surprisingly, however, the community of laugh-makers at the time was decidedly split on the issue of performing on radio to live, laughing audiences.

As *Radio Mirror* explained, "Standing before a mike and hoping their efforts were going over, instead of watching the reception on the faces of their followers, was too much of a risk, in their way of thinking. Cantor, Jolson, Fred Allen, Ed Wynn watch their studio audiences enjoy them and hope the invisible listeners feel the same way. And, obviously their shows are peppier because the mob is around them. After all, the most important thing is that they be given every facility for their best work."

But a dilemma arose among veteran stage comedians like Cantor and Wynn, who were accustomed to including visual gags in their stage acts, and apparently didn't take the time to consider how their clowning would play on radio. They often wore costumes, mugged for the studio/theatre audience, and insisted on including sight gags to keep the visitors in front of them laughing along, thus eliminating as much dead air as possible. This was a reasonable argument (not to mention that it helped with the proper timing of each joke), but there were pitfalls. While a comedian could score points for inviting home listeners to feel more a part of the laugh fest, his antics for the benefit of the theatre-goers only were obviously lost on the millions at home who had no use for funny faces or sight gags on a radio show.

In addition, there were those in the broadcasting business who didn't welcome adapting to the sound of a studio audience reacting to the comedy. John Carlisle, director of programming for CBS, grumbled, "To sit by a radio receiver and hear laughter without knowing what provoked it is extremely annoying. So annoying, in fact, that some comedians would do better to work without a studio audience." That was fine with Fred Allen, for one, who also found audience laughter distracting, even when it was coming from his *own* audience (George Burns joked, "I think Fred Allen didn't even want people listening.")

Allen himself put it as bluntly as possible when he proclaimed that "all comedians should be prohibited by law from laughing at their own jokes, thus insuring a one hundred per cent lull. All studio audiences should be equipped with woolen mittens. Their applause would then be seen and not heard and those who listen at home would not be disturbed."

The debate continued throughout the year, even as a growing number of listeners clamored to get free tickets to see their favorite broadcasts in person.

To further cloud the issue, some comedians seemed to experience a change of heart, in both directions. Cantor, who could be held responsible for opening this can of worms over the reaction to his spontaneous "hats and scarves" skit on his program, made a 180-degree turn of opinion in early 1934. In a curious column he wrote for *Variety* that January, he insisted "I don't care how smart or conscientious the radio performer may be, with a visible audience in front of him he is tempted to play to the elephant's tail. The laughter and applause on the average hour program, with a studio audience present, runs about four minutes. The sponsor is paying for that time and the listening public should get entertainment during those four minutes instead of laughter, a good part of which puzzles, and prolonged applause which irritates."

He also disputed the argument that radio comedians used live laughter to help with their timing, adding that any comedian "would be 100% better off concentrating on that audience listening in throughout the country...The comedy would be more imaginative, more creative. The studio audiences are nice people, but they're a nuisance." Cantor was apparently in an especially grumpy mood the day he wrote the piece, adding, "Don't let any comedian tell you that he needs the audience's reaction in order to time his gags. That's the bunk. It is merely soothing syrup for the guy's vanity." Most of his contemporaries disagreed.

When asked to compare working in film and on radio, Cantor said, "In the movies, you can always depend on re-takes. It is easier, I think, to make a good picture than a good radio program. But I have a warm spot in my heart for radio because of the knowledge that I am actually in the homes of people I might never reach through my stage or film work."

Ultimately, it was the advertising agencies, who effectively controlled radio on behalf of the sponsors they represented, warmed to the idea of live audiences on the air. "Advertising agency men appear not to share Eddie Cantor's viewpoint with regard to radio programs performed before audiences," *Variety* reported. "While some actors take the same slant espoused by Cantor, the agency group feels that the objections to an invited audience do not offset the advantages."

In April, a group of some of the top radio comedians gathered for an informal luncheon to discuss the pros and cons of having live audiences attend comedy programs. Present were Jack Pearl, Jack Benny, Jimmy Durante, and two Marx Brothers, Groucho and Chico. Eddie Cantor and Ed Wynn were absent, but both had already made their feelings on the matter well-known.

During the meeting, Pearl said he highly favored a live audience. Jack Benny and Chico Marx agreed. Groucho was on the fence initially, and, the report continued, "Durante claimed that the invisible audience only should be considered, and that an audience in the studio was frequently distracting to the comedian."

Benny admitted that he was initially indifferent to broadcasting before a studio audience, but had recently warmed to the idea of admitting visitors, as long as it did not interfere with overall theatre attendance.

Groucho, while acknowledging that most radio comedians still had a soft spot for their days of performing onstage, agreed with Durante's position. "I would prefer to have no visible audience," he said. "That enables the comedian to concentrate entirely on the listening audience, as well as eliminating the use of make-up and the nuisance of procuring tickets for relatives and friends."

Chico, however, offered an interesting counterpoint to Groucho's comment, relating an anecdote highlighting a side of his brother not obviously apparent to the public. "While we have always banned visitors at the studio," Chico said, "recently it was decided to transport the act to the stage of the Playhouse. At the very first performance the improvement in Groucho's technique was apparent to me. The visible audience obviously stimulated him and for the first time I really saw the old Groucho of the footlights. His actor's blood was roused and he gave the best performance he has ever given on the air."

While not present at the meeting, George Burns had told an interviewer only a few weeks before, "We never have [studio] audiences listening to us when we broadcast because we're afraid that if radio listeners heard laughter coming over the air they might think that Gracie is just clever instead of crazy."

Actually, that excuse didn't stand up well to logic, the critics, or sponsors. *Radio Digest* suggested, "It would help…if George and Gracie had a studio audience to get the laughs started. A joke usually sounds funnier if you hear somebody laugh at it first. You're encouraged, and you don't feel so ashamed if someone looks aghast at your ingenuousness. Gracie has always objected to having a studio audience and, while it's more of her business than ours, we hope she changes her mind…"

The more believable reason was simply that Gracie suffered from terrifying mike fright, revealing:

> "When I played in vaudeville I often wished that the floor would sink under my feet. When I had to make my first appearance over the radio I suffered from mike

fright. I still do. My hands get cold and my face gets hot. Other comediennes have audiences when they broadcast. I couldn't. I'm afraid. I'd be sure that they were laughing at me instead of with me, and I couldn't stand it. At least in the theatre the footlights separate us, and I can't see them, but it would be torture to me to watch their faces and think, 'I know this isn't going over.' I was that way even when I was a child- afraid of everything. I tried to pretend not to be afraid."

Once she and George relented, and began performing their program in front of an audience, Gracie coped by avoiding making eye contact with the attendees. "Gracie never worked to the audience or, later, to the camera," George recalled. "In radio, for example, most performers kept the house lights on during their shows so they could watch the reaction of the audience. Our first few years [on radio] we didn't even let anyone in the studio, and when our sponsor finally demanded that we did, we kept the house dark when we were on the air."

George himself came to enjoy performing their radio show to a live audience. As vaudeville veterans, the experience obviously wasn't new to them, but being on radio did make a difference. In the end, the advantages outweighed the drawbacks:

"We find it much easier to work before an audience. However, we use the studio visitors only as a gauge of what listeners may be doing. The studio audience enables us to judge the pauses for laughs. Amos 'n' Andy, as we all know, invite no studio guests, but our case is different. Their characters are so believable that they do not need an audience. Their lines are not the punchy type; by that I mean the listening audience can relax when in tune with them, but to get laughs the radio comedian must 'punch.' It's the laughs that give the comedian's

1934

audience a chance to relax, because they must be attentive to hear the gags."

By the way, the staggeringly popular *Amos & Andy* show, on the NBC network since 1929, avoided the issue altogether by simply refusing to have a studio audience until 1943.

Groucho Marx, in another interview, again expressed his objections to the studio audience trend. When asked what he considered the worst influence exerted on radio by the stage, he answered, "The habit of playing before audiences. However, that evil is being rapidly eliminated in the theatre. Have you seen a Broadway show lately?" Did he then consider studio audiences a detriment to radio? "Certainly," he said. "But at that I don't think they are any more of a detriment than the programs are."

And how did the listening public feel about the issue?

A number of published letters to *The New York Times* reflected a range of opinions. A man from Wilkes-Barre, Pennsylvania wrote: "...the noise, raucous laughter and applause caused by the studio audiences spoil many radio programs. The programs of Jack Pearl, Jack Benny, Jimmy Durante, Ed Wynn, Eddie Cantor, Marx Brothers et al. are spoiled by the so-called necessary studio audiences...The studio audience too many times spoils the lines of the joke or whatever is being said."

A man from Schenectady agreed, objecting to "the distracting, boisterous and continued interruptions that completely shatter every 'audienced [sic] radio program.' Antics and facial grimaces or physical contortions do not reach the silent audiences. If they consist of the stock in trade of the performers, then the sponsor and its artists should return to vaudeville. Long noses, big eyes, funny hats and comical wardrobes are the vintage of burlesque and not radio."

But a woman from Long Beach, New York wasn't bothered by hearing laughter and applause coming out of her radio speaker. "I am most emphatically on the affirmative side, in spite of the noise, raucous laughter and applause which seems to disconcert some listeners to the point of distraction. I have never yet found it necessary to dial these programs out. Though they do not necessarily add to my enjoyment of the programs, they certainly do not detract from it." She also posited a rather odd theory that different programs had different quality audiences. "The Phil Baker and Jack Benny audiences seem to know how and when to laugh better than, say, the Ed Wynn audiences. That is something I cannot even attempt to explain…"

An editorial in *Radioland* included a pointed comment aimed at Eddie Cantor's misgivings on the issue:

> "Columbia Broadcasting System inaugurated its Radio Playhouse the other day and fell in line with the present demand that network programs be seen as well as heard at the point of origin. Eddie Cantor, who not long ago was quite hurt over the necessity of broadcasting before an audience, seems to be leading a lost cause—but we haven't noticed Eddie choking off any applause on that Sunday hour."

Radio Mirror magazine also weighed in on the matter, noting in a June editorial that in its own mail from readers, "three out of five letters take up the subject of audiences being used as background atmosphere on the air. And the opinions are about equally divided…So that the only solution is to follow the method which seems to make the broadcast most realistic, which puts the performer most at ease and which will satisfy the greater number of those tuner-inners [across the country]."

By the following year, the tide of studio laughter had already become too strong to turn back. New York City had ample theatres and auditoriums of various seating capacities serving as homes to radio's most popular programs (although most audience members were guests of the program sponsors and the stars, so tickets for the general public were tricky to secure, at best). Perhaps not everyone was happy, but radio comedians were at least hearing instant feedback for their efforts, which can only be a good thing, despite the disapproval of those who seemed to prefer listening to—and performing—comedy in a silent vacuum. The concept and practice of a comedian spouting off jokes to dead air was quickly becoming obsolete.

Meanwhile, radio sales continued to soar, with the total number in the United States reaching the 18,000,000 mark, according to a joint survey conducted by Radio Retailing and CBS. It is estimated that the sale of sets in 1933 alone reached 3,806,000, an increase of 45 per cent over 1932.

Will Rogers kept a busy schedule at this time, spreading himself between his films, writing his syndicated column, world travels, and radio appearances. Author's collection.

April 6 - W.C. Fields stars in *You're Telling Me*.

Fields appears here as Sam Bisbee, a small-town optometrist and inventor of various outlandish devices in search of financial backing. One of his inventions, a puncture-proof automobile tire, does catch the interest of a major tire company in the city. Fortune seems assured, until his demonstration for the company's board meets with disaster, in the form of Sam shooting out the tires of a police car parked in front of the company building, mistaking it for his own vehicle.

Back at home, on "the other side of the tracks" in Crystal Springs, his daughter is in love with a snobbish rich family's well-meaning son, leading to a culture clash that appears to doom the romance.

While on the train home from his ill-fated tire demonstration, a despondent Sam proves equally inept at attempting suicide by drinking a bottle of iodine. After giving up on the plan, he meets a beautiful young woman (Adrienne Ames), whom he mistakes for being on the verge of ending her own life as well. In truth, she is Princess Marie Lescaboura, of an unnamed European country (Sam cheerfully dismisses her title as a sham). The two bare their souls to each other, leaving Marie suitably moved enough by Sam's plight to arrange a visit to his home, before she returns to her country. Rumors fly throughout Crystal Springs—thanks to two gossips on the train— that Sam and Marie are having an affair. Each re-telling of the rumor becomes increasingly lurid as it's passed on. Before long, Sam has become a local pariah just as Marie arrives in town, amid much pomp and considerable fawning by the mayor and locals. She tells of how Sam had saved her life "during the war," and, accordingly, he should be treated as a hero. She even convinces the mayor to invite Sam to officially open the town's new golf course.

This turn of events allows Fields to repeat his fabulous golf routine, seen here in its most refined form, and assisted by Tammany Young as his caddie. All ends well in the story, as the tire company executives arrive to make an offer for his invention, and the love-struck young couple finally get their parents' blessing to marry.

1934

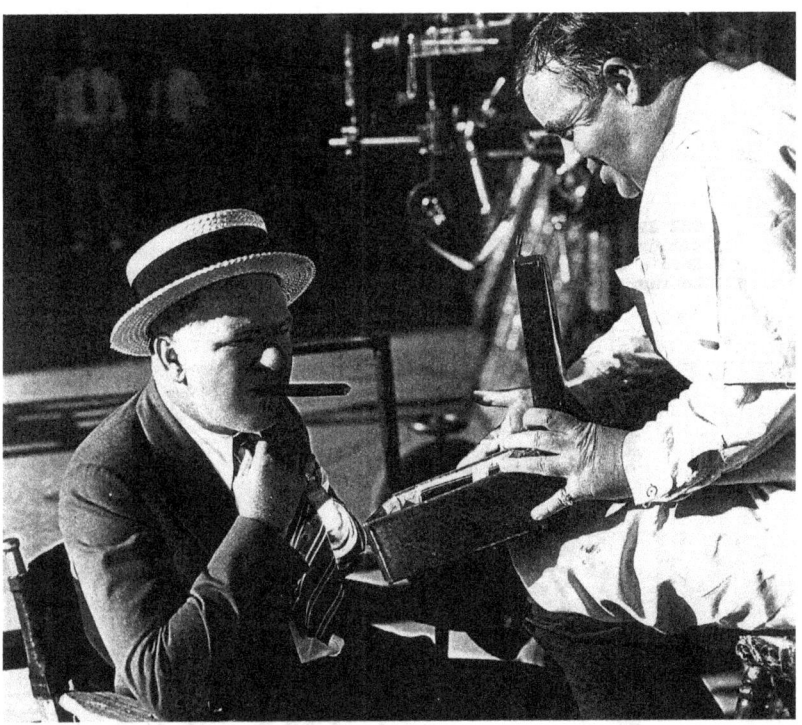

Fields makes a few final adjustments before shooting a scene for *You're Telling Me*, aided by friend and frequent foil, Tammany Young. Author's collection.

Perhaps the most endearing aspect of *You're Telling Me* is Sam's close, but strictly platonic, friendship with Marie, as he encourages her to keep up "that princess stuff." They develop quite a beautiful friendship, and demonstrate a genuine fondness for each other that's certainly rarity for a Fields' film; his onscreen marriages, usually to scornful, shrewish wives, are always played for laughs, and his younger children serve only as sources of angst for him. Here, we see him value the young princess Marie as a dear friend—an unexpected but refreshing turn (his later relationship with Gloria Jean in *Never Give A Sucker an Even Break* also strikes a sweet note due their characters' uncle-niece relationship). This alone makes *You're Telling Me* a special entry in the already special canon of Fields' features throughout the 1930s.

April 13 - The first Ritz Brothers film, *Hotel Anchovy*, premieres.

Even with a total of twenty films to their credit—fourteen of which were released in the 1930s—Al, Jimmy, and Harry Ritz were known by the public primarily as stage performers who undoubtedly knew their way around knockabout slapstick and novelty dance numbers.

They made the short *Hotel Anchovy* for Educational Pictures, released through 20th Century Fox. Its success prompted the studio to sign them to play comic relief roles, primarily in musical numbers, for Fox features. They were eventually given their own starring series of films, beginning with *Life Begins in College,* in 1937.

Print ad for *Life Begins in College.* Author's collection.

While the Ritz Brothers have sometimes been compared to that other family trio, the Marx Brothers, the onscreen Marxes boasted three distinct personalities (even when fourth brother Zeppo was present), whereas the Ritz Brothers looked very much alike, and performed their famed comic song & dance routines in perfect sync with each other, but with little to distinguish one brother from another. However, bug-eyed Harry Ritz did possess a more natural comedic flair, and came to be considered the leader of the trio.

1934

May 5 - The Three Stooges star in *Woman Haters*, their first short subject for Columbia Pictures.

Moe Howard, Curly Howard, and Larry Fine created their own style of unabashed knockabout slapstick and stylized violence that, while never very appealing to the intellectual set, has maintained its popularity to the present day (and, it has often been noted, with overwhelmingly male audiences).

The Stooges were originally teamed with comedian Ted Healy in an energetic, rough & tumble act onstage, back when Shemp Howard was part of the team.

Moe and Healy had known each other since their early teens, and first appeared with the other Stooges (with Curly replacing older brother Shemp) in a handful of films for MGM, until the Stooges finally left Healy and set out on their own, due in part to Healy's self-destructive alcoholism.

"When sober," Moe wrote, "Ted was the essence of refinement; while under the influence, he became a foul-mouthed, vicious character. Liquor had killed his father and uncle and had destroyed his sister's life. When Ted was young, I remember that he made a pledge never to touch liquor, after having seen the consequences of its effects on his family. The strain of his life in show business got him started, and once he started drinking he was never able to stop."

Healy was notorious off-stage for his quick temper and generally unpleasant disposition, but for audiences, he epitomized the brash, flippant smart-aleck vaudeville comic. He had his ample share of fans, including an up & coming Milton Berle, who spoke of how he patterned his own style after Healy.

Healy, not surprisingly, could get especially rough on the Stooges during their more violently comic scenes, and his overall demeanor gave him a more mean-spirited edge than Moe's cartoonish infliction of wrath upon his fellow stooges (watching Healy's scenes today, there is something about his slapping the others that is more likely to induce as gasp than a belly-laugh).

Free of Healy, and with a new contract with Columbia, it took a few films—beginning with *Woman Haters*—for the Stooges to fully develop their screen personas. Interestingly, and perhaps to the annoyance of some viewers, all of the dialogue in *Woman Haters* is spoken in rhyme, which was just one of several gimmicks short film comedies were experimenting with at the time. In addition, Larry takes on a rare lead role here; his predicament as a reluctant groom-to-be, facing peer pressure from his fellow members of the Woman Haters Club, serves as the center of attention for most of the film. Moreover, Curly isn't even referred to as "Curly" yet, but by his real name, Jerry.

With Columbia as their new home, and contracted to produce eight two-reelers per year, the team took a fairly quick route in developing the characters as we know them today. *Woman Haters*, followed by *Punch Drunks* and *Men in Black*, all contributed to establishing their classic screen personas, with *Men in Black* earning them their only Oscar nomination (although it was *Punch Drunks* that was added to the National Film Registry in 2002.)

The three and only Stooges. Author's collection.

The casual observer might assume the chaos of a typical Stooges film is the result of hodge-podge ideas and violent gags whipped up on the spot, but Larry Fine's description of the team's work ethic should quell that assumption: "We rehearsed a short three weeks before we shot it, which no other people did, even in features. We didn't just take a script and shoot it. We went to the studio every day, went through the routines, and tried to improve it and improve it. And I think it paid off... They're still shown after forty years. That's a lot longer than a lot of marriages last around here."

Moe once explained their strategy from their pre-film vaudeville days, which they continued to utilize in movies. "Our three rules for working were watch, listen and plan. We watched the tempo of the act, listened to the other member when one was in the spotlight, and planned our routines. There was a lot more to it than just going up and telling funny stories and smacking each other around. We checked the slapstick carefully in order not to overdo it. If comedy goes on too long, the audience begins to think about it. We aimed not to give anyone time to think."

The team would produce a remarkable total of 191 shorts and appear in two dozen features (in either a starring or supporting capacity) between 1934 and 1958.

June 13 - The Hays Production Code restrictions go into effect.

For anyone who appreciates, or advocates, unrestrained creative freedom, this date can be considered the beginning of a Dark Age in Hollywood history, one that lasted a good twenty-five years. The moral content of films, dating back to the earliest silent days, hadn't been much of a problem for the industry; common sense ruled decisions regarding appropriate language, violence, sexual imagery, etc. Despite the mythic images of the 1920s as a freewheeling, hedonistic, booze and drug-fueled decade (the stock market crash was to provide a sobering change of course), the films of the major studios did not often indulge in material that would likely offend the average filmgoer. European films worked within somewhat wider parameters, but mainstream American films as a whole were hardly in danger of becoming cinematic burlesque shows.

Nevertheless, by the early 1930s, Hollywood's image had begun to suffer, thanks to moralists who relished the idea of painting Tinsel Town as the modern-day incarnation of Sodom & Gomorrah. Headline-grabbing scandals and a number of increasingly risqué films (for that time) created a movement to place a written code of moral standards in films, including a list of words that were not to be uttered onscreen, and themes or issues to be avoided that might offend audiences. Many state legislatures began instituting their own laws, but that resulted in different states often allowing or rejecting different scenes or language in a given film, with no uniform standard. What was a film distributor to do?

In 1922, an effort to ease mounting pressure and threats of federal government censorship caused the studio heads to appoint Will H. Hays, former Postmaster General and chairman of the Republican National Committee. Hays was a devout Catholic, and the code he designed was influenced by the tenets of the Catholic Church, thus creating an undeniably strict set of rules. The code, announced in 1930, was not well-enforced at first, as studios gingerly stepped around some of the more ludicrous and/or stifling rules that would require extensive script re-writes, the re-editing of scenes, and even changing the artwork on promotional posters. The studios preferred to censor themselves than have a governing body dictate film content for them.

On June 13, 1934, the Production Code Administration and its regulatory policies went into full effect, and led by former public relations man Joseph Breen (who, like Hays, was conservative enough to allow little tolerance for the alleged moral decay of American films). Breen ran the day-to-day operations of enforcing the Code. The most prominent of its rules was the requirement that all feature films, beginning on July 1, would need to obtain a certificate of approval before being released to the public.

The set of guidelines was strict to the point of being draconian. Producers and their studios had little choice but to comply, or risk protests, boycotts, and economic fallout if they didn't. Every script was to be submitted to the Hays Office experts on censorship. They would identify the scenes and/or dialogue likely to offend, and the producer would be expected to make changes in the

1934

script before a film could be released. With few exceptions, they would comply, while making the somewhat sniveling excuse that Hollywood's self-imposed censorship was necessary due to the competition among studios, which had created a temptation to veer towards sensationalism, thus neglecting good taste.

But there was outrage nonetheless.

An extended and harshly critical piece by writer Eric Ergenbright in *The New Movie* magazine tackled the new reality of Hollywood:

> "Censorship, both official and unofficial, hangs like a storm cloud over the picture industry, ready to hurl down its torrents of wrath whenever a taboo is violated. Producers, writers, directors and stars are in a continual agony of apprehension. Will the barbers resent that scene in the beauty parlor? Will the censorship board delete that joke about the farmer's daughter? Will the Associated Banana Venders sue for millions if the banana-eating hero is shown with a tummy-ache? There's never a picture filmed which isn't preceded by a host of conferences—and there's never a conference which doesn't bewail and consider the dangers of breaking some taboo."

For anyone mistaking Political Correctness as a phenomenon of just the past few decades, the Hays Code was an earlier, and considerably more disturbing example of P.C. run amuck. It wasn't just sex or nudity in films (or, more often, the mere suggestion of same) that was being quashed; horror films that were deemed too frightening or violent were ordered to be toned down. Certain criminal acts could not be depicted, or even mentioned. The list was a long one. Any potential religious controversy was to be avoided, and no religion was to be referred to in such a way that could be interpreted as a slight. Birth control or illegitimacy were not to be spoken of, either.

In addition, ethnic groups in the U.S. were to be spared any form of negative portrayal. The logic of this, however, became stretched and twisted beyond reason. For instance, the crime drama *Scarface* had to be extensively re-shot and edited to wipe away the implication that the title character was of Italian heritage. "The Hays Office taboo experts," continued Ergenbright, "finally convinced Howard Hughes, the producer, that countless law-abiding Italians would be mortally insulted. In the final version, 'Scarface' was a man of undetermined nationality…By habitually showing Mexicans and Italians as illiterate criminals, Frenchmen as "Oo-la-la-ing" fops, Englishmen as 'Silly awsses' and Germans as beer-swilling militarists, Hollywood came near losing its foreign market."

The unfortunate exception to this, of course, was the Hays Office's attitude toward depictions of black people on screen. Some films were released in two versions, one for theatres north of the Mason-Dixon line, and another for the South. In *Hold Your Man*, Jean Harlow and Clark Gable are seen being married by a black preacher in prints distributed in the north, but they are married by a white minister in prints sent to the south.

Hollywood also treated the issue of Prohibition with a weak spine, deeming the controversy too volatile, even with its repeal on December 5, 1933, after nearly fourteen years. Organizations that had wanted to see Prohibition remain intact protested depictions of people drinking liquor. The Hays Office promised that such scenes would only be allowed if demanded by the plot.

There were to be continued pockets of resistance to the Code throughout the industry, but most studios shied from making waves that might hurt profitability for films that had already become significant investments. Some in the business, however, threw their hands up in exasperation. Veteran screenwriter Anita Loos was among them. She had been writing and re-writing her adaptation of the Clark Gable-Joan Crawford film *Chained*, when the situation brought her to the breaking point. "What's the use?" she said. "The censors have made it impossible to deal honestly with any screen subject."

1934

How did the Code affect comedy specifically? In hindsight, certain examples of naughty dialogue or risqué sight gags of the pre-code era would have gotten the kibosh had the new standards been enforced just a few years earlier. For instance, a line uttered by Groucho in *Animal Crackers* ("We took some pictures of the native girls, but they weren't developed. But we're going back again in a couple of weeks!") would never have gotten past the Hays office. The speakeasy scenes in the brothers' *Horsefeathers* also probably wouldn't have made it into the film, had it been completed and sent for review in 1934 instead of the year it was released, 1932. It's likely those scenes would have had to be re-shot, using a different setting.

There were many instances in Hal Roach's short films starring Thelma Todd and ZaSu Pitts (or Patsy Kelly), in which Thelma would somehow temporarily lose her clothes, to be briefly seen wearing very little. The gorgeous Todd managed to appear in some state of undress in nearly every film of that Roach series. These scenes would no doubt have been excised after stricter enforcement of the Code. It's also doubtful that a scene in *Meet the Baron*, featuring about two dozen young women removing their lingerie and then taking a communal shower, with water spray strategically protecting their privacy (such as it was), would have been edited before viewing by audiences.

Perceived offenses veered into the realm of the ridiculous. It was reported that comedian and actor Roscoe Ates, who had overcome a speech impediment as a teen, but who often used his stutter for comic effect in performance, suffered at the hands of stutterers who resented his lighthearted use of the condition. The Hays Office heard from parents and teachers who reported that school children had taken to imitating him, and thus had acquired their own permanent speech impediments!

Some restrictions had financial interests as their motivations. No critical commentary or unflattering depiction of other nations, governments, or cultures was allowed, for fear the film in question would receive a ban in a given country, which would hurt overseas business.

The Hays Office justified some sections of the code with examples of American comedies that had insulted cultures elsewhere. Harold Lloyd's inclusion of Chinese villains in *Welcome Danger* was enough to kill the market for his work in China, serving as a lesson to film comedians who dared to portray any ethnic group in a negative light. And Eddie Cantor's *The Kid from Spain* was met with anger in Mexico over a comical bullfight sequence, with Cantor as a bogus matador.

Robert Woolsey expressed his frustration at the restrictive nature of the Code on the comedy he and partner Bert Wheeler had been offering to audiences. "We have a children audience. Nothing gets by the censors. They're tougher on us than they are on Fascist newspapers in Spain." His dour assessment also prompted him to refer to the post-code Wheeler & Woolsey films as "synthetic, like bathtub gin."

The comedian who suffered the most from the effects of the Code was, not surprisingly, Mae West. With such restrictions on dialogue now being enforced with an iron hand, her screenplays, upon being submitted for approval, were heavily edited, causing her to water down her trademark sexual innuendoes. *The New Movie Magazine* piece decried that "Mae West's second opus, *I'm No Angel*, found the censors recovered from the daze into which they had been thrown by *She Done Him Wrong*, and they proceeded to tear it limb from limb. Never was a picture, with the possible exception of *Hell's Angels*, so mangled—yet no two boards agreed on their cuts. What to do about it? Hollywood has given up trying to find the answer."

West resorted to deliberately including lines that she knew would be excised, in order to retain other lines that seemed more innocuous in comparison. Nevertheless, much of the suggestive material that her audiences had come to expect from her had to be discarded, thus weakening the very screen character that had made her a hit in movie theatres just a year earlier. In *Go West, Young Man* (adapted by West from the play *Personal Appearance* by Gladys George) released in November of 1936, she plays a movie star stranded in a remote country boardinghouse. In its review, *Photoplay* lamented, "Gone are the days when Mae West was young and free with her contempt for movie censors. Deliberately, Mae tones down her robust technique in favor of a better story and strong support…"

Variety said, "Miss West, in her own way, is excellent in the role Miss George created on the stage. Miss George was not hindered by the limitations of screen censorship; hence the play's sock tag isn't half as punchy in the film, nor are other lines or situations up to the same potency."

The review suggested, however, that turning up the character's sex appeal quotient wasn't necessarily a good thing for the comedian's longevity. "Miss West's swagger, the hands-on-hip business, and various devilish expressions are in almost constant evidence; too much so possibly because it tires a bit and no longer is quite the novelty it once was."

After such a meteoric rise to the top in 1933, the combination of censorship and West's own one-note screen image, with repeated allusions to sex and overall naughtiness, brought about a fairly swift decline for her career. Fickle audiences have long demonstrated how they can quickly tire of a screen character, even while returning time and again for another, without feeling jaded.

July 13 - W.C. Fields stars in *The Old Fashioned Way*.

This film, continuing Fields' impressive run of successes in 1934 alone, is an adaptation from his 1927 lost silent film, *Two Flaming Youths*. Paramount chose this story over a script submitted by former Hal Roach workhorse script writer, H.M. "Beanie" Walker, who left Roach Studios in 1932 after sixteen years writing titles for the studios' silent films, and dialogue for nearly all of the talkies.

The story presents Fields as The Great McGonigal, owner and manager of a repertory theatre ensemble performing the vintage melodrama *The Drunkard* on tour. McGonigal, of course, has a reputation for skipping out on hotel bills and other debts, and in fact, we first see him as he's trying to board a train while evading the sheriff. They do meet face-to-face, but only after Fields has lit the sheriff's warrant on fire, and then lights his own cigar off the flaming piece of paper, before hustling onto the departing train.

Once the troupe has arrived in a town called Bellefontaine to perform the play at the local opera house, he must contend with a number of distracting individuals: a dour rooming house owner who has past experience with his antics, an eccentric local aspiring singer who fairly tortures him with her singing audition, and her son (Baby LeRoy) who gives him no end of humiliation at the dinner table by hurling mashed potatoes at his face and dipping his pocket watch in molasses. Fields famously gets his revenge, after the room is clear of the adults, by kicking the toddler on his rump, and strolling away, whistling a merry tune.

Not all Fields fans realized that he was a superb juggler in his early stage career, but thankfully his extraordinary skills are preserved in a scene in *The Old Fashioned Way*. Despite encouragement from Paramount executives who knew of his talents, he resisted juggling in the film, fearful that his slower reflexes would set him up for embarrassment. The storyline, however, is especially compatible with the inclusion of a juggling routine, so he acquiesced, knowing that it could be the last opportunity to commit his remarkable talents to film. One would be hard-pressed to detect any loss of speed or dexterity while watching the scene, as Fields juggles balls, flips a walking cane on his toe, and balances cigar boxes that seem to defy gravity.

November 30 - Laurel & Hardy release *Babes in Toyland*.

Also known as *The March of the Wooden Soldiers* and, decades after its release, a holiday season favorite on television, this film doesn't necessarily rank among Laurel & Hardy's best, but the story behind its development and production provides a glimpse into the team's relationship (particularly Stan's) with their boss, Hal Roach.

In this musical fable featuring Mother Goose characters, with a musical score by Victor Herbert, Stan and Ollie play Stannie Dum and Ollie Dee. Roach's original idea, however, was to have them to play Simple Simon and the Pie Man. That's where a severe rift between Roach and Stan came to the fore.

1934

Poster for the film, with its alternate title. Author's collection.

As Roach told the story, he went to New York to buy the film rights to the original stage incarnation of *Babes in Toyland*, even though, in his opinion, the production he saw showed more interest in new lighting effects than in offering a cohesive plot.

"So I wrote the story on the train journey back.
Hardy was the pie man and Laurel was Simple Simon.
The heavy was the spider who wanted to destroy Toyland,
and his way of destroying Toyland was to put hate into the
wooden soldiers. And he engaged Laurel and Hardy to

separate love and kindness from hate. This is the story I wrote. But because I wrote it, Laurel said, 'Oh, this is no good. It's not funny.' And we argued—and all the time they're getting paid! Finally I said, 'Laurel, you take over.' And he said, 'We're not funny without the Derby hats.' And I said, 'Derby hats are nothing to do with it.'"

That specific point of contention about derbies may seem immaterial, but Stan once explained his long-time partiality to derbies: "The derby hat has always seemed to be part of a comic's makeup for as far back as I can remember. I'm sure that's why Chaplin wore one. [Derbies] gave us something we felt these two characters needed, a kind of phony dignity. There's nothing funnier than a guy being dignified and dumb."

Indeed, in countless scenes of Stan and/or Ollie falling into a mud puddle, a pond, from atop a ladder, etc., the two immediately—almost reflexively—reach for their hats and fix them atop their heads once again, even as they might remain seated in the muck or destruction they've just created—as if the derbies would somehow help restore both their physical and emotional equilibrium.

Roach continued the story behind *Babes In Toyland*:

"I finally gave up; they went out and made a picture that was a very bad picture. It did not do business, and it should have been one of the greatest pictures ever made in my humble opinion. They brought these goons in from the forest to destroy Toyland, and the P.T.A. of America condemned the picture because that would scare the children. Instead of being a picture for children, it was condemned! Laurel just couldn't take it that somebody else was writing the story. So soon after that we parted company, because it was just too much. I mean I couldn't afford it…"

1934

With Stan nearing the end of his contract, a resentful Roach simply chose not to renew it. Part of his justification was that the studio was moving away from two-reelers and into features, which required stronger storylines. And Stan, as Roach was always quick to claim, was a brilliant gagman but dreadful at storyline construction. "Seventy-five percent, 80 percent of the basic plots of their things were mine," he contended. "Now we were gone from two-reelers and were into feature pictures, and Laurel in story construction was just impossible. His things were—hell, a ten year old kid could have written better…"

He may have been displeased with the final version of *Babes in Toyland*, but it quickly became a favorite among audiences and critics as well. *Picture Play* raved:

> "A musical fairy tale is unheard of in films except the incomparable Silly Symphonies, but here is one, full-length and chockfull of charm, gayety, humor and some of Victor Herbert's unforgettable music…Though intended for children, it shrewdly presents those adult comics, Laurel and Hardy, at their best as they skillfully perform in the spirit of juvenile make-believe while supplying their own particular brand of grown-up fun. They deserve no end of credit for this, and equally, too, does producer Hal Roach share honors for giving us a picture that is as wholesome as a Christmas tree and will give as much joy as long as the film holds together…"

Variety was equally enthused:

> "If Hal Roach aimed at the production of a purely juvenile picture to which children might conceivably drag their elders, he has succeeded in a measure beyond others who have sought to enter this realm. It's packed

with laughs and thrills and is endowed with that glamour of mysticism which marks juvenile literature…[It is] a gorgeous fairy tale which gives everything to Laurel & Hardy, and to which, in return, they give their happiest best."

The review concluded with the prophetic comment, "This picture may not be consistently big box office, but it is the best juvenile product to date and deserves the long life it will have."

Regardless, in March of 1935, the studio announced Stan's termination. "The motion picture team of Laurel and Hardy, comedians, has been broken up after seven years. Hal Roach, producer of their pictures, announced today that Stan Laurel, the bewildered, sad-faced half of the combination, had not signed a new contract. 'Inability to agree on stories,' was the reason given. The producer said Oliver Hardy would remain at the studio as the star of a series of domestic comedies."

Roach held considerable control over the future of the team. Because they had been working for him under separate contracts, this left open the possibility of replacing one or another as circumstances dictated, although Roach did not regard the team's enormous popularity lightly. Only three weeks later, after he and Stan had a proper airing of their creative differences, they reached a truce, and Stan re-signed with his boss. "The movie team of Laurel & Hardy was back in the flickers today," it was reported. "Stan Laurel, who had 'story' trouble with Hal Roach, producer of the comedians' pictures, patched up the difficulties today and signed a new contract. Oliver Hardy, his teammate, was all smiles as Laurel, who writes the gags for their films, emerged from Roach's office with the announcement that they were to go to work at once on a picture."

Despite the lingering hard feelings that still simmered between Roach and Stan (who would be "fired" and then just as quickly re-hired on more than one subsequent occasion), the mutual admiration between Stan and Ollie never wavered. They were each asked separately about the other, beginning with Stan, for an issue of *The New Movie Magazine* that spring.

"Hardy inspires me. He is like the character he portrays because of certain individual traits. To me he is refreshing, so darned human! His humor lies in the funny way he thinks. I can look at him and know just what he is thinking. His moods are very funny to me, the moods of a born comedian.'

Ollie's take on his partner:

"Laurel is the most unselfish man that ever lived and the funniest man in the world, as a comedian, as a writer, and as a human being. He is so distinctive that he stands absolutely alone. He doesn't depend upon funny clothes to make him funny, he is funny in himself. And I have sense enough to stand back and let him be funny.'"

August 2 - Clark & McCullough star in *Odor in the Court*.

This is considered to be one of the team's finest and most chaotic shorts, with lots of snappy dialogue written by Bobby Clark. He and McCullough play lawyers, Blackstone & Blodgett (McCullough's character was named Blodgett in most of their films), who, desperate to find a client, agree to take on a husband's divorce case. They enter the courtroom accompanied with a marching band and flag-waving crowd. Clark dominates the proceedings with nonsensical interruptions that infuriate both the judge and the opposing lawyer. His tactics include blackmailing the attorney (who happens to be engaged to the judge's daughter) with a compromising photograph that he and Blodgett had set up with the aid of their secretary. Incredibly, they succeed in obtaining the divorce decree for their client, who is also spared having to pay alimony. The blaring marching band then happily leads everyone out of the courtroom—just the kind of boisterous nonsense at which the team excelled.

November 30 - W.C. Fields stars in *It's a Gift*.

Before embarking on *It's a Gift*, one of his nearly perfect feature efforts, Fields took a departure from his familiar, contemporary settings to assume the role of Mr. Macawber in *David Copperfield*. As portrayed by Fields, Macawber is a cheerful family man who loves children and takes in the young Copperfield as part of the family, until a spell in debtor's prison prompts Macawber and the family to leave town and start anew, but without the boy.

For *It's A Gift*, Fields was back on more familiar and terrain, i.e. battling the world, including his own family, but primarily in self-defense. As small town grocery store owner Harold Bissonette, he isn't absent from the screen for much more than sixty seconds of the film's entire running time. There isn't much plot, other than that of Bissonette planning to use a family inheritance to buy an orange grove in California. This leaves a lot of room for the film to provide several classic if unrelated sequences, including an early scene of Fields hopelessly trying to shave in the bathroom while his daughter monopolizes the mirror (borrowed from his 1927 silent film *The Potters*), his attempt to rest on his back porch hammock despite frequent interruptions (duplicated from his 1926 feature *It's the Old Army Game*), and fending off an elderly blind and deaf customer wreaking havoc in his grocery store.

"Two phases of W. C. Fields's remarkable talent are currently on view," *Picture Play* began its report, adding:

> "If you would enjoy his skill in portraying character,
> then by all means see his Micawber in 'David Copperfield.'
> Not only does he make Dickens's immortal creation a
> human being and not a caricature, as many players have
> done, but he qualifies as a dramatic actor of skill and
> restraint... If, however, you are content to laugh at
> Mr. Fields solely as a comedian, you must not think
> of missing him in his Paramount offering. Thinnest of
> stories, it is really a series of lengthy episodes which

permit Mr. Fields to continue his monologue without interruption of plot and with little interference from other players. Mr. Fields is the whole show."

Fields with an unlikely companion, indeed his character's only friend, in *It's A Gift*. Author's collection.

Photoplay happily announced, "It's a gift! W.C. Fields makes this one long laugh from start to finish. In his favorite role—that of a henpecked husband—he starts with his family for sunny California and an orange grove. And the laughs pyramid with each of his successive absurdly amusing adventures!"

Andre Sennwald in *The New York Times* noted that "with the one exception of Charlie Chaplin, there is nobody but Mr. Fields who could manage the episode with the blind and deaf man in the store so as to make it seem genuinely and inescapably funny instead of just a trifle revolting."

1935

January 4 - Bob Hope begins his first radio gig, joining *The Intimate Revue Show*.

Hope was yet another vaudeville comedian who, due to his friendly but wisecracking demeanor, seemed a natural for radio. He was also dabbling in films at the time, having made three unsuccessful shorts for three different studios in 1934, and would make six more throughout 1935 and '36. His real film success would have to wait a bit longer, but in the meantime, radio exerted its pull on him just as it had with so many others in just the previous few years.

His gig on NBC's *The Intimate Revue* (starring James Melton and Jane Froman) came about as a result of his popular guest turns on Rudy Vallee's show, but *The Intimate Revue* lasted only three months. Hope returned later in the year on CBS in *The Atlantic Family*, which ran a full year, and he would host still more musical variety programs over the next two years.

Like his more experienced peers who had already made the transition from vaudeville to radio, Hope appreciated the advantage of performing over the airwaves. "Radio was a medium where, every week, more people would hear my jokes than had seen my vaudeville act in ten years on the Gus Sun Time [vaudeville circuit.]"

April 16 - *Fibber McGee & Molly* **premieres on radio.**

The situation comedy format continued to gain popularity with the radio-listening public in a short span of time, overtaking vaudeville-style jokes that had no connection to the gags preceding or following them. Fred Allen and Jack Benny, playing themselves, began constructing thin storylines to sustain the gags on their respective programs, while *Fibber McGee & Molly*, like *The Goldberg's* and *Amos & Andy*, presented purely fictional characters, to great audience response.

Jim and Marion Jordan. Courtesy of Martin Grams.

1935

Jim and Marian Jordan spent three years in vaudeville as a harmony singing team, and began their radio career as such, but found themselves faced daunted by too much competition from too many other singers. They tentatively ventured into comedy at a small station in Chicago in 1924. Once they started to click on the air, making enough money to sustain them, the couple left vaudeville altogether, and starred on the program *The Grab Bag*, in which they acted out gags they had clipped out of humor magazines, impersonating several characters at a time.

Radio Stars said of the Jordans, "[They] are one of the few radio teams which bases its act upon the theory that its listeners have some intelligence… They've seen radio comedy grow up from infantile gags, blue-printed and hurled straight into the laps of the listeners, to humor which is more deft and subtle, more adult."

Jim Jordan gave credit where it was due for the trend toward more mature comedy on radio. "Radio audiences are smarter now," he said, "thanks to the work of comedians like Fred Allen and Jack Benny. [Audiences are] educated to expect something more than the old-time minstrel question-and-answer gags, and we're trying to give them that type of humor-smart, but not too smart. We're playing up to our audiences, instead of down to 'em, which was the accepted formula in the old days."

Each Fibber McGee script was first written by Don Quinn, a former commercial artist who had difficulty finding work in his field during the Depression, but managed to get himself hired writing for Olsen and Johnson.

For *Fibber McGee and Molly*, Quinn would send each rough draft to the Jordans, who would consult with him on necessary improvements, after which he would write further drafts himself, often straight through the night. "And even then," he said at the time, "we sometimes make last minute changes. I keep just one program ahead. I used to try and get three or four up in advance, but found that the script was very much fresher when it was prepared only a week ahead."

The Jordans worked an average of at least eighteen hours on each program, including rehearsals and script supervisions. A favorite recurring gag has

Fibber searching for something throughout the house that leads him to open the door of his overstuffed closet. The crashing avalanche of household items tumbling out of the small space became the program's trademark. The only line closest to a catchphrase to emerge would be Molly's admonition, "T'ain't funny, McGee!" but they were careful to use it sparingly, to avoid the fate that had fallen upon the likes of Jack Pearl and others.

As situational comedy on radio gained popularity in the mid-1930s, a contrary argument asserted that not every radio comedian necessarily thrived with the more structured, sketch-style format. *Radio Mirror* pointed out:

> "They told us Jack Benny and Fred Allen were setting the styles in comedy this year - that the others would have to change their acts from gags to skits or be lost in the shuffle. So what? So Jack Pearl changed and lost the following Baron Munchausen had - and Cantor gives us exactly the same old fast and furious type of script he always has - and tops them all in the Crosley rating after the first sample. Rubinoff and Parkyakakas are still on the air, and still in Cantor's hair."

June 14 - Clark & McCullough's last film, *Alibi Bye Bye*, is released.

While the team's film output did not include many entries that most observers would consider comedy masterpieces, *Alibi Bye Bye*, like their *Odor in the Court* the previous year, comes close, especially in the short's final ten minutes. It's a shame that this was to be the last film Clark & McCullough would ever produce (although that wasn't necessarily the plan at the time).

In the story, the team work as "alibi photographers" Flash & Blodgett in Atlantic City. Their studio includes a number of backdrops depicting various popular American tourist destinations, allowing anyone who happened to be in Atlantic City for more tawdry forms of entertainment, to pose in front of a chosen backdrop of a national landmark, to serve as photographic proof that they've been to an undeniably wholesome locale during their time away from home.

Unbeknownst to each other, a husband (Bud Jamison, stalwart supporting player for The Three Stooges) claiming to be on a hunting trip, has arrived in town for some naughty fun with a friend and a couple of girls, while his wife, unbeknownst to him, *also* arrives in Atlantic City to spend the weekend with her friend. The husband poses at Flash and Blodgett's studio for a photo in front of a hunting lodge backdrop, while the wife later does the same in front of the Capitol building in Washington, D.C. To complicate matters, both are staying at the same hotel.

Complications ensue, as Flash and Blodgett attempt to deliver the photos to their clients, involving a truly dizzying sequence involving a half-dozen characters hustling between four rooms on the same hotel corridor, and escaping each other's notice within split seconds, as the doors open and slam shut with uncanny precision timing, just quickly enough for everyone to keep missing a glimpse of each other. It's a truly breathtaking and quite hilarious comedy sequence, but one that has, like the team itself, been relegated to relative obscurity in the ensuing decades (fortunately, at this writing, *Alibi Bye Bye* is available to view on YouTube).

July 26 - W.C. Fields' ***Man on the Flying Trapeze*** **premieres.**

This film continued Fields' winning streak, as he remained careful to present his screen character not merely as someone at odds with the world just for the sake of it, but as a hapless victim of life's constant little jabs. In this story, he plays an office clerk who, after years of reliable service, dares to ask for an afternoon off, but when his request is denied, comes prepared with the phony excuse that his mother-in-law has died. News of her supposed demise spreads through town, until Fields is exposed for his lie and is fired. His troubles only continue to mount from that point on.

Picture Play magazine admired Fields' deft touch of mixing comedy and a bit of understated pathos.

"While it is no different from other films starring the great comic, it follows a pattern that he has made peculiarly his own, ironic, penetratingly human comedy. Always, however, Mr. Fields does more than provoke laughter. He symbolizes the millions of commonplace men, their futile, drab lives and their yearning to escape…Now all this is not the most original material in the world, but as played by Mr. Fields it is hilariously funny and curiously touching."

August 15 - Will Rogers dies in plane crash, age 55.

Rogers was an avid flyer, and close friend of famous pilot Wiley Post. In the 1920s and '30s, aviators were full-fledged celebrities, not unlike the first generation of NASA's Mercury astronauts in the early1960s. Charles Lindberg, of course, was the most famous aviator of all, but Amelia Earhart and Post had also won the affection and respect of the public. In 1930, Post became the first pilot to fly around the world (with a navigator), and, three years later, he repeated the feat, flying solo. In 1932, Earhart became the first woman to fly solo across the Atlantic (and, of course, would attempt her fateful around-the-world flight in 1937).

Before their flight, Rogers had asked Post to fly him to Alaska, for the purposes of gathering material for his newspaper column. Post was working on a project that would create a flight route from the west coast of the U.S. to Russia. While taking off at one of their stops near Fairbanks, their plane crashed into a lake, killing them both instantly.

W.C. Fields said of his friend and former *Ziegfeld Follies* co-star, "Rogers was the nearest thing to Lincoln that I have ever known. His death was a terrible blow to me."

Rogers' popularity, especially for his gentle political humor that poked fun at both Democrats and Republicans in Washington, has rarely, if ever, been equaled in quite the same way. One testament to his legacy can found just about every day on the cable news networks, during reports and interviews from the second floor Statuary Hall, near the House of Representatives, where TV reporters file their on-air reports. Look carefully, and you'll notice a bronze statue of Rogers visible in the background, created by sculptor Jo Davidson and donated by the Oklahoma legislature in 1939. Rogers is the only entertainer represented by a statue in the hall, otherwise populated by former statesmen and high achievers from public life.

September - Double features overtake movie theatres.

A major new strategy for film studios and theatres began to take a firm hold with the announcement that all but one RKO theatre in the greater New York area would become double-feature houses (that exception being the Palace on Broadway, which continued to show one feature film at a time). Just days earlier, sixty-five Lowe's chain theatres in the area announced their new policy of showing double-bill features as well, their one exception being the State Theatre.

The *New York Times* reported, "The State, like RKO's Palace, will adhere to the single-feature and stage-show policy. The announcement yesterday from RKO said the change of policy had been prompted by the success of its trial last week in the RKO Albee in Brooklyn. The majority of RKO houses will show *Accent on Youth* and *The Daring Young Man*. Some will show *The Man on the Flying Trapeze* with W.C. Fields, and *Hard Rock Harrigan*."

November 15 - The Marx Brothers' *A Night at the Opera* **premieres.**

After releasing one feature per year for Paramount for the previous five years, all of which did well financially, the studio still opted not to offer a new contract, so the brothers as screen comedians had to sit out 1934. According to Harpo, "The Marx Brothers had been in a rut. Our last three pictures, *Monkey Business, Horse Feathers* and *Duck Soup*, were all the same kind of patchwork of gags and blackouts. We were making a pleasant amount of loot but we were standing still. One more picture of this type and the law of diminishing returns would set in and we'd be on our way out."

His assessment smacked of pessimism usually attributed to Groucho, but Harpo's idea of a solution, however, was reasonable enough: "What we needed was a good, strong producer who'd give us a change of pace."

Word had been going around the industry that the brothers' value was waning. *The New York Times* painted this dreary picture at the time: "After the lethargic welcome given to such pieces as *Duck Soup* and *Horsefeathers*, made by Paramount, other lots viewed the four Marxes—now reduced to three now that one has become an agent—with a degree of disinterest."

The brothers finally landed the gig, thanks to Chico. He had become friends with fellow card player and MGM production head, Irving Thalberg, who didn't know much about the mechanics of comedy films (nor did anyone else of importance at MGM), but was definite in his views of what a top-notch, quality MGM comedy film should be.

For the Marxes' first Metro effort, Thalberg insisted that the brothers' characters not only interact with the romantic leads, but actually *care* about them, rather than virtually ignore them, as they had with the lead couples in their Paramount films. By giving their characters more to do, other than insulting and/or playing pranks on innocent victims, the producer reasoned, audiences would find the Marxes more endearing, and that would help strengthen the comedy even more, once the brothers unleashed their mayhem on truly deserving opponents.

As Groucho wrote years later, Thalberg promised: "I'll make a picture with you fellows with half as many laughs—but I'll put a legitimate story in it and I'll bet it will gross twice as much as *Duck Soup*."

The Marxes apparently accepted this way of thinking with nary an argument, which one might have expected them to put forth in the interest of getting *more* laughs, not fewer. Encouraged nonetheless, they asked to hire their favorite writers, George S. Kaufman and Morrie Ryskind, to write the script. The writing team had just won the Pulitzer Prize for *Of Thee I Sing* the previous year (the brothers originally suggested starring in the film adaptation, but better sense prevailed, and they were talked out of it). Kaufman reluctantly traveled from his beloved New York City to Hollywood to work on the script for a brief time, but returned to New York as soon as he could, leaving Ryskind to continue polishing the script, and regularly presenting portions to Thalberg as his writing progressed.

"I'd go to [Thalberg's] office with about seven pages of the script and read them," Ryskind recalled. "I would never get a giggle out of him. He just looked. Now I knew it couldn't be that bad. After all at least once in a while, let's say every two pages, there must have been a funny joke! But he didn't laugh once! Yet, when I was through reading he would tell me, 'I think that's some of the funniest stuff I've ever heard.' And he meant it. I could never figure that out."

In acknowledgment of the team's earlier successes on stage, Thalberg also suggested a method for them to test the new material before live audiences. The comedy routines were to be polished during a west coast stage tour in which the brothers, and a troupe of about twenty, performed a half-dozen key scenes intended for the film, during which the creative team would measure audience reactions, timing the laughs with stopwatches, and fix the script accordingly.

When asked after the tour what he thought of the process, Harpo gushed, "Terrific. I can't understand why it hasn't been done before…George Kaufman, Morrie Ryskind, and another fellow who worked on the story went along with us. Al Boasberg is his name. They went with us. Sat through every show. We gave four shows a day for twenty-five days. Played Salt Lake, Seattle, Portland, Santa Monica—the old Pantages route. They made notes on every show. When a line didn't get the laugh we expected, we changed it or threw it out… It was tough work. We were rehearsing all the time… This tryout on the road didn't cost [Thalberg] anything. We didn't make any money out of the show, but it paid for the costumes, scenery and time. That includes four weeks of rehearsals, too."

Harpo hadn't realized that the idea of testing key scenes on tour prior to filming had, in fact, been done before, by none other than Eddie Cantor, as he prepared material before shooting his 1932 feature *The Kid from Spain* (which boasted credits including Leo McCarey as director, *Duck Soup* writers Kalmar & Ruby, and choreography by Busby Berkeley). Cantor, like the brothers, toured the west coast for about six weeks, beginning in San Francisco. As *Variety* reported, "Cantor believes the stage tryout [for] a film comedy, to set laughs for timing, etc., is essential to a film reproduction." It's curious that the practice never became commonplace.

Sam Wood was to serve as director of *A Night at the Opera*, much to Groucho's dismay. The comedian didn't like him, claiming that Wood didn't understand comedy, especially *their* comedy. The results, however, speak quite well for Wood's ability to get the best from the top-notch words and actions of the script. By the time the Marxes returned to the studio from the road tour, the film's key scenes had already been worked out, so rehearsals on the set were almost unnecessary. "In a day we'd shoot a scene that ordinarily would have taken three or four days," Harpo said. "And that means something when your production cost is $10,000 a day. We shot the picture in forty days and only needed one day for retakes."

The finished film boasts high production values typical of MGM at the time, with extensive musical numbers, and two talented singers, Alan Jones (Ricardo) and Kitty Carlisle (Rosa), doing their own singing.

The story opens in Milan, where Otis B. Driftwood (Groucho) has arranged for wealthy widow Mrs. Claypool (Margaret Dumont) to invest in the New York Opera Company. Her substantial donation would allow the company manager, Gottlieb, to hire world-famous Italian tenor Lassparri to sing in New York. In the meantime, aspiring star Ricardo Baroni, relegated to the chorus, has agreed to have his friend Fiorello (Chico) serve as his manager. Ricardo and female star Rosa are in love, but Lassparri intends to make Rosa his own. His treachery is exhibited when he repeatedly hits his dresser, Tomasso (Harpo) with a whip whenever angered.

Groucho mistakes Chico to be Lassparri's manager, and the two engage in the classic "contract scene," in which they dispense of the mind-bending clauses of legalese in the contracts by simply tearing them out. In the end,

Groucho thinks he's accomplished his task of signing Lassparri to sail to New York.

Harpo, Chico, and Ricardo manage to stowaway on the ship, in Driftwood's steamer trunk. This, of course, leads to the famous stateroom sceneHere, Groucho's closet-sized stateroom, already crowded with him and the three others, somehow attracts at least a dozen more people—chambermaids, plumbers, and a manicurist are among those who, as the scene progresses, inexplicably arrive at his door and proceed to pack themselves in like sardines. When Mrs. Claypool arrives in the corridor and opens the door, they all come tumbling out as if stuffed into Fibber McGee's closet. The scene's creation has been credited to Al Boasberg, who specialized as a script doctor, fixing up existing scripts with additional gags and routines.

The legendary stateroom scene. Author's collection.

Ricardo and Rosa briefly reunite, while the others are caught and sent to the brig, but escape and arrive in New York disguised as three famous aviators. Once discovered, they escape and hideout in Driftwood's hotel room. The suspicious police sergeant tries keeping a close eye on the situation, but gets befuddled as the Marxes pull off an elaborate switcheroo on him, dodging between two adjoining hotel rooms.

Ricardo and Lassparri then have a confrontation, after which Gottlieb fires both Rosa and Driftwood. The brothers then proceed to sabotage the opening night of *Il trovatore* by any means possible, including substituting the orchestra's sheet music with that for "Take Me Out to the Ballgame." They also abduct Lassparri, allowing for Ricardo to take his place onstage. Ricardo is a hit with the audience, while Lassparri returns to boos and thrown fruit, as Ricardo sings his heart out in an encore duet with Rosa.

On the set, with (l. to r.) Chico, Sam Wood, and George S. Kaufman. Author's collection.

Kitty Carlisle recalled her time working with the brothers. "Groucho paid me the compliment of asking my opinion about the jokes. He was a worrier of the three. He would read me a line deadpan and ask, 'Is that funny?' When I'd shake my head he'd go away, only to come back with another deadpan reading. He did it over and over, till he finally came up with a good one and I burst out laughing."

While *A Night at the Opera* enjoyed its lofty status among comedy fans and film historians for several decades, a debate has also emerged among Marx aficionados. A common assessment today is that the Thalberg/MGM approach to comedy filmmaking was *not* a good fit for the brothers. Back at Paramount, their features gave audiences ample servings of Marx anarchy in each film, interrupted only by an occasional musical love song sung by a lead romantic couple nobody really cared about. Expressing compassion for vulnerable folks around them was simply not what the Marxes were about.

Director Sam Wood keeps a close eye on the Marxes shortly before chaos ensues. Author's collection.

This isn't an entirely new assessment. Upon the film's release, critic Andre Sennwald, after expressing his dour feelings about another popular comedy team ("Laughter is a difficult quantity to measure. One man's comedy may be another man's Wheeler and Woolsey"), he noted his reservation about the new creative turn the Marxes had taken.

"Although *A Night at the Opera* is vastly superior fun, my impression is that several of the earlier Marx carnivals have provided more continuous merriment than their current madhouse. That, I suspect, is because with age I grow more resentful of the half-witted romantic business that insinuates itself into even the best film entertainment. I am jealous of every minute that Groucho, Harpo and Chico are missing from the screen while the lovers bleat of the sweet emotion and grow cow-eyed in its service."

Furthermore, evaluations of the team and their films in more recent decades have consistently ranked *Duck Soup* above *A Night at the Opera*. For instance, *Entertainment Weekly*'s list of the top all-time comedy films placed *Duck Soup* at #7, and *Opera* at #31. The book *The 50 Funniest Movies of All Time*, by Kathryn Bernheimer and published in 1999, put *Duck Soup* at #3, but had no spot on the list for *Opera* at all. The following year, the American Film Institute's 100 Funniest Films of all time also ranked *Duck Soup* at #3, *A Day at the Races* at #59, and *Monkey Business* at #73, but no place for *A Night at the Opera*. However, the film was added to the National Film Registry in 1993, following the addition of *Duck Soup* in 1990.

December 13 - Olsen & Johnson's revue *Everything Goes* opens.

The team, fond of presenting all-out, breakneck comedy, and from several directions within the theatre at once, first presented this 15-scene revue at the Roxy in New York. *Billboard*'s main objection was to the show's title, closely resembling the Cole Porter hit *Anything Goes*. "Outside of that, however, the show's a comedy wow, with the two chief comedians going crazy all over the theatre, and the customers shrieking in the aisles. Olsen and Johnson are the two funniest guys, for this reporter's money, in show business today." The sketches followed each other in rapid succession, with only a few breaks to allow for a sister singing act, a one-man band, and a dancer.

Newspaper ad for *Everything Goes*. Author's collection.

The team later took *Everything Goes* on the road, and, while stopped in Arizona, happened upon a local festival called "Helzapoppin." They decided to add an extra 'l' and make it the new name of the show from that point on (more about *Hellzapoppin'* later).

December 16 - Thelma Todd dies

The year ended on a tragic note, with the sudden and suspicious death of Thelma Todd.

Earlier in the year, Thelma Todd's Sidewalk Café opened for business on the Pacific Coast Highway as a restaurant/nightclub, becoming a popular night spot for Hollywood types, plus those of a somewhat less savory nature.

Thelma herself did not actually own the establishment; her erstwhile lover, director Roland West, bought the property several years earlier. Thelma, who loved the location by the ocean as well as the Hollywood community who frequented the restaurant, happily agreed to front the operation as its hostess. Gangsters reportedly sought to acquire a piece of the restaurant in order to turn part of it into a gambling establishment. Although she wasn't an owner, Thelma's objections held considerable sway with West, who must have been torn by the two sides pulling him in opposite directions.

On the morning of December 16, after having been missing since her night with friends at the Trocodero night club, Todd was found dead in her garage, sitting in her car, from what the coroner determined to be carbon monoxide poisoning. While it was ruled accidental, there were a number of details that didn't add up. Some suspected suicide, but those who mingled with Thelma at the Trocadero didn't notice anything unusual about her behavior, especially nothing resembling depression or distress. Several suspects have been considered for murder in the decades since, and West may have succumbed to intimidating pressure from those determined to remove resistance to their plans, but the case has never been solved. Thelma was only 29 years old.

Her popularity as a comic actress, despite the fact that she had yet to secure a true starring role in a full-length feature, warranted the news of her death to be reported on the front page of *The New York Times* on December 18.

Nearly two months after her death, Roach studios released *The Bohemian Girl*, but with virtually all of Thelma's presence either edited out, or re-shot. She is still briefly visible in part of a musical number, "Heart of the Gypsy," with her singing voice dubbed. Her last short subject with Patsy Kelly, *The All-American Toothache*, was also released in 1936, albeit with a heavy heart, and most probably for Roach to fill the order for the team's eight shorts that year.

There's no telling how far her career could have continued on its upward trajectory, possibly including starring roles in comedy features, a la Carole

1935

Lombard. Fortunately, we are still able to enjoy Thelma's beauty, comic timing, and appealing energy in nearly 100 films over a span of only eight years.

1936

The year began with many comedy favorites cavorting on various New York theatre stages, steadily solidifying reputations that would last for decades.

A new edition of *George White's Scandals*, featuring Bert Lahr, Willie Howard, Cliff Edwards, and Rudy Vallee, had just opened on Christmas night of '35. Howard had become a stage star along with his partner and brother, Eugene. They played vaudeville as openly Jewish performers, often donning the Yiddish dialect for their fast-moving comedy patter and songs. They spent several years between 1912 and 1922 as stars in *The Passing Show*, and joined *Scandals* in 1926. Willie continued performing solo from 1936 onward.

Billboard gushed of Lahr and Howard's contributions to the new *Scandals*:

> "There should be a law passed immediately requiring every revue to enlist the services of Messrs. Howard and Lahr. Between them they make much of the evening a laugh fest of hilarious low comedy. Mr. Lahr works hard and well and proves, among other things, that he can be excruciatingly funny when he simply gives a number on the telephone. And Mr. Howard, as is

his habit, also does yeoman service displaying his great versatility and taking another step toward establishing himself as the foremost comedian of the stage."

Much of the material with which the comics are supplied is, to be nice about it, on the ragged edge of respectability; some of it is also funny, but some of it is not."

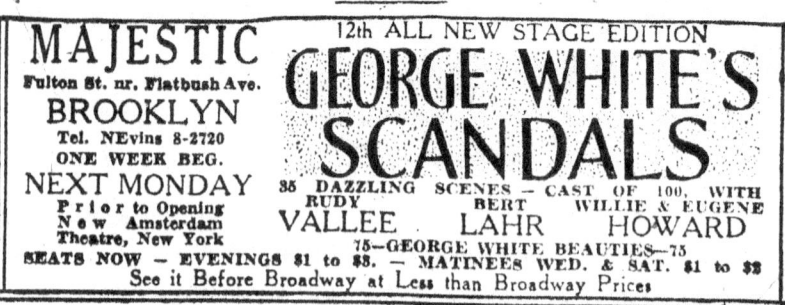

A top-notch cast like this was common on the New York stage throughout the decade. Author's collection.

Elsewhere on the New York stage, at the Loew's State theatre, Burns & Allen were proving that their success on radio hadn't put a dent in their talents to keep audiences elated with their live act, which had long-ago become second nature. During this run, the team slightly blurred the lines between straight vaudeville and revue, by appearing in the other acts as well, rather than simply introducing them (this had become Ed Wynn's usual *modus operandi*). Record-breaking capacity shows all week necessitated adding more performances each day, with as many as five shows daily, even six on Saturdays. *Billboard*'s review could scarcely contain its joy:

> "[The] draw is Burns and Allen with their intimate revue, which is grand entertainment and only runs 49 minutes to permit the playing of so many shows. The show is

charmingly intimate, with the headliners working in each and every act and making it definitely take the form of a revue.
Burns and Allen in working this show, are the gift of the year to vaude, especially Gracie. She's a tireless little worker and so able a comedienne. To her falls the job of mistress of ceremonies and the way she introduces each act and butts in on them is a joy to behold. Of course, George and Gracie still carry on with their comedy cross-fire, and it's even better now, and also still use their dancing bits in hauling off a joke."

At the same time, a new edition of *The Ziegfeld Follies*, with headliner Fannie Brice, and with support by Bob Hope, began promisingly. "As for Miss Brice," *Billboard* reported, "it is enough to say that she has never been better. That is praise indeed." However, the run was abruptly halted after a week, as Brice battled laryngitis, as well as a series of other illnesses. The show would re-open that autumn with her, but with Hope replaced by Bobby Clark.

February 5 - Charlie Chaplin releases his last silent film feature, *Modern Times*.

By 1936, the term "talkie" had pretty much disappeared. Movies weren't "talkies" anymore, they were simply movies (or, the more common term at the time, "pictures"). Charlie Chaplin's refusal—or inability—to come to terms with talkies resulted in his making only two films throughout the entire decade: *City Lights*, and this, his last non-speaking film feature, *Modern Times*. He did make some concessions to sound here. Along with the music soundtrack (composed by Chaplin), sound effects are used more frequently, and in a more robust way, than those of typical comedies of the silent era. And, there is in fact some dialogue in the film. More precisely, it consists of a handful of orders barked by the factory manager to his employees (via a two-way closed circuit TV system, no less!) But Chaplin remained adamant in his position that he didn't want his Little Tramp to speak, fearing it would ruin the character. His creative dilemma had not found any resolution since the release of *City Lights*. "I had thought of possible voices for the tramp," he later wrote in his memoirs, "whether he should speak in monosyllables or just mumble. But it was no use. If I talked, I would become like any other comedian. These were the melancholy problems that confronted me."

Some of the more heavy-handed film historians through the years have claimed that *Modern Times* was Chaplin's grandiose statement about the nature of a newly-industrialized society, and its effects on the common man. Well, yes and no. First of all, the germ of the idea was not quite so profound. "I was riding in my car one day and saw a mass of people coming out of a factory, punching time-clocks," he explained, "and was overwhelmed with the knowledge that the theme note of modern times is mass production. I wondered what would happen to the progress of the mechanical age if one person decided to act like a bull in a china shop."

Chaplin's longtime friend and fellow comedy genius, Stan Laurel, detested pretentious interpretations of comedy by film critics and scholars. "Anyone who thinks *Modern Times* has got a big message is just putting it there himself," Laurel insisted. "Charlie knew that the pressures of modern life and factory life would be good for a lot of *laughs*, and that's why he did the film, not because he wanted to diagnose the industrial revolution or some goddamned thing."

It is also evident that *Modern Times* is, if anything, more about life during the Great Depression than it is about the growth spurt of industry in the early decades of the century. Indeed, only about the first quarter of the film's running time takes place in the factory. The often-used film clip of Chaplin getting wound through a set of giant gears is certainly a great visual treat, but anyone new to the film today might be surprised by the story's turn from the factory to that of Charlie's character befriending a girl in need (played by the enchanting Paulette Goddard, Chaplin's girlfriend at the time).

"*Modern Times* was a great success," he wrote, "but again I was faced with the depressing question: should I make another silent picture? I knew I'd be taking a great chance if I did. The whole of Hollywood had deserted silent pictures and I was the only one left. I had been lucky so far, but to continue with a feeling that the art of pantomime was gradually becoming obsolete was a discouraging thought…"

In September, he made it official, announcing that he was putting the Little Tramp to rest.

New York Times critic Frank Nugent wrote, "Charles Chaplin's announcement last week that he would never again appear on the screen as the pantomimic little tramp with the derby hat, baggy trousers, oversized shoes and flexible cane was sudden but scarcely surprising. King Canute discovered he could not check the tide and it was inevitable that King Charlot realize he could not stem the tide of sound. 'Modern Times' must have brought that realization home, must have convinced him it was hopeless even to attempt to compromise with progress."

Nugent noted that the success of *City Lights* was due in part to the fact that a good number of moviegoers in 1931 had not yet rejoiced, or even welcomed, the sound revolution, and saw Chaplin as the last stalwart who could provide them with more of what they had known and loved for years, i.e. silent storytelling. He concluded:

"And so, when we analyze the passing of the greatest personality the screen has ever known—for Charles Chaplin's little tramp was the colossus of the cinema—we see it vanquished by the microphone, by an animated cartoon and by that inevitable machine of destruction variously known as change, time or progress. There probably is a human equation, too. Mr. Chaplin is 48 now, not quite ready for a wheelchair, but still forgiven if he chooses to forego his death-defying whirls around a skating rink for the possibly equally hazardous task of producing a co-starring venture with Paulette Goddard."

Modern Times as added to the National Film Registry in 1989.

At the same time Chaplin released his last film of the decade, his friendly rival Buster Keaton was making a modest turnaround at Educational Pictures. After the disappointing attempt by MGM to pair him with Durante in three features, Keaton left the studio, only to get shut out of the other major Hollywood lots. His drinking problem worsened, but he managed to get hired for a couple of modest films in England and France.

Upon returning to Hollywood and desperate for a salary, he signed with Educational Pictures to star in 16 two-reelers. These low-budget shorts show Keaton past his prime, but he was given greater control over the comedy content of the films, which marked a small but significant victory for him.

March 25 - Paul McCullough dies, age 52.

It's plain to see, in the more than thirty Clark & McCullough two-reelers, that the straight man of the team, McCullough, rarely had much to do on-camera, other than cackling at Clark's one-liners (usually directed at a third party), or acting as assistant to help carry out his partner's plans. Some have speculated that McCullough's diminished role had brought about a deep depression by this time in 1936, while others have suggested that the depression came first, causing Clark and their associates to lighten McCullough's load, thus focusing the comedic business almost squarely on Clark.

The team released *Alibi Bye Bye*, which was to be their last, and arguably best short for RKO, in June of 1935. After leaving the studio, they took to the road on tour. But by the end of the year, McCullough was exhausted and extremely depressed. He checked himself into a sanatorium on the outskirts of Boston. On the day he left the facility, his close friend Frank T. Ford picked him up to drive McCullough to his Brookline home. McCullough asked to stop in Medford for a shave. While in the barber shop, he grabbed a razor from the barber, and slit his own throat and wrists. He died two days later. The incident shocked the entertainment community, and Clark, naturally shaken by his partner's death, ceased performing altogether for the next six months.

1936

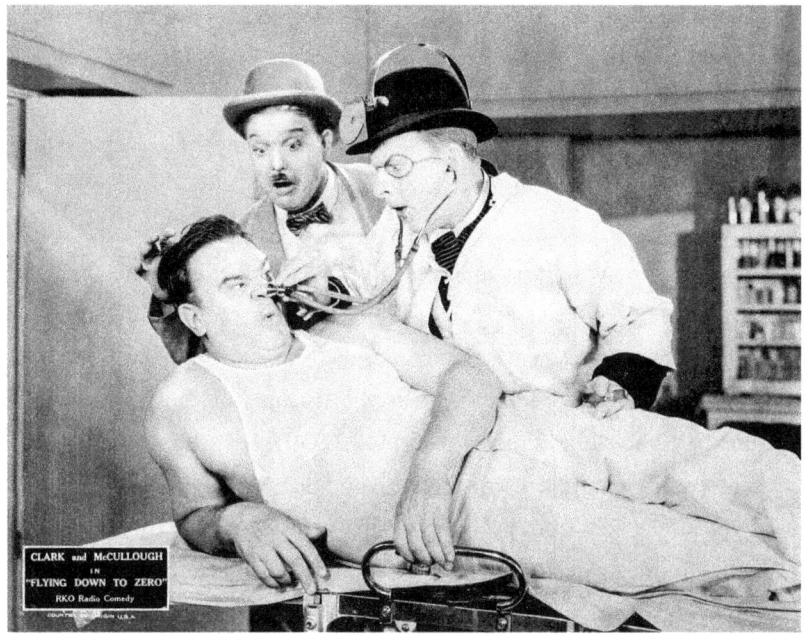

Clark & McCullough in *Flying Down to Zero* (1935).
Courtesy of Steve Cox.

July 7 - Ed Wynn appears on RCA experimental TV broadcast.

With the stage, radio, and sound films at the service of comedians in the 1930s, yet another potential mass medium, television, was swiftly creeping into the public consciousness.

Several inventors, working independently of each other, made considerable progress developing television in the 1920s. The most prominent of these was young Scotsman John Logie Baird, who first demonstrated the transmission of live, moving silhouette images from a transmitter to a receiver. Baird gave the first of his public demonstrations in 1925. Word of this reached the U.S. in January of 1926. *The New York Times* reported from London, "John L. Baird, who has perfected television after years of research, has been giving practical demonstrations here..." Just days later, on January 26, Baird demonstrated his apparatus for members of the Royal Institution, and for the press.

In the same period, American Charles Francis Jenkins began transmitting moving images through the air as well, across Washington, D.C., over a distance of about five miles.

Even with the medium at this primitive stage, the general public, including those in show business, kept track of television's development and potential.

The first major television breakthrough in America came on April 27, 1927, when engineers at AT&T Labs achieved the first live inter-city television transmission by wire. The experiment linked Commerce Secretary (and future president) Herbert Hoover in Washington, D.C, and AT&T president Walter Gifford in New York, about 230 miles away.

The experiment took place in two stages: first with a transmission by wire, using telephone lines from Washington, D.C. to New York City, and then an over-the-air broadcast from the AT&T transmitter and studio in Whippany, New Jersey, to New York.

One of the several individuals participating in the Whippany broadcast was a vaudeville comedian identified by history only as A. Dolan, who performed a monologue in an Irish brogue, sporting side whiskers and a broken pipe. He then left his place in front of the transmitter but appeared a few minutes later in black face, telling jokes in a black dialect. By doing so, he became the first comedian ever to appear on a television transmission, "And in its possibilities," wrote journalist Orrin Dunlop of the demonstration, "an observer compares it with the Fred Ott sneeze of more than thirty years ago, the first piece of comedy recorded in the movies."

It was Philo Farnsworth's development of all-electronic television, replacing Baird's mechanical invention, that jump-started the industry. Within the next couple of years, a handful of current stars and stars-to-be, such as Claudette Colbert, Jimmy Durante, and Al Jolson, found themselves, at various times, in front of crude television equipment, and under intensely hot lights, as part of experimental tests. The likes of Sophie Tucker, Ted Healy, and Milton Berle did likewise.

In his autobiography, Berle recalled his brief first time in front of a television camera, in 1929. F.A. Sanabria, owner of the United States Television Corporation in Chicago, asked Berle and Trixie Friganza to perform a portion of his stand-up routine as part of an experimental transmission. "My instructions were to do eight minutes and keep it clean, and don't move around too much. Of the actual broadcast, all I can remember is a small room and fierce heat from the lights and the heavy make-up we had to wear. We were part of history, but I don't think either of us made history. The broadcast was sent out to maybe twelve people in Sanabria's company who had sets."

On July 7, 1936, RCA conducted a more high-profile experimental broadcast, touted as television's "first planned show," for invited guests and RCA licencees, who viewed the performance on specially-prepared receivers at Radio City (the ten-kilowatt transmitter atop the Empire State Building had opened just a week before).

The broadcast consisted of a mix of short newsreel films, an outdoor ballet performance by the Radio City Music Hall Ballet, a fashion show, a comedy team performing in blackface, the Pickens Sisters singing and performing a comedic opera routine, and finally Wynn. As one of the highest-paid radio comedians, Wynn spoke often about his eager impatience for the true arrival of television, hoping to "try to prove to the radio audience that if they think I am funny now, they will like me twice as well in television. I'm not saying this to be vain; I'm speaking purely from a professional viewpoint."

The experimental RCA transmission was filmed by Pathe News Inc., which set up a film camera about ten feet behind the studio TV camera (consequently, several of the acts were almost totally blocked from view of the film camera by the television equipment). For his turn before the cameras on this occasion, Wynn awkwardly stepped in front of the camera, claiming that he had just been asked to participate in the production a half hour earlier, and thus had no prepared material. "I don't know what to say," he shrugged. Whether or not this was merely an act is difficult to determine. Finally, his longtime announcer, Graham McNamee, appeared, seemingly to Wynn's relief, and the two got into their usual radio banter and visual riddles before the broadcast was brought to a close.

Wynn's peers also considered the future of television as a means of mass entertainment. In November, Eddie Cantor would announce his intentions to begin memorizing his lines for radio, rather than relying on reading his scripts in front of the microphone each week. "Television will not be such a revolutionary change for the actor with stage and screen experience," he said, "but it will be a hard task-master for those radio artists whose personalities have remained hidden behind the unseeing 'mike'."

* * *

Meanwhile, changes were afoot in the film industry. By 1936, double-features had become the order of the day from movie theatre owners, and, by extension, by the studios, thus endangering the future of shorts—especially comedy shorts. Production companies that had been specializing in the twenty-minute films began to disappear. Even Hal Roach Studios had to succumb to the trend in order to survive.

The Roach studio was riding a wave of success and creative activity at the time. Located in Culver City, just a mile from its distributor, MGM, the Roach lot employed between 600 and 700 that year, and *The New York Times* noted that "sixty-eight of these employees have been with him fifteen years or longer. Some even date back to the old days when his studio was a converted home in downtown Los Angeles."

The *Times* also reported: "The double-feature mania which has gripped the nation has killed one of the cinema's most flourishing institutions, the slap-sick comedy factory. Most of them have given up the ghost. Hal Roach, however, has adapted himself to the times by renouncing the two-reelers for the more respected multiple-reel films…"

As much as Roach loved the two-reeler format, he had equal distain for producing comedy features, and for a specific reason. "Making comedy you have to go up; you can't do your funniest gag first or you die on the way," he explained. "So you must keep on being funny as you go along. Well, a two-reeler was almost an ideal length, because you didn't have to go too far to get to the finish. When you got into feature pictures that meant an hour and a half, so you had to go three times further than you did in a two-reeler. Therefore, you had to have a very fine story. I mean something that holds together besides just the comedy. There was no better gag man, with the exception of Chaplin, than Stan Laurel. But in the construction of a picture that ran for an hour and a half, the construction thing is something that he was very incapable of doing."

By the end of 1936, Roach had reluctantly given up producing two-reelers. Laurel & Hardy filmed their last short, *Thicker Than Water* the previous year, before moving to features. The series that began as a vehicle for ZaSu Pitts and Thelma Todd, and went through changes culminating (after Todd's death) with the pairing of Patsy Kelly and Lyda Roberti, was also discontinued. Roach experimented with putting Our Gang into features with *General Spanky*, which takes place during the Civil War, but it was not a box office success. Roach saw he had little choice but to give up producing shorts altogether.

September 14 - *The Ziegfeld Follies of 1936* stars Fannie Brice and Bobby Clark.

The *Follies*, a lavish, annual production from 1907 through 1931, was by this point heading to its permanent closing curtain. Bobby Clark, six months after losing his comedy partner Paul McCullough to suicide, replaced Bob Hope for the autumn addition. Clark provided a kinetic energy to the proceedings that had far surpassed that of Hope earlier in the year. There was no question, however, that Fannie Brice remained the true star of the show.

"...Miss Brice is the personification of 'The Follies,' and that enterprise is still, to all intents and purposes, the property of Miss Brice," *The New York Times* declared. "As general utility comic—and it takes a general utility comic to stay on the same stage with Miss Brice—there is Bobby Clark, playing now alone. Bobby Clark is Bobby Clark, changeless, agile, wry. Last evening's audience wondered whether he would make that old, cigar-dropping entrance, now that his partner has gone; he made the entrance. He is in most of the sketches and so most of the sketches are good in that mad Brice-Clark mood that is of 'The Follies."...For the alumni—'Baby Snooks' is still Miss Brice's confusion to Hollywood..."

The two top stars energized the last official *Ziegfeld Follies* edition. Author's collection.

1936

Fannie Brice in 1936. Courtesy of Martin Grams.

September 6 - *My Man Godfrey,* **starring Carole Lombard and William Powell, is released.**

This screwball classic already had a lot going for it even before the first frame of film passed through the camera. The script was co-written by one of the Marx Brothers' top writers, Morrie Ryskind. The director was Leo McCarey, one of the greatest comedy directors in film history, who boasted a long list of credits working with Laurel & Hardy, the Marx Brothers, and W.C. Fields, to name just a few. Lombard was not only strikingly beautiful, but an actress of remarkable versatility, alternating between comedy and drama with ease. Indeed, she was a comic actress and bathing beauty for Mack Sennett between 1927 and 1929, taking part in the usual Sennett slapstick in a dozen two-reelers. *My Man Godfrey* would confirm her status as major comic actress, just two years after her breakthrough role in Howard Hawks' *Twentieth Century* co-starring John Barrymore.

Powell at the time had seen his career take off with his success in *The Thin Man* movie series with Myrna Loy. The first film of the series, released in May of 1934, was a critical and box office smash, and received Academy Award nominations for Best Picture, Direction, and Screenplay. The follow-up, *After the Thin Man* was released on Christmas Day of 1936.

In *My Man Godfrey*, written Ryskind and Eric Hatch (from Hatch's novel), Lombard plays Irene, a flighty, high-spirited daughter in a wealthy, eccentric family. Taking part in an elaborate scavenger hunt at a high-society party, she finds a required "forgotten man" (Powell) at a riverside shanty town and brings him to a party. Once Godfrey berates the wealthy snobs in attendance, the infatuated Irene offers him a job as the family butler. He proceeds to inject a bit of sanity into the household full of eccentrics, and reluctantly falls in love with Irene in the process. As was the case in most of her comedy roles, Lombard here forsakes glamour in the interest of getting laughs, and she is nothing short of hilarious in doing so. Her performance here rightly won her an Oscar nomination.

Picture Play called *My Man Godfrey* "a triumph of wit, humor, and goofy fun. It is the best of its kind since *Twentieth Century*. With neither let-up nor let-down, it goes madly, mirthfully on, leaving one gasping and wondering what the eccentric characters will be up to next. And it's all original and fresh, too…"

As for the leads, the review described Lombard's performance as "truly amazing" and that Powell is equally extraordinary. "His acting is modest, reticent, and convincing both as a tramp and an earnest servant. And in spite of Miss Lombard's tempests and tantrums she remains beautiful, charming, and likable. If that isn't a feat I don't know what is."

Print ad for *My Man Godfrey* at Radio City Music Hall in New York. Author's collection.

Frank Nugent, reviewing for *The New York Times*, chose similar words, calling the film "the daffiest comedy of the year…there may be a sober moment or two in the picture; there may be a few lines of the script that do not pack a laugh. Somehow we cannot remember them. It's nonsense, of course, but it's something to relish on a damp September morn."

My Man Godfrey was added to the National Film Registry in 1999.

October 4 - Joe Penner returns to radio.

After becoming a national star in 1933, then abruptly walking away from his program in June of 1935, Penner's successful three-week vaudeville tour in the New York area in the spring of 1936 gave him renewed confidence to return to radio, but on his own terms. After auditioning for sponsor Cocomalt, he put together the program called *The Park Avenue Penners* (known as *The Joe Penner Show*), and signed the contract in record time. He also hired former Jack Benny writer Harry Conn to write the scripts, at $1,500 each week—the same salary as Penner himself!

Newspaper ads for the new 1936 radio season. Author's collection.

Conn followed Penner's instructions to produce scripts that were more flexible, giving the comedian more to do than simply repeat his famous but worn-out shtick. The show aired throughout 1937, to be canceled in June of the following year.

1936

Penner remained on the air via different sponsors until April of 1940, but with diminishing returns as time wore on. He died of a heart attack in 1941 at the age of 36.

December 8 - David Freedman dies at age 38.

Freedman was, at the time of his death, pursuing a lawsuit against his former employer, Eddie Cantor, claiming that when Cantor initially hired Freedman in 1931, he promised the writer ten percent of Cantor's current and future earnings from radio. Cantor denied that such a contract, either written or verbal, existed. It was during the height of the legal proceedings when news of Freedman's death resulted in a mistrial. More significantly, to the entertainment world and to the public, which had, over time, become familiar with Freedman's name (if not his face), it meant the loss of radio's top comedy writer. His death was blamed by some on the enormous amount of work he had to maintain for several comedians simultaneously, and on a weekly basis, for years on end. Fred Sammis, editor of *Radio Mirror*, wrote an editorial in which he laid the blame of Freedman's death squarely on the unforgiving workload he had to deal with, due to the lack of top comedy writers in radio.

> "He worked himself to death and died in his sleep, not yet forty, from exhaustion. In the past five years, Freedman wrote for practically every comedian who has had a radio program. Often his jokes were so much in demand that Freedman worked twenty hours without pause. His office was the top floor of a triplex apartment. It was a bare room containing only his typewriter, a small table, and one or two chairs. The ceiling was a skylight of heavy glass. No one, not even his best friends, ever went up to that top floor. Dave worked there isolated from every human being."

Sammis then offered a surprising assertion that despite Freedman's extraordinary income from his multiple employers, he died with virtually no money in the bank. "Though fame and huge salaries were the fruits of his toil, when Dave died he had practically no estate. The men who knew him best told me that he left only $5,000 in cash to his widow and his children."

Sammis concluded by quoting an unnamed comedian as saying, "You know how hard we try to avoid a bad program. But at times they're inevitable. They wouldn't come as often if there were more Dave Freedmans."

December 17 - Edgar Bergen and Charlie McCarthy debut on the Rudy Vallee Show.

Bergen had been practicing ventriloquism since his pre-teen years, and, in 1919, when he was sixteen, paid a Chicago wood craftsman, Theodore Mack, $36 to create the dummy out of white pine, one that would eventually come to be named Charlie McCarthy. That first incarnation resembled a scruffy street-urchin or corner newspaper boy, and, once Bergen left Northwestern University, the dummy became his partner in vaudeville, beginning in 1922.

Bergen slogged through vaudeville with his wooden companion for more than fifteen years before clicking with several influential individuals who wanted to see the "team" succeed. Bergen and Charlie (who by this time was sporting a tuxedo, top hat, and monocle) became the darling of high society parties. At one such affair hosted by society patron Elsa Maxwell, the famed playwright and actor Noel Coward positively fawned over Bergen and his comedy material (which Bergen wrote himself). Coward's endorsement helped Bergen land a gig at Rockefeller Center's Rainbow Room for $400 a week. Later, when comedian Ken Murray attended a Bergen-McCarthy show, Murray insisted to Bergen that the act was worth twice that salary, and talked Bergen into demanding the raise, which he got.

A talent scout for Rudy Vallee also caught the act, and recommended the team for Vallee's radio show. Their first appearance resulted in an immediate and enthusiastic public response, prompting Vallee to invite them back the following week, and shortly thereafter he offered a three-year contract.

Variety reflected the public's response to Bergen's radio debut with this rave:

"Standard in vaudeville and now doing his stuff in nightclubs, Edgar Bergen makes the jump into radio with non-chalant ease. He talks to himself and the replies make for amusing entertainment. His dummy bears the name of Charlie McCarthy, and is a saucy little fellow. Humor is situational and character-bred rather than gaggy...It represents the culmination of years of theatre-trained work. An artiste-in the old and best meaning."

The up-and-coming "team" of Bergen & McCarthy.
Courtesy of Martin Grams.

The irony of a ventriloquist becoming a hit on radio is not to be overlooked. After all, the whole point of a ventriloquist's performance is to present his partner as a living, breathing person, one who speaks while the lips of the human half of the team remain still. Even though Bergen freely admitted that he wasn't especially skilled in that regard, his wit and ability to ad-lib (giving most of the punchlines to Charlie, of course), in conjunction with having created such a popular smart-alecky "boy," ensured his success with live audiences. But radio? *The New York Times* observed, "Of all the legendary radio improbabilities, such as jugglers, magicians, dancers, etc., the ventriloquist does not lag far behind. For, with the ventriloquist, too, much of the illusion depends upon the truism that 'seeing is believing.' That is the way the radio showmen have reasoned up to now. And so it remained for Rudy Vallee… to bring this unique 'team' to the microphone…[Bergen's] material is fresh and sparkles with humor and spontaneity."

Print ad for *The Goldwyn Follies*. Author's collection.

Vallee had taken a chance, but whatever apprehension he may have felt before that first broadcast with Bergen and McCarthy quickly vanished with his listeners' response to the team. "Edgar Bergen did a thing no one thought possible in radio," *Radio Mirror* commented, "by scoring a sensational hit with a ventriloquist act on Rudy Vallee's variety hour."

Samuel Goldwyn of MGM heard the team on the program as well, and signed Bergen (and Charlie) just before they became a national sensation. Goldwyn is reputed to have said, "Sign those two guys. They're marvelous." At that time, Bergen was receiving $300 a week; the Goldwyn contract called for $15,000 for him and Charlie to appear in the picture *The Goldwyn Follies*. Bergen specified that there was to be no option on his future services.

Vallee was as enamored of Charlie McCarthy as the millions who tuned in to the program each week. "Imitation may be the sincerest form of flattery," he said, "but not when it comes to Charlie. The public will brook no competition there. There are no imitators, and there never will be, for the simple reason that the public will not tolerate one. It has humanized the little fellow and taken him completely to its heart. This, needless to say, has worked terrific hardship upon the ventriloquist's art, no matter how skilled the performer may be."

As Bergen said, "I write my own spot on the radio. I write 75 percent of the dialogue. No one understands Charlie as I do."

* * *

Elsewhere on radio, the art of the running gag was about to come to full bloom with the now legendary Jack Benny-Fred Allen "feud." In early December, a study of various popularity polls led broadcasters to report that Allen topped a nation-wide telephone survey of one-hour shows. In the half-hour category, Benny ranked No.1, with Eddie Cantor second, and Burns &Allen third.

George & Gracie's own running gag a few years earlier, you'll recall, in which she would turn up on unlikely broadcasts searching for her brother, had to be discontinued, due to the personal strife the joke had been causing real-life George Allen.

The running gag that was to become the Fred Allen-Jack Benny feud came from even more organic origins, when, on Allen's December 30 broadcast, a young violin protégé named Stewart Canin played a challenging selection (Allen, in his autobiography, identified it as "The Flight of the Bumble Bee" by Rimsky-Korsakov, while Benny, in his own memoirs, felt obliged to correct that, stating that Canin in fact played "The Bee" by Dvorak). After the number was over, Allen referenced how poor Benny's playing was in comparison. "I said…he should hang his head in symphonic shame and pluck the horsehairs out of his bow and return them to the tail of the stallion from which they had been taken." Benny was listening to the show, and on his program the following week, had a few remarks of his own for Allen. He then volunteered to play "The Bee" on Allen's show. Allen took him up on it, although neither reported the results of the challenge.

While the feud began spontaneously, and gained momentum via a trade-off of ad libs, the response by delighted listeners prompted the two comedians to meet, along with their writers, to plan out a strategy for future broadcasts. "It was all cold and calculated," Benny said, "and the sky was the limit. Or rather, the mud was the limit."

However, Benny also recognized that hurling vicious insults at Allen was not very well-suited to his own radio character. The on-air Jack Benny was usually the target of jibes from his supporting players. Allen was better known for his caustic sense of humor, but he was also wary of being perceived as someone attempting to hitch a ride on Benny's top-rated standing among radio comedians at the time. "The Jack Benny program was the highest-rated show in radio at the time," he wrote. "With our smaller audience it would take an academy award display of intestinal fortitude to ask Jack to participate in a feud with me. I would be hitching my gaggin' to a star." Perhaps Allen's recollection failed to include that his own show had just been rated the most popular of hour-long programs on the air (but Benny had the strongest overall numbers).

Allen did note, with some justifiable pride, that until that point, "radio was a calm and tranquil medium…fraught with politeness. No voice was ever raised in public. When Jack and I started to ignore precedent and bellow censored Billingsgate at each other, the radio audience perked up."

The popular Allen-Benny feud continued on the screen in *Love Thy Neighbor* (1940). Courtesy of Steve Cox.

The feud continued for years, with several highlights along the way, including what was meant to be a climactic, and presumably physical, battle on the air between the two men in March of 1937. After trading a spirited round of insults and ad-libs, the two challenged each other to fisticuffs in the hallway. A musical number followed, after which they returned, laughing, reminiscing, and even singing to each other. It seemed the feud was over, but yet another confrontation was to take place on Allen's show several years later. Allen, trying out a new (fictional) game show with Benny as a contestant, had Benny's pants forcibly removed in front of the audience, producing mass fits of hysterical laughter. "Allen, you haven't seen the end of me!" the de-bagged Benny protested, to which Allen replied, "It won't be long now!"

As much as Allen was revered by his fellow comedians and writers as a brilliant satirist, he was known by his friends as a basically unhappy man. George Burns wrote, "Fred Allen played a sarcastic, bitter, sometimes morbid, miserable, dejected, unhappy, sad comedian named Fred Allen. He was perfect for the part. The thing I always noticed about Fred was that he just wasn't happy unless he wasn't happy…[He] was radio's most popular pessimist. He was the kind of person who would look for the dark cloud inside the silver lining."

Allen and Jack Benny were close friends away from the microphone, and admired each other's talents, but even Benny had a hard time figuring him out. They enjoyed each other's company, especially when reminiscing about their days as struggling vaudevillians. "But when you got him off vaudeville, Allen became somebody else, a bitter and frustrated and unhappy man. I couldn't understand him. He couldn't understand me." Allen had become phenomenally successful, had a famously strong marriage to Portland, lived a clean, modest life, and commanded the respect of the nation's greatest humorists. "What was wrong?" Benny pondered. "He thought there was something so silly about my feeling good all the time when I took a morning walk and inhaled the fresh air, or relished a cold glass of spring water, or enjoyed a good story told by one of my friends, especially, for example, Fred himself."

December 25 - *The Show Is On* opens on Broadway, starring Beatrice Lillie and Bert Lahr.

Christmas brought a treat to comedy fans in the form of this revue. Those collaborating on it comprised a Who's Who of comedy and music giants of the

1936

time, with sketches written by the recently-deceased Dave Freedman (with one sketch by Moss Hart), songs and additional music by Hoagy Carmichael, George & Ira Gershwin, Harold Arlen, and Richard Rogers and others. Vincente Minnelli directed. The show ran for 236 performances, with Beatrice Lillie and Bert Lahr as the obvious selling points. As Brooks Atkinson celebrated in *The New York Times*:

> "B. L. are their initials. Beatrice Lillie and Bert Lahr are their names. Since Christmas night they have been warming the old Winter Garden with the sunniest comedy it has contained in a musical revue laconically entitled *The Show Is On*...Being gifted with a magnetic comic spirit [Lillie] can afford to be subtle, and she is, making something irresistibly hilarious out of minute incidents in her pantomime."

At one point, it was reported, Lillie sat atop a prop moon, maneuvered by crane above the stage and first few rows of the audience, tossing away her garters. In the sketch by Moss Hart, she parodied John Gielgud performing *Hamlet*.

As for Lahr's talents, some of which were put to use in his "Song of the Woodman":

> "Lahr's sense of humor is a robustious [sic]one that bursts with low comedy dynamics and prances crazily through any sort of scene. After working pretty seriously at his trade of merrymaking, he can take almost anything in his stride today. He is flamboyantly comic as the dim-witted movie star who talks himself into an income-tax fine; he is abdominally comic as the conventional 'Dutch' comedian in a burlesque show... Lahr has become a satirist with a comic strength that virtually annihilates the subject of his material."

Program for *The Show Is On*. Author's collection.

Variety was also pleased, calling the show "perhaps the best revue in years," and giving Lillie a slight edge over Lahr. "Not that Lahr does not put over some comedy punches, for he has generous assignments with Miss Lillie alone, and with others. But the pint-sized fun-maker from London lands more surely." Dave Freedman, who died just two weeks before opening night, was also remembered in *Variety*'s review. "Posthumous credit goes to Dave Freedman. It would have been a great satisfaction had he been able to watch his sketches click in succession."

1937

As radio's popularity continued to grow exponentially, so did the salaries of its top stars. The average Joe (or Joan) even today would be quite content with the paychecks the top radio comedians were receiving over eighty years ago. For instance:

During Eddie Cantor's first year on the air in 1931, he earned $2,500 per weekly broadcast. As of March of '37, he was reported to be the highest paid radio star with a regular show, estimated at $15,000 for each half-hour program. As was the case with most of his contemporaries, he needed to pay his writers and supporting cast out of his salary, but, *The New York Times* pointed out, "this still leaves a neat penny for Mr. and Mrs. Cantor and the five daughters."

Burns & Allen's salary at the time reached $10,000 per broadcast, which also had to be dispersed throughout the cast and orchestra.

Jack Benny brought in $9,500 per broadcast, followed by the likes of Fred Allen, Al Jolson, and Ed Wynn, all earning between $5,000–$6,000.

The New York Times saw the radio star's job as quite cushy, and full of possibilities. "Surely, aside from the other comforts that broadcasting has provided for the performer who once was obliged to tour the country to find an audience, it has also lent him the Midas touch. For in addition to the fabulous salaries earned at the microphone it has opened the door to that twin art, the cinema. And with television in the offing there will be new worlds to conquer, and possibly new sponsors to pay even larger bills!"

April 16 - Laurel & Hardy star in *Way Out West*.

The second film produced by Stan Laurel for Hal Roach (the first being *Our Relations* the previous year; the "producer" title was largely ceremonial), shows the team in peak form.

Set in the Old West, the simple plot has Stan and Ollie on their way to Brushwood Gulch to deliver a gold mine deed to the young daughter of the deceased mine owner. They haven't met the girl, Mary Roberts, and are easily fooled by nasty saloon owner, Finn (James Finlayson, of course) and his girlfriend, Lola (Sharon Lynn). Upon meeting the real Mary, and realizing they've given the deed to the wrong people, Stan and Ollie spend the rest of the film attempting to get the deed back from Finn's safe.

Stan and Ollie meet the scheming saloon owner Finlayson.
Author's collection.

1937

The slapstick sequences here are among the team's best, as are the two musical interludes performed by Stan & Ollie themselves—first a dance routine, later a song—and each number is delightful. Comedy highlights, and there are many, include their late-night attempts to retrieve the stolen deed from Finlayson's upstairs safe, and Stan's uncontrollable laughing fit during a bedroom chase scene, during which Lola inadvertently tickles him while trying to retrieve the deed hidden under Stan's shirt.

May 9 - Edgar Bergen becomes host of *The Chase & Sanborn Variety Hour*.

Bergen's popular appearances on Rudy Vallee's program soon led to his own weekly, one-hour time slot. The new program, along with his personal appearances with Charlie, had money virtually pouring into Bergen's bank account. The show earned him $2,500 a week, but he also received another $1,000 a week in royalties for various Charlie McCarthy dolls, books, and toys. A weeklong gig in Los Angeles brought in $17,000, and their appearance in *The Goldwyn Follies* film paid $15,000.

Bergen's *Chase and Sanborn Variety Hour* included a roster of regulars that brought the weekly payroll to over $20,000: Don Ameche, Dorothy Lamour, Nelson Eddy, orchestra conductor Werner Janssen, and, perhaps most surprising, a certain film comedian named W.C. Fields, who was still slowly recovering from the myriad of illnesses. A painful sacroiliac, pneumonia, and vertigo conspired to plague him for the previous eighteen months, keeping him off movie sets.

Fields claimed he never had much interest in radio's entertainment value, and didn't listen to it with any regularity, but at one point during his hospitalization, he began to experience double vision, making it impossible for him to read. With books, newspapers, and magazines rendered useless as entertainment, and in an attempt to save his very sanity, he turned to radio for his contact with the world at large. In doing so, he tuned in to the programs of Jack Benny, Burns & Allen, and others whom the public had already been enjoying for several years. Fields found himself glued to the radio to hear his comedy peers, especially Benny. With increasing enthusiasm, he looked forward to hearing Benny's program each Sunday night (a few years later, he would write a pair of personal letters to Benny, dated just two weeks apart, with each praising the show, and Fields even including a sketch for use in Benny's program, should it pass muster: "…I listen to the program so assiduously every week that I am beginning to feel part of it…If you feel [the sketch] is 'worth the candle' when you are sometime stuck for Rochester dialogue, use it."

By the time the opportunity to actually take part in radio arrived, Fields was hooked, and he accepted Edgar Bergen's invitation to be on the Chase & Sanborn show. It proved a good fit for Fields, who was still only able to take on work that wouldn't be physically taxing on him. His feud with Charlie McCarthy, during which they'd swap stinging insults at each other, proved a massive hit with listeners.

By this point in his career, Fields had established himself as a true comedy titan, and was receiving praise along the lines of this pronouncement in *Picture Play* the previous year: "Now he is an institution, comparable to no other comedian, and suggesting no one in his characterization of a likable scoundrel. While critics hymn praises of Chaplin's universality, they must not forget that Mr. Fields is supremely powerful because of his ineluctable Americanism."

As Bergen later recalled, "When I had my own show I brought W.C. Fields in, I would meet [him] on a Monday and we would talk about what we would do. Fields could write good jokes, but would forget them. His memory was bad. He'd start reading a joke and he wouldn't know what the payoff was until he got to it. So he couldn't lean on it. He wrote some lovely jokes and we would put toppers on them, which were real good. But he'd try to cut them out because he didn't think they were very funny. Well, if there were any jokes we thought were really funny, we'd say, 'Bill, that was one of your own jokes.' And he'd say, 'Oh, it is?' We never had an argument. We protected him whatever condition he was in. Sure, he'd ad-lib, but Bill never said anything too dirty. We got into a little trouble when we had Mae West, but even that would be dull by today's standards."

Bergen also called Fields "the most talented man I ever worked with anywhere. He could read a joke somebody wrote for him. He could write his own joke and deliver it masterfully. And he was a master of pantomime—which had no part in radio of course, except for the occasional benefit of our studio audience."

"Sometimes," Fields reported, "I get a letter complaining about the insinuations I make regarding Charlie McCarthy's parentage, but I've got a plan for that. In the future, I'm going to ask that all complaints be accompanied by ten empty packages of Chase & Sanborn. Listeners get the feeling that Charlie is human, and so does everyone around the studio. Sometimes I get it myself, when I catch Edgar Bergen and Charlie off in a corner enjoying a heart-to-heart talk with themselves. All I know is that the more I hate [Charlie], the more I love him. But I won't know he's human until he bites me!"

A *Radio Stars* editorial proclaimed:

"Never did a radio program whiz so quickly to top
ranking as the *Chase and Sanborn Variety Hour*...
It would be unfair to single out one particular member
of the cast as the outstanding reason for the program's
success. All have been exceptionally entertaining...
When you have so able and acknowledged a group of
performers that it's impossible to select any one as the
best, then you most decidedly have an outstanding
radio program."

Radio Mirror concurred, warning that "*The Chase & Sanborn Program* is a multiple threat not only to programs which are on the air at the same time on other networks, but to all variety programs and all comedians. From now on, they'll all have to measure up to the entertainment concocted and served by the Messrs. Don Ameche, W. C. Fields, Edgar Bergen, Charlie McCarthy and Werner Janssen, Miss Dorothy Lamour, and assorted guests."

Comparing how he had been treated by the management of various entertainment venues, Fields ranked them in order, from worst to best. "In the circus they knocked you over the head with a tent stake. In burlesque, they didn't even speak. In vaudeville, there was a little politeness, in musical comedy, they were very polite, and in pictures, they were kinder still. And now, in radio, I don't know whether they're kidding me or not. I've never been handled so gently."

While Bergen & McCarthy were riding high, there were still comedians who, while acclaimed for their work on the stage and screen, continued to struggle translating in radio, often because they were simply too reliant on visual gags and/or mugging (making faces) for the studio audience. We've discussed how likes of Cantor and Wynn eventually learned the consequences of playing more to the audience in front of them than to their radio listeners. As Wynn began planning a new program, *Gulliver the Traveler* in February, he announced, as part of a New Year's resolution, "I promise to remember I am performing for my listeners, not my studio audience."

Bert Lahr, however, was another beloved comedian who apparently *hadn't* learned that lesson yet. On the stage, he was totally at home, where few could match his ability to keep audiences convulsed, most recently in *The Show Is On*. He was asked to host the radio program *Manhattan Merry-go-round* on NBC, which had been primarily a music program before Lahr exerted his influence. The reviewer for *Radio Mirror* was less than impressed with the results.

> "Bert Lahr is a very funny man behind foot-lights. On the air he is not funny at all. Rowdy he is, and noisy, and awfully energetic, but hard work doesn't invariably produce good humor. Bert -and it pains me to say so -also commits the cardinal radio sin. He makes no bones of playing to his visible audience instead of his invisible one. On the air he's been

known to run through his repertoire of comical faces, panicking the people in the studio but leaving you and me distinctly chilly. Other comedians do the same thing—but they don't do it as openly as Bert does."

June 11 - The Marx Brothers' *A Day at the Races* premieres.

As a follow-up to *A Night at the Opera*, Producer Irving Thalberg decided to stick with his successful formula, i.e. to fashion a storyline in which the Marxes would make an effort to help a young, likeable (and musical) romantic couple, add a few big production numbers, and, oh yes, include a few carefully worked-out comedy set pieces, all to be polished during a road tour of live performances.

This time, however, a cruel fate intervened. Thalberg died of pneumonia during production, at the age of thirty-seven, and with him went much of the Marx Brothers' enthusiasm for making movies. This was especially the case with Groucho, who summed it up when he wrote, "After Thalberg's death my interest in the movies waned. I continued to appear in them, but my heart was in the Highlands. The fun had gone out of picture-making. I was like an old pug, still going through the motions, but now doing it solely for the money."

The self-described "old pug" was only 47 years old at the time, and *A Day at the Races* was only the brothers' seventh film to date.

In the story, Dr. Hugo Z. Hackenbush (Groucho) is called upon by wealthy Emily Upjohn (Margaret Dumont) to treat her during her stay at the Standish Sanitarium. Unbeknownst to his only human patient, Hackenbush is actually a veterinarian. The young owner of the struggling sanitarium, July Standish, is resisting an attempt by a banker and his accomplices to take over the facility and convert it into a casino. Her boyfriend Gil (Allan Jones) has purchased a racehorse, hoping it will win a big race, the proceeds of which would go to help save the sanitarium. His friend Chico—a sanitarium employee, God help us—and jockey Stuffy (Harpo) resolve to help Gil, by hook or by crook, of course.

A Day at the Races is usually considered somewhat of the lesser sibling of *A Night at the Opera*. It suffers from slower pacing, diminished energy, and, like its predecessor, too much plot, but it still contains several memorable scenes. Some have attributed its lesser overall impact to Thalberg's premature death, although the key comedy scenes had already been worked out and polished during the road tour, and were ready by the time filming began.

And what memorable scenes they are! Among the best of these is the Groucho-Chico "Tootsie Fruitsie Ice Cream" confrontation at the racetrack, one of the more elaborate and visual of the many set pieces the two had shared on film to that point. In the scene, Chico has Groucho completely baffled as he coerces him into buying stacks of horse racing guides in order to decode the name of the favored horse in an upcoming race. Groucho is also hilarious in a solo bit, during which he drives Whitmore to apoplexy both on the phone and via intercom simultaneously, in an attempt to keep Whitmore from discovering his true past. In another scene, the three brothers wreak havoc during their medical exam of Margaret Dumont. And, of course, there's a climactic horse race, with Harpo the jockey causing mischief mid-race. His win ensures a happy future of the sanitarium, and of the young couple.

June 18 - Al Boasberg dies at 44.

One of the most respected and in-demand comedy writers of the era, Boasberg, at the time of his sudden death, was earning $1,000 a week from Jack Benny as a script doctor. In commenting on the loss, Benny said, "I considered Al Boasberg one of the greatest gag men who ever lived—and in addition I considered him one of my very best friends." Years later, Benny wrote, "He was a good man. The last time I saw him was when we signed a new contract for two more years. Same terms, a thousand a week. Well, he went home that night, went to sleep and died." The two men had also begun discussing a new character for Benny's program, that of his wisecracking assistant, Rochester.

1937

November 21 - Bergen and Charlie McCarthy top poll.

Program survey of more than thirty cities placed Edgar Bergen & Charlie McCarthy as most popular program among hour-long programs. Within six months of the program's debut, Bergen led runner-up *Major Bowes' Amateur Hour* by nine points, after the two were tied during the summer. As for half-hour programs, Jack Benny led Eddie Cantor by nine points, followed by Burns & Allen, Al Jolson, and Phil Baker. *Amos & Andy*, still led the 15-minute programs, of course, followed by newsman Lowell Thomas, and *Lum & Abner*.

November 26 - Carole Lombard and Fredric March star in *Nothing Sacred*.

A scathing satire on the newspaper business, and its willingness to sacrifice the truth in favor of publicity and sensational stories, *Nothing Sacred* provides another showcase for Carol Lombard's supreme talents as a comic actress (and Frederick March holds his own as well). The film is as relevant, and funny, today as it was when it premiered on this date in 1937.

Misdiagnosed with a fatal disease, Hazel Flagg (Lombard) wishes to visit New York before she dies. The ever-opportunistic newspaperman March, trying to help his paper recover from an embarrassing hoax, brings her to the city. Hazel later discovers that she is indeed healthy, but continues to allow the newspaper to roll out the red carpet and report on her last days with feverish gusto. Eventually, however, her growing guilt forces her to confess to March, but too much is already at stake, so they continue the deception together.

Nothing Sacred continued Lombard's hot streak as a comic actress. Even without her later roles, including those in dramas, her performances in *Twentieth Century*, *My Man Godfrey*, and *Nothing Sacred* easily established her as the 1930s' queen of screwball comedies.

This elegant portrait of Carole Lombard belies her talents as a screwball comedian, who could take pratfalls with the best of them. Author's collection.

Imagine how perfect she would have been opposite Cary Grant in *Bringing Up Baby*, released the following year; Katherine Hepburn in that role looks woefully out of her element in comedy, at least at that point in her career (although she does take a number of pratfalls like a trouper). Lombard undoubtedly would have done wonders with it.

Nothing Sacred also capped off a good year for screenwriter Ben Hecht, whose annual pay from Goldwyn, at $260,000 a year, made him the highest paid writer in Hollywood.

1937

December 12 - Mae West performs sketch on the Charlie McCarthy Show, sparks national outrage.

After rocketing to the top of the popularity polls and ratings, it seemed that the Bergen/McCarthy act could do no wrong on its weekly program. Strictly speaking, this would still hold true even after the December 12 broadcast, as it was Bergen's on-air guest who triggered the controversy, not Bergen himself.

One of the sketches that evening featured West, Bergen, and Don Ameche, performing a spoof of the Adam & Eve story, written specifically for West by Arch Oboler. The sketch portrays Adam as a laconic husband and Eve as his bored, impatient mate, looking for some excitement, and an opportunity to "expand my personality." She even provokes the serpent in the Garden of Eden to pick forbidden apples for her, which she then makes into applesauce for Adam and herself. As Oboler explained, "Instead of going on the premise that the snake tempted Eve, it occurred to me, since Miss West was such a dominant woman, to have Eve tempt the snake."

Listening to the sketch today, it is not especially hilarious, and even the studio audience offered only a handful of hearty laughs throughout the eight-minute segment (the biggest laugh was in response to a comparatively innocuous joke about a dance craze at the time called "The Big Apple"). But the sketch is, predictably, full of the kind of double-entendres and sexual innuendoes long-associated with West. To provide some added punch for radio, her inflections magnified the suggestiveness of the dialogue still further.

Protests poured in to NBC, prompting Chase & Sanborn's advertising agency, J. Walter Thompson, to publicly apologize. In the words of the agency's president, Stanley Resor, "We wish to express our deepest regret that the program broadcast Sunday night, Dec. 12, gave offense to anyone. Obviously, the whole purpose of these broadcasts is to afford wholesome entertainment. These programs, over a period of eight years, are evidence of this. The script of this feature of the broadcast was our responsibility. It was a mistake and we can assure the public at large that the same mistake will not be made again."

It was to no avail. *The Catholic News* commented, "Last Sunday night, with the introduction of Mae West into the program, the Chase & Sanborn hour descended into the mire."

West was no stranger to the heavy hand of censorship and overly-sensitive morals police (and, at least once, the *actual* police). The Hays office had been taking the bite out of her film work for the past several years, in the interest of maintaining ever-so-high moral standards. But even *she* couldn't have prepared for the outrage ignited by the Adam & Eve sketch. "Once again," *The New York Times* lamented, "Mae West finds herself the storm center of the amusement world."

With the deluge of protests continuing from all over the country, a number of knee-jerk reactions were set in motion, as enumerated in the *Times*.

1. A legion of decency crusade against radio suggestiveness, similar in scope and purpose to campaign against the motion picture industry in 1934.

2. Closer surveillance by motion picture producers over radio activities of their stars.

3. Possible postponement of release date for Miss West's new picture, listed for early January showing, until public indignation cools.

4. A complaint lodged with the FCC by the Reverend Dr. Maurice S. Sheehy, head of the Catholic University's Religion Department, labeling Miss West's remarks as 'filthy, sacrilegious and irreverent."

Finally, in the most draconian measure of all, NBC instituted a total ban on the mere mention of her name on the air, announcing:

> "Reference to the name of Mae West, film actress, whose role in an 'Adam and Eve' sketch over the WEAF network on Dec. 12 was critically received by many listeners, has been banned by the National Broadcasting Company on any of its fifteen managed and operated stations throughout the country. A.H. Morton, general manager of the N.B.C. station group, has ordered that no script utilized as a basis of broadcast programs over these stations shall contain any reference to

1937

Miss West, nor shall her name be mentioned by entertainers or others."

There were also more than 100 other WEAF-WJZ network stations for which NBC had no direct control over programs, but "no program 'built' by the broadcasting company, or any program from a station or studio of the company, will contain the actress's name."

The ban was to remain in force for *twelve years*.

Mae West enjoying her relatively brief height of popularity.
Courtesy of Steve Cox.

The repercussions of the scandalous broadcast suddenly had those in the broadcasting business identifying with their counterparts in the movie industry, who had already been living under the stern hand of the Hays Office. "As a result," reported the *Times*, "the two entertainment mediums have been drawn together for their mutual protection…The Hays office is apprehensive lest the purity folks be inclined to charge the crime up to [Hollywood]. That the public's reaction will be reflected in the reception accorded Miss West's newest endeavor, *Every Day's a Holiday*, is conceded, and the industry is laying low, hoping that any interest of the Legion of Decency will be confined to the single film."

Every Day's a Holiday would be West's final film for Paramount.

Indeed, the ruthless efficiency of the Hays Office throughout the previous five years had trained writers and producers to immediately quash any slightest potential transgression of the code, in an effort to create the appearance of serenity on the surface. Objectionable material had been obliterated. The public was safe. "The tranquility that has persisted for so long has made the outburst provoked by Miss West's broadcast the more startling."

It was noted at the time that neither West nor her representatives issued any statement of apology or regret for the tempest. "What the attitude of her producers is can only be surmised from a remark made by a studio executive. 'You don't hear any shooting from the boys in the street, do you?' he queried. 'West's public likes that stuff.'"

Just as a side note, a rumor began making the rounds a few weeks after the broadcast that West had been scheduled to appear on Kate Smith's show to present her side of the controversy. The report turned out to be a hoax; it's difficult enough to picture the two women in the same room together, let alone imagining Smith giving West air time to discuss the scandal.

1938

Mae West's notorious guest appearance notwithstanding, the Edgar Bergen/ Charlie McCarthy team continued to enjoy riding a crest of popularity well into 1938. It was reported that there had been some concern the act might easily lose popularity and go the way of many passing fads. The concern caused MGM to switch the release dates of *The Adventures of Marco Polo* with *The Goldwyn Follies*, in which Bergen and Charlie were featured. The studio wanted to milk as much cash out of the team as possible, before the bubble burst.

What actually happened, with the sustained popularity of the act, and with Charlie voted the leading personality on radio, was that producers began looking for acts of that ilk—be they talking horses, singing dolls, or other such novelties with promise.

Bergen and McCarthy first appeared on Rudy Vallee's program in December of 1936. A little more than a year later, Bergen was demanding $100,000 a picture. And, along with the gig in Los Angeles for which he was paid $17,000 for a week, he earned $5,000 and expenses for a five-minute appearance in San Francisco.

As *The New York Times* noted, "An interesting phase of Bergen's career is the subjugation of his own personality by the public in favor of Charlie's. All fan mail is addressed to the impudent Mr. McCarthy and Bergen says that he is never welcome at gatherings unless he brings his dummy along. Bergen must be careful of his treatment of Charlie on the air, for in the past his harsh handling of the little doll has brought a deluge of mail upbraiding him for his cruelty." Even professional show biz columnists and reporters fell into the somewhat disturbing habit of invariably referring to McCarthy as if he were a real, flesh & blood person. Charlie even "wrote" some guest columns for major newspapers and fan magazines (one can only assume that Bergen served as ghost writer).

February 1 - Abbott & Costello first appear as regulars on *The Kate Smith Hour*.

A new comedy team making the rounds in burlesque seemed to sneak up on an unsuspecting but receptive public in 1936, when Bud Abbott and Lou Costello staked their claim in the comedy world. Abbott was a well-known and highly respected straight man who had worked with many comedians in burlesque, including performing with his wife Betty, and was admired for his encyclopedic knowledge of comedy routines. Costello was several years younger, and eager to find the best straight man for his often undisciplined rough & tumble antics. They had seen each other perform several times and eventually decided they would be a good match. Their success together was immediate, and soon their stage career would take them to a national audience via radio, when they became regulars on Kate Smith's show.

On March 24, they performed "Who's On First" on the air for the first time, and the resulting buzz about them in the press gained momentum. *Radio Mirror* proclaimed, "Radio Rose of the Month goes to two new comedians, Bud Abbott and Lou Costello of the Kate Smith program. Their insane comedy reminds one of [comedy team] Tom Howard and George Shelton, but their material is fresher and their delivery clever."

It isn't widely known that within a few months of their radio debut, the team was being considered by MGM to star in a musical comedy film,

Honolulu. They were even screen-tested, but their roles eventually went to George Burns and Gracie Allen (it would be their last motion picture together). Warner Brothers also expressed an interest in Abbott & Costello, who spent the summer of 1938 playing the Steel Pier in Atlantic City.

Kate Smith wasn't done discovering new stage acts that would prove a smash on her show. Vaudeville may have been on life-support by 1937, and most show business observers had declared it dead long before then, but that didn't stop new talent from being discovered, and subsequently whisked away to the Big Time, be it on radio or elsewhere.

Not long after Abbott & Costello's debut broadcast, a young comedian named Henry (professionally "Henny") Youngman also began making a name for himself onstage. Youngman had been writing jokes for Milton Berle, who was only two years older, but who had vastly more experience, having been in show business since childhood. Berle became Youngman's comedy mentor, buying his jokes, and coaching him on the fine points of stand-up comedy, although he knew not to tinker with the rising star's rapid-fire way with one-liners.

Youngman caught Smith's attention in the Yacht Club in New York, shortly after which she gave him a regular gig on her program.

"A funster of his type draws laughs rather than applause when there's a click," *Billboard* reported, "but there are frequent occasions when Youngman's sock is so terrific that he gets both laughs and applause — the latter so spontaneous as to definitely impress as an emotional outlet of appreciation that the clappers find it impossible to dam."

September 22 - *Hellzapoppin*, starring Olsen & Johnson, opens.

The Golden Decade was a busy one for Olsen & Johnson, as they alternated between the stage and starring in low-budget films, mostly for RKO. On this date, the expanded version (by one hour) of their revue *Everything Goes*, now with the Schubert's backing and with the new title *Hellzapoppin*, opened a the 46th Street Theatre, and took Broadway by storm.

The show was rarely identical from one performance to another, but it never strayed from its nature of a vaudeville show on steroids, or hallucinogens, or both. With so many surreal gags bombarding the audience each night—often from within the audience itself—several stood out among theatre-goers and critics alike.

The show kicked off by running a gag newsreel-style film in which a myriad of sounds and utterances would appear to come from the mouths of F.D.R., New York's Mayor LaGuardia, Mussolini, and Hitler. Olsen and Johnson then appeared, set to preside over the chaos. One woman made regular appearances wandering up and down the orchestra aisles calling for "Oscar! Oscar!" A man carrying a potted plant also appeared from time to time, in search of the plant's rightful owner. Each time he reappeared throughout the performance, the plant would be considerably taller. Various fruits and other objects sometimes went airborne into the audience as well.

Brooks Atkinson, reviewing the show for *The New York Times*, seemed in turns perplexed, amused, and even dismayed by the onstage presentation:

> "Folks, it is going to be a little difficult to describe this one… Anything goes in 'Hellzapoppin' — noise, vulgarity, practical joking — and about every third number is foolish enough for guffawing.
>
> Very prominent in the proceedings are Olsen and Johnson, a pair of college cut-ups now well on toward middle life without much flowering of their culture. As far as they are concerned, it is house-cleaning day in vaudeville…
> There is no relief even in the intermission. For that is the time when a clown starts paddling up the aisle and haunting unwary customers…this is mainly a helter-skelter assembly of low-comedy gags to an ear-splitting sound accompaniment—some of it ugly, all of it fast…"

1938

Mischa Auer joins the anarchy in the film version of *Hellzapoppin* (1941). Courtesy of Steve Cox.

Atkinson concluded his assessment with an interesting comparison. "*I'll Say She Is* was funnier these many years ago because the Marx Brothers were in it. But if you can imagine a demented vaudeville brawl without the Marx Brothers, *Hellzapoppin'* is it, and a good part of it is loud, low and funny."

Variety was more willing to accept the revue for what it was:

"Olsen and Johnson, plus a dash of the Shuberts and a large sprig from the old NVA [National Vaudeville Artists] roster, total the maddest cocktail fed the New York theatre since Clayton, Jackson and Durante first wrecked the Palace stage

some years back. Its heavy hoke, zany slapstick and blank-cartridge explosions must leave the audience quite shell-shocked; if only moderately received, it will at least be heard during its Broadway run…
As is, it's entertaining, very racy, fast, loud…
From start to finish, 'Hellzapoppin' makes no pretentions of being anything else but lowest of vaude's low comedy."

As of May of the following year, the show had become not only the Shubert's greatest success, but one of Broadway's top-selling shows ever to that point, taking in a million dollars. "Eventually it is expected another edition of the show will go on, since the Messrs. Olsen and Johnson have props stored in San Francisco and will polish them off toward that good day."

The show was adapted on the screen in 1941, with mixed results. While it offered a good helping of the show's surreal, bombastic energy, the team took a back seat for much of it to Martha Raye.

* * *

As the new radio season got underway in the autumn of 1938, the leading comedians saw no impetus to fix what wasn't broken in their respective programs. Jack Benny, Edgar Bergen, Fred Allen, and Fibber McGee all retained their sponsors and time slots. Burns & Allen took on a new sponsor, with a raise to $12,000 a week. Joe Penner also found a new sponsor and pay hike. Eddie Cantor experienced a drop in ratings when he moved to an earlier time slot on Monday nights the previous season, but he preferred the earlier hour for the show so children could hear it before bedtime (the program included, ironically, Camel cigarette commercials).

Six years into his program, Fred Allen continued to assume about 90% of the weekly writing duties. He brought a number of writers to his employ to that point, but always ended up re-writing and polishing the scripts himself, staying true to his philosophy that creating and presenting situational and

1938

character-based comedy was preferably to that of random gags. He even continued to type the scripts himself, being unable to find a secretary who could not only type, but toss in new, quality gags while doing so.

In a *Radio Stars* feature story on Allen, it was stressed that despite his lofty position as one of the most respected and well-liked comedians of the day, "nothing in his dress, looks or life suggests the Broadway atmosphere, the wise-cracker or the big shot…In the space of one year, Fred and Portland stepped out socially, by actual count, twice…While most stars of his magnitude live in swank apartments or penthouses, Fred, in New York, lives simply in an apartment hotel. In Hollywood, there was no mansion with swimming pool, but a simple bungalow. He has no chauffeur -not even a car; no maids nor butlers."

Sept. 27 - *The Pepsodent Show*, starring Bob Hope, debuts.

Hope's appearance in *The Big Broadcast of 1938*, featuring W.C. Fields, is notable for introducing what would become his theme song, "Thanks For the Memory". The film as a whole was not well-received, but Hope's presence led to a 1938 contract with Pepsodent for the NBC program that helped him achieve a higher level of stardom.

Upon signing the ten-year contract, he defied the ongoing trend away from rat-a-tat-tat one-liners by radio comedians, and stubbornly determined that his own style needed to consist of an almost unwieldy supply of short & sweet gags, told in his famously swift delivery. He employed a battery of eight writers, the most of any radio comedian of the time. "All these comedy minds were necessary," he said, "if I was going to carry out my plan, which was almost unheard of at that time. It was to go on the air every week with topical jokes written right up to airtime. And some even after. Even if they weren't all good, they would give the *Pepsodent* show an immediacy that I find missing today…We had to be good or else. It was life or death, sink or swim, and I knew I needed as many life preservers as possible or we'd all go down with the ship."

Bob Hope. Courtesy of Steve Cox.

He also brought on the hyperactive, bug-eyed Jerry Colonna as his sidekick, bantering with him for a while after the opening monologue, allowing Colonna to take on a number of eccentric characters.

September 30 - Marx Brothers in *Room Service*.

Room Service was a Broadway hit, written by John Murray and Alan Boretz, and starring Eddie Albert, Sam Levene, and Yiddish theatre star Alexander Asro. It ran for 500 performances. The fast-paced story centers on a small time producer desperately scrambling to avoid himself and his cast from getting thrown out of a hotel for non-payment of the bill, while also awaiting money from a new backer for the show.

RKO bought the film rights for a then-record $255,000 as a vehicle for the Marx Brothers. At the time, it was intended to be the first of three films in which they were to star for the studio.

Upon signing to do the film (with the help of Zeppo, their agent), the brothers called upon veteran Marx writer Morrie Ryskind to adapt the dialogue and action to fit their established characters. It proved to be difficult task, and one met with only marginal success. "I had misgivings about this," Ryskind said, "because, and I explained this to them, I felt the only good things for the team were those things written expressly for them…In itself it was a very funny play but their characters had to be there, for I knew that when an audience came to see the Marx Brothers, it was them they came to see, not a film…My job was to adapt and sometimes that means leaving the thing alone. But in this case I had to add three characters who weren't in the play."

The director was William Seiter, who did a fine job for Laurel & Hardy with *Sons of the Desert*.

The film premiered just over two months after the Broadway production closed. Up-and-coming starlets Ann Miller (who was only fifteen at the time, but lied about her age to get hired) and Lucille Ball had minor roles. It turned out to be the only Marx Brothers film for RKO, losing over $300,000. The team would return to MGM the following year.

October 31 - Robert Woolsey dies.

Woolsey had been in failing health, due to kidney disease, and his death came as both a professional and personal blow to his comedy partner of the previous decade, Bert Wheeler.

December - Bergen/McCarthy, Jack Benny lead polls.

A year-end popularity poll of radio programs produced fairly predictable results for both hour-long and half-hour comedy offerings.

> Popularity Poll - Hour-long shows:
> 1. Bergen/McCarthy (had led polls for previous 15 months)
> 2. Radio Theatre
> 3. Bing Crosby "Music Hall"
> 4. Vallee Varieties
> 5. Town Hall Tonight (Fred Allen)
>
> Half-hour shows:
> 1. Jack Benny
> 2. Al Jolson
> 3. "Big Town" w/ Edward G. Robinson
> 4. Burns & Allen
> 5. Eddie Cantor

Meanwhile, *The Goldbergs* continued on its merry way as it approached its tenth anniversary. Gertrude Berg was still writing each and every script herself, and had long ago won the hearts of listeners as the Goldberg family matriarch. A journalist for *Radio Stars,* observing a recent broadcast, relayed how both Berg and the rest of the cast (including Roslyn Silber and Everett Sloane as Goldberg siblings Rosie and Sammy) still displayed an emotional investment and authenticity in playing their respective characters.

> "Despite the artificial studio atmosphere, lack of make-up, costumes and scenery, a witness to the broadcast would soon forget that he was watching actors and actresses, so expressive are their faces, words and gestures. So completely do they

'put their hearts' into their work that they are one with the characters they portray."

Elsewhere on radio, W.C. Fields' return to films after a long medical leave didn't mean he was about to abandon the microphone. He found work on *Your Hit Parade*, providing a bit of patter in between musical numbers.

> "Fields hasn't lost any of his microphone appeal in the year he's been absent from radio, and these Saturday night sessions are pure delight....Everybody in Hollywood is looking forward to the day when Fields' new movie, *You Can't Cheat an Honest Man*, is completed. In it he co-stars with his old enemy, Charlie McCarthy, and the result certainly ought to be something to see."

The logistics of having him on the show proved awkward. The program's orchestra transmitted from New York, while Fields contributed his segments from Hollywood. So, studio audiences on each coast could only be present for their half of each broadcast, while listeing to the other half on loudspeakers. There was talk about moving the entire program to Hollywood, but, due to problems with the material, plus a sinking feeling that disaster was looming, Fields quit the show before that could happen.

1939

A good number of film critics and historians, to this day, still consider 1939 to be the greatest year in Hollywood's history, in terms of the stellar list of titles released. No fewer than ten films were nominated for the Academy Award for Best Picture: *Gone With the Wind* (the winner), *Goodbye, Mr. Chips, Dark Victory, Love Affair, Mr. Smith Goes to Washington, Ninotchka* (the only comedy nominated), *Of Mice and Men, Stagecoach, The Wizard of Oz,* and *Wuthering Heights.*

Other films destined for classic status released that year include *The Hound of the Baskervilles, Gunga Din,* and *The Hunchback of Notre Dame.* Overall, it was an extraordinary output for a single calendar year, but at the same time, the overall health of film *comedy* was quickly deteriorating. There were happy exceptions, of course, but ominous changes were in the air.

February 17 - *You Can't Cheat an Honest Man,* starring W.C. Fields, premieres.

Fields, now signed with Universal Studios, was about to give audiences four outstanding film comedies in a row within the next three years. Unfortunately, he also denied them the opportunity of seeing him as the title character in one of the Oscar-nominated films listed above, *The Wizard of Oz*, starring Judy Garland.

Producer Mervyn LeRoy named Ed Wynn as his choice to play the Wizard, while LeRoy's assistant Arthur Freed, as well as E. Y. Harburg, preferred Fields for the role. LeRoy approached Wynn first with the offer, but Wynn turned it down, considering it too small a part. The studio then offered Fields a reported $150,000 to play the Wizard, but Fields was too busy writing the screenplay for *You Can't Cheat An Honest Man*. Of course, the role ultimately went to Frank Morgan, who made his somewhat brief appearance in the film memorable all the same.

It behooves us to acknowledge here that while we can only speculate how the Wizard's scenes may have played out with either Wynn or Fields in the part, audiences were still treated to what would become Bert Lahr's most famous and beloved role as the Cowardly Lion. His co-stars Jack Hailey and hoofer Ray Bolger, despite their own considerable talents, had to take a back seat to Lahr's untouchable performance.

Getting back to Fields, his battles with Paramount executives over creative control of his films continued now that he was at Universal Studios. In a letter to studio executive Cliff Work, Fields attempted to explain why it had always been difficult for him to collaborate with others on his own material. "The work I'm doing on the screen differs from that of anyone else. My comedy is of a peculiar nature. Naturally no writers have developed along the lines of my type of comedy and that is why I have differences with writers, supervisors and directors alike. I am misunderstood mostly by these departments but the customers and the critics seem to get my point O.K."

You Can't Cheat an Honest Man co-stars Edgar Bergen and his wooden sidekick Charlie McCarthy, giving Fields and his hand-carved nemesis a chance to continue their popular radio feud on the silver screen.

The plot has Fields as Larson E. Whipsnade, the owner of an itinerant circus perpetually struggling to stay one step ahead of the law (shades of *The Old-Fashioned Way*). Bergen and McCarthy comprise the act called the "Disappearing Little Rajah," but their pay is long overdue, and they consider leaving the circus altogether—that is, until Bergen meets Whipsnade's beautiful daughter (Constance Moore). The two hit it off, although she feels obligated to marry a wealthy, snobbish socialite, with the hope that he would then help in alleviating Whipsnade's financial woes. All turns out well in the end, of course, with the loving couple, and Whipsnade, escaping the high society snobs, including the presumed groom-to-be.

Fields posing for *You Can't Cheat an Honest Man*. Author's collection.

Highlights include Fields at his daughter's high society wedding reception, where he turns a friendly ping-pong game into a fierce competition (played in fast motion to great effect).

"W.C. Fields and Charlie MacCarthy [sic]continue their world-famous feud in this insanely mad picture which is hilariously entertaining, although it suffers from lack of story. The picture moves rapidly when Fields is on the screen and he rushes from one gag to another, some old, some new, all delightfully Fieldsien…Charlie and Edgar have some swell scenes together, one, particularly, when they get caught in a balloon, though it is Mortimer Snerd, a ventriloquial bumpkin, who shares Bergen's lap with Charlie, and who steals the scene from both of them."

Charlie's wisecracks tend to grow tiresome by the second half of the film, but Fields shines throughout. Furthermore, it is while viewing *You Can't Cheat an Honest Man* that the fundamental issue regarding Bergen & McCarthy, and the nature of ventriloquism itself, becomes more conspicuous than it had during the "team's" radio broadcasts. In the film, whenever we see the two chatting alone with each other, or with a third person present, Charlie is treated as if he is a real, living person. At one point, Fields' daughter, searching the carnival grounds for Bergen, asks someone "Have you seen Edgar and Charlie?" as if she actually considers Charlie as a sentient being (why would she not simply ask if anyone had seen *Edgar*?) However, when Fields appears, and launches into his usual repartee with Charlie, his insults include constant references to the fact that Charlie is, of course, carved from wood ("Shut up, or I'll throw a woodpecker on ya," and "You termite's flophouse"), thus sending us back to reality, with all suspension of disbelief eradicated. Yet a little later, we see another scene of Bergen and Charlie alone together, where they become two real people again. This constant whiplash can become somewhat tedious (at least it does for *this* viewer).

1939

An intriguing news item appeared in *The New York Times* in early May, teasing Fields fans with the idea of his return to Broadway, but that the plan had encountered a delay: "The bring-W.C. Fields-back-to-Broadway appears to have struck a minor snag," the report began. "The authors of his show, George S. Kaufman and Moss Hart, would like to open it in December; Mr. Fields prefers to wait until next spring. It seems several other performers slated for the star's supporting cast may not be available in the spring of 1940. Discussions go forward." Unfortunately, the project never materialized, but, considering how Groucho often preferred his own ad-libbed lines over Kaufman's in the stage versions of *The Cocoanuts* and *Animal Crackers*, who's to say how much of a Kaufman-Hart play would have survived the changes Fields would have inevitably suggested, or demanded?

April 30 - The New York World's Fair opens, formally introduces television to the public.

In a major milestone for the entertainment world, and for the world in general, the opening of the World's Fair in New York served as the platform for NBC president David Sarnoff's official introduction of television to America, drawing crowds to witness demonstrations in the RCA pavilion. Of course, TV was hardly sprung on an unsuspecting public. Ever since inventors like John Logie Baird began to make headlines with their demonstrations of crude television in the mid-1920s, newspapers and magazines kept constant track of the new medium's development. Broadcasting executives, entertainers, and journalists tended to get ahead of themselves—or, rather, ahead of television's technological progress—with predictions and dreams of what the medium might bring to themselves, and to the public at large.

It was reported in May of 1937, two years before the World's Fair opening, that producer Samuel Goldwyn, for one, saw the prospect of television intimidating enough to the motion picture industry that he announced all of his film productions, from that point on, would be released in technicolor. As it turns out, he didn't adhere to that vow quite as soon as he promised, and television may or may not have influenced his announcement. Still, those in show business pondered what the arrival of the new medium would mean to the status quo.

The World's Fair opening ceremonies, including the arrival and speech by President Roosevelt, were broadcast by relaying the images to atop the Empire State Building. A single camera was positioned on the newsreel platform, about fifty feet from the speakers at the microphones.

Crowds at the Fair watched the televised coverage of the ceremonies on a dozen television receivers with 9" x 12" screens on exhibit at the RCA building. Special screens were also installed for the public at Radio City Music Hall.

The curious public comes face-to-face with television for the first time. Author's collection.

The event was acknowledged by broadcasters as the beginning of a new industry, the aim of which is to take Americans "sight-seeing by radio." Most of those involved marked down April 30, 1939, as having the same significance as that of Nov. 2, 1910, when the radio "craze" started.

The next day, *The New York Times* reported, "Science presented television as a new deal in communication yesterday as President Roosevelt spoke in the Court of Peace at the opening of the World's Fair. For the first time a President of the United States faced a tele-camera, which for the first time took its place on the platform with a battery of newsreel cameras overlooking a historic scene." Television receivers went on sale in several New York stores the next day.

Regular broadcasts began airing from studios at Radio City, on Wednesdays and Fridays from 8 to 9 p.m., with outdoor pick-ups at the Fair on Wednesday, Thursday, and Friday afternoons.

Most comedians, like Cantor and Wynn, were eager to take their skills to the new medium. Those who felt protected standing behind the radio microphone weren't quite so enthused. Not long after the "official" unveiling of television at the Fair, Rudy Vallee spoke with some trepidation about a future with television. "No one knows what television will do to any of us," he said, "but it is safe to say that it will wipe many entertainers off the map, just as talkies put many of the silent stars into the discard overnight. And I am sure of one thing, that the motion pictures will supply 80 or 90 percent of the television show of tomorrow. Long-distance television will be a hungrier monster than ever broadcasting was."

June 19 - *The Streets of Paris* opens on Broadway, starring Bobby Clark and Abbott & Costello.

The revue, produced by Olsen & Johnson and Lee Schubert, presented a mix of musical numbers and comedy sketches, and most famously introduced Abbott & Costello to the "legit" stage, even as they had already amassed great popularity on Kate Smith's show. Bobby Clark shared top billing, and the newly-discovered Brazilian bombshell, Carmen Miranda, treated New Yorkers to her exotic song stylings and captivating presence.

Bud & Lou's first appearance in the show was in a sketch called "Customs," in which they arrive at the customs counter upon returning from

France by ship. While waiting for the customs inspector, they launch into several of their popular routines, making just slight alterations to "Hole in the Wall," "Mustard," and "You're 40 Years Old" (routines they were to later preserve in their films).

In later scenes, the two performed the "Find-the-Lemon" table routine, and "Rest Cure" (also known as "Crazy House"), in which Lou checks into a sanitarium to provide quiet relief for his nerves, only to be interrupted by a steady flow of crazy patients.

The final sketch of the show, "That's Music," had Bud and Lou together with Clark, taking place in a Paris music shop.

Brooks Atkinson, reviewing in *The New York Times*, reported, "Although they are calling it *The Streets of Paris*, the vagabonds of Broadway should feel at home. For the revue that went off at the Broadhurst last evening is "Paris-a-poppen' with the emphasis on knockabout fooling….Out of vaudeville and motion-picture stage shows someone has had the wisdom to bring Lou Costello and Bud Abbott to town with some remarkably gusty stuff. They belong to the traditional school of mountebanks that pairs a dazed clown with an abusive straight man, and throw water freely in its most inspired moments."

Unfortunately, Atkinson's deadline prevented him from seeing the highlight of the show. "Out of deference to press time, your correspondent was unable to remain for a sketch that puts Bobby Clark and Costello and Abbott on the stage at the same moment, which out to be worth some sort of prize. For Costello and Abbott are also pretty funny fellows in low comedy antics."

Variety found the show's comedy to be first-rate, and also cited *Hellzapoppin'* as its inspiration. "It's a toss-up as to who provides the most fun, Abbott & Costello or Clark…Show's top fun has the team in something called 'Rest Cure' which panicked the first-nighters. Here is real Olsen & Johnson stuff and the travesty was probably written by them. There are pistol shots galore and the type of nutty nonsense that makes *Hellzapoppin'* the most popular revue in a generation."

1939

Bud and Lou made a bit of history on July 19, by making their television debut on a program called *So This is New York*, less than two months after NBC began its television operations.

The Streets of Paris closed at the Broadhurst on February 10, 1940, after 274 performances. It then went on the road until that May, and finally took up residence, through the efforts of producer Mike Todd, at the World's Fair, with Gypsy Rose Lee replacing Carmen Miranda.

October 20 - Marx Brothers' *At the Circus* premieres.

By 1939, a mere ten years since their feature film debut in *The Cocoanuts*, the Marx Brothers' hearts just weren't in it anymore. This can't all be attributed to the death of Irving Thalberg in 1937; there simply didn't seem to be anyone supervising MGM's output who knew or cared about what to do with the Marxes. In a year that saw the studio the release of a number of now-classic epic dramas, the brothers, who had reached their commercial peak just a few years before, were being given short shrift. Instead of a team of writers who knew their characters and style of dialogue, i.e. Kaufman & Ryskind, Ruby & Kalmar, and others, the studio dropped the task of writing the Marx scripts onto the lap of one young writer, Irving Brecher.

True, Brecher had already proven himself as a radio writer for *Community Sing*, one of Milton Berle's attempts at success on the air. As Berle was negotiating his deal to host the show, he noticed an ad placed by Brecher in *Variety*:

"IRV. S. BRECHER - Positively Berle-proof gags—
Gags so bad even Milton Berle won't steal them"

Amused by the ad, Berle contacted the writer, who was only 23 at the time, and working in his uncle's movie theatre. Berle gave him a starting salary of $35 a week as a gag writer, which grew to ten times that figure after Berle signed on to host *Community Sing*. The two began as collaborators, but

Brecher's jokes began to outnumber those of his boss. He also phased out the vaudeville-style jokes, replacing them with more situational and character-driven material, as Harry Conn had done to such great success for Jack Benny's early seasons on the air.

Berle's confidence in Brecher grew so that he would soon forego reviewing the script until rehearsals. He also doubled Brecher's salary to $700 a week.

Before long, Brecher moved on to MGM, and found himself recruited for the daunting assignment of writing a Marx Brothers script.

"[Producer] Mervyn LeRoy asked me to write a Marx Brothers film," he recalled, "which I did, called *At The Circus.* And then I wrote a second one, *Go West,* and that was enough for me. 'Cause I'd written both of them by myself... nobody'd ever done that. And I paid the price—I wound up with a tic. And the depression of writing a film for the Marx Brothers, who were wonderful people and friends of mine, but left all the decision-making about 'is this script okay or not?' to Groucho."

The Marxes in *At the Circus.* Author's collection.

1939

Buster Keaton returned to MGM in 1939 not as a star, but as a gagman, and did his best to offer some of his comic genius to the brothers. They actually could have used all the help they could get for *At the Circus* and *Go West*, but they weren't impressed with Keaton's suggestions.

Keaton had just completed starring in a series of 10 two-reelers at Columbia, but he had growing tired of working with the limited budgets he was given. Each of the films was shot in about three days' time, using existing sets and props, and weren't given much care in the planning or marketing. They were even thrown in for free to theaters with the studio's major feature releases.

"Several times I urged Harry Cohn, president of Columbia, to let me spend a little more time and money," Keaton said. "I explained that on a larger budget I could turn out two-reelers that he could sell instead of giving away as part of a package. Cohn, whose company was doing great without my suggestions, wasn't interested. And making those 'cheaters' was the way I supported myself and my family from 1935 to 1940." He then made his unlikely return to MGM, only to get the somewhat icy reception from the Marxes.

He didn't take it personally, as the brothers weren't in the most receptive, or attentive, of moods during their final two films for the studio anyway. "It was an event when you can get all three of them on the set at the same time," Keaton recalled. "The minute you started a picture with the Marx Brothers, you hired three assistant directors, one for each Marx Brother. You had two of them while you went out to look for the third one and the first two would disappear."

* * *

In contrast to the declining quality of film comedy as 1939, the first generation of top-notch *radio* comedians were still enjoying both creative and popular highs.

Jack Benny's popularity was still growing, thanks in part to his skilled cast of supporting players. Fred Allen was still pouring over every word and syllable of his scripts, rehearsing and revising each one with his cast and writers (and then rewriting himself, right up to air time).

Burns & Allen were also following the same preparations that had been bringing them success for the previous eight years: George would have each of his writers prepare a script for the upcoming broadcast. He would then take the best of each and work with the team to shape them into a coherent story. Gracie wouldn't see the finished product until the rehearsal earlier on the day of the broadcast.

Amos & Andy, while not the ratings powerhouse it was earlier in the decade, still continued to hum along to great popularity. Freeman Gosden and Charles Correll had created, by the program's tenth anniversary, about 125 characters, any of whom would come and go as the men deemed appropriate for any given episode. The only difference came with the surprising addition of part-time player Madaline Lee as Andy's secretary, Genevieve Blue. With that one exception, the two creators continued to play all of the parts on the show themselves. They would, as always, begin writing each day after lunch, with Correll typing as Gosden paced the floor (only due to the fact that Correll's typing skills were the better between the two). The collaboration remained equal, with the only rehearsal of the material being a brief run-through as they completed each script.

Also in 1939, Red Skelton, a newer addition to the roster of radio comedy stars, became another clown whose reliance on visual humor in burlesque, vaudeville, and movies needed to be steered into the more restrictive world of purely aural comedy. He scored a bit hit with listeners as a guest on Rudy Vallee's show (who else?) in August of 1937, which led to his modest NBC program *Avalon Time*, first originating in Cincinnati before moving to the network's Chicago studios.

Skelton and wife Edna Stillwell, who had been writing much of his onstage routines, co-wrote and performed most of the program's sketches, with the rest assigned to a writing team, averaging a total of three sketches per show.

Despite the success of a few newer comedians on radio at the time,

Vallee himself had begun to take note of a slowing in the stream of younger comedians well-suited to radio. "Especially it is hard to find good comedians," he said, "possibly because good comedians are born, not made, and they are not born by the carload."

Even the proven comedians in other arenas, such as vaudeville, weren't necessarily destined to make radio their home for the long-term. Milton Berle's collaboration with writer Irving Brecher on the *Community Sing* program was all well and good for about a year, but Berle also came to the realization that radio was too restrictive a medium for his style. "I got my biggest laughs when I did the warm-up before the show," he said. "Then I could work on the studio audience without a script, doing material I had tested out on stages and in nightclubs. But reading from a script didn't feel as good for me. I was too used to winging it in front of a live audience, feeling them out, working them. A script ties you down, and radio, being a medium for the ears, not the eyes, was not the best exposure for a visual comedian. I did okay, but I never felt I was getting across my best."

He felt more comfortable back on the stage, where he was simultaneously starring on Broadway in *See My Lawyer*. However, even the Broadway stage was experiencing a shortage of comedy in late 1939. Berle wrote an open letter to *The New York Times*, printed on New Year's Eve, expressing his hope to see an increase in lighthearted Broadway productions. His comments served as a gentle nudge to encourage readers to attend his own show, noting that *See My Lawyer* was one of only four or five light comedies running on Broadway, out of more than thirty major shows.

> "In view of the worrisome life most of us lead, and because of the routine that we must necessarily encounter during most of our life, I believe that our minds should be completely at ease when we go out to have a good time, when we go to a Broadway show. And what makes you forget your troubles more than laughter?"

Back in the real world, there was more than enough motivation to seek out any humorous solace from the state of affairs. The 1930s had seen the increasing influence of anti-Semitism in the political and social arenas. The rise in popularity of Fascist and Nazi ideas and philosophies in Europe gained support in the U.S. (culminating in a Nazi rally held in Madison Square Garden on February 20, 1939). Also distressing was the support of Germany by the likes of much-admired American figures as Henry Ford, Charles Lindberg, and radio preacher Father Charles Coughlin. On radio, the most obviously Jewish-themed entertainment program, *The Goldbergs*, reached its own ten-year anniversary, and it might have been expected to receive more than its share of hostile, anti-Semitic mail. Surprisingly, that didn't appear to be the case. As reported in *Radio Stars*:

> "In spite of the anti- Semitic propaganda that has seeped across the Atlantic from the Fascist nations of Europe, *The Goldbergs* continue a serene course with no trace of an attack on racial grounds. Small repercussions were expected to pop up in the fan mail. So far, the expectations have been groundless. On the contrary, the letter files of Gertrude Berg, creator of *The Goldbergs*, include warm tributes from Protestant, Catholic and Jew alike, praising her for the spirit of toleration she is indirectly spreading by her sympathetic, comic treatment of a simple Jewish family."

December - The Three Stooges film *You Nazty Spy*.

While *The Goldbergs* on radio seemed secure against the rise of anti-Semitism in the U.S., and the chaos spreading throughout Europe as a result of Hitler's aggression, the least likely of movie comedy teams at the time were the first to create a searing parody of the growing crisis.

1939

This striking shot of the Stooges provides a fascinating contrast of them both in and out of character. Author's collection.

The Three Stooges films aren't often credited with possessing much in the way of social or political significance, nor were they ever meant to, but *You Nazty Spy* was quite daring for its day. The team, and their director, Jules White, filmed the parody of Hitler and Mussolini in one week in early December. It was released on January 19, 1940, nine months before Chaplin released *The Great Dictator* (although Chaplin's plans for his film had already been in the works by the time *You Nazty Spy* began filming).

Longtime comedy writers and Stooge associates Clyde Bruckman, who had worked with Buster Keaton on *Sherlock Junior* and *The General*, and Felix Adler (gagman for the Laurel & Hardy features *Our Relations* and *Way out West*) are credited with the script for *You Nazty Spy*.

The story takes place in the fictional country of Moronica. When munitions executives conclude that they can only save their business by waging a war, they call upon wallpaper hangers Moe, Larry, and Curly to take over after Moronica's peaceful king is overthrown. Moe assumes the likeness of Hitler (after he unwittingly sticks a piece of black tape under his nose), while Curly takes on Mussolini. Larry is appointed the Minister of Propaganda. Moe's balcony speech to the masses devolves into ranting pseudo-German, as Larry holds up signs reading "Cheers" and "Applause" to the crowd.

The film's political nature is all the more striking considering how it flagrantly defied the Motion Picture Production Code, which had been enforced throughout the previous five years. One of the code's articles stated, "The history, institution, prominent people and citizenry of all nations shall be presented fairly. No picture shall be produced that tends to incite bigotry or hatred among peoples of different races, religions or national origins." While that edict seems intended on protecting the dignity of ordinary citizens, it was apparently to include ruthless dictators as well.

One reason these offenses may have survived the final edit of the film could lie in the fact that the Hays Office did not give shorts the scrupulous attention normally given to features, so the film was released without controversy, and even prompted the production of the only Three Stooges sequel, *I'll Never Heil Again*.

As a side note, it behooves us to mention, at this point in the chronology, the ultimate fate of the Stooges former boss, Ted Healy. As we've noted earlier, Healy's drinking problem continued to get the better of him on an increasingly regular basis throughout his adult life, and it apparently triggered a violent incident in December of 1937, at the popular Trocadero nightclub in Los Angeles. As with most scandalous incidents in Hollywood during that era, the details have remained sketchy, with conflicting versions making it difficult to determine exactly what happened. Basically, witnesses claimed that while celebrating the birth of his first child, an inebriated Healy took offense to a congratulatory comment, for which he called actor Albert "Cubby" Broccoli (future James Bond producer) outside. A violent confrontation followed, leaving Healy battered and bruised.

Ted Healy biographer Bill Cassara decries the rumors that have swirled around the incident in the decades since. Some versions of the story include the claim that Pat DiCicco, former husband of Thelma Todd and gangster wanna-be, was present, as was actor Wallace Beery. Reports differ on whether the scuffle took place inside the club, outside, or a little of both, and who actually inflicted the most damage on Healy. Theories also have persisted through the years that the Los Angeles coroner was paid off by the powerful MGM publicity department to declare alcoholism, not injuries from the assault, as the cause of death. No one was ever brought up on charges. According to Cassara:

> "Broccoli claimed that Healy tried to punch him, and Broccoli defended himself by punching him back. Healy eventually went home after a doctor looked at his wound. Once home, he went into convulsions and died. Prior to this, the family doctor tended to him but there was nothing he could do. The good doctor declined to sign a death certificate (the correct professional move) and let the coroner determine cause of death. After an autopsy, the medical examiner discovered Healy died of acute toxic nephritis caused by acute and chronic alcoholism. He declared no injury to the skull or brain caused by the blow resulting in the laceration. The case was closed, and it was deemed a 'natural death.'"

Cassara also considers the theories about the MGM cover-up "ridiculous."

It was a sad, but perhaps inevitable, end to Healy's life, during which he brought about almost as much consternation to those who knew him personally as he did laughter to the general public. History has shown us that the Three Stooges probably wouldn't have made their mark on slapstick comedy had they not left Healy and set out on their own in 1934.

1940 and beyond

The 1940s began with movies and radio still at the forefront of American entertainment, and with a new companion, television, still working its kinks out, but showing great promise. The first few years of the decade served as a transition period for a good number of the major comedy stars, and not necessarily in a good way. It's almost as if New Year's Day, 1940, signaled a surprisingly abrupt end of the golden years of film comedy, like a speeding car suddenly running out of gas and sputtering, before hitting a brick wall. It may seem overly simplistic to suggest that the turning of a simple calendar page to mark the beginning of the 1940s could so starkly represent the extinguishing of the brilliant comedy flame, one that had shone so brightly for the preceding ten years. Yet it really was just about that sharp of a decline. Some might argue that the peak of the Golden Age occurred even earlier, perhaps about halfway through the 1930s, but as we've seen, top-quality comedy output did indeed continue throughout the full remainder of the decade.

Then, however, things changed, and quickly.

Firstly, many legendary comedians, who were well on their way to successful careers back in 1930, had passed away at young ages by decade's end, or shortly thereafter. By way of review, the list includes:

Roscoe Arbuckle - died of a heart attack, June 29, 1933, age 46.

Will Rogers - died in a plane crash, August of 1935, age 55.

Thelma Todd - died under mysterious circumstances, December of 1935, age 29.

Paul McCullough - died by his own hand, March 25, 1936, age 52.

Dave Freeman -died December 8, 1936, age 38.

Al Boasberg - died in June, 1937, age 44.

Ted Healy - died from alcoholism December, 1937, age 41.

Robert Woolsey - succumbed to kidney failure in 1938, age 50.

Charley Chase - died of a heart attack in 1940, age 47.

Joe Penner - died of a heart attack in January of 1941, age 36.

As untimely as those deaths were, most of the popular film comedians of the Golden Decade were, thankfully, still very much with us as we entered the 1940s. The problem was that a combination of circumstances—poor treatment by big movie studios, lackluster material, changing public tastes, and, oh yes, a world war—disrupted much of the finest comedians' familiar high standards of quality output. There were exceptions, of course, and occasional bursts of top-notch creative work were still to come, but these were becoming few and far between.

In addition, a few of the silent-era giants, like Harold Lloyd and producer Mack Sennett, had left the industry altogether by 1940 (Lloyd released his fifth and final release of the 1930s, *Professor Beware*, in 1938).

Laurel & Hardy, who kept the quality of their output throughout the 1930s astoundingly high, released the last of their top-notch films, *A Chump at Oxford* and *Saps at Sea*, in 1940, before leaving Hal Roach Studios and joining 20th Century Fox. Creatively, it was a disastrous turn of events for the team. Fox studio executives promptly denied Stan any sort of creative control over the comedy material. The result was a handful of poorly-made features written and directed by those who didn't have the understanding of Laurel & Hardy's comedy. "We had no say in those films, and it sure looked it," Stan said. "We had done too many films in our own way for us to keep taking anything like that, so we gave up the ghost. It was sickening."

Fields in *Never Give a Sucker an Even Break*, just after turning to the camera to inform us, "this was supposed to take place in a saloon, but the censor cut it out. It'll play just as well." Author's collection.

The Marx Brothers' 1940 MGM release, *Go West*, continued a creative decline for the brothers. It was not a film to compare favorably with their earlier MGM films, *A Night at the Opera* and *A Day at the Races*, released just a few years earlier. Their subsequent efforts, *The Big Store* in 1941, and *A Night in Casablanca* (United Artists) in 1946 continued that drop in quality—although, as always, there were individual scenes that aspired to the team's anarchy from a few years before (the final film in which they appeared together, *Love Happy*, in 1949, was mostly a Harpo vehicle, with support from Chico, and a voiceover narration and brief on-camera cameo by Groucho).

The one comedian who still managed to release some of his best work was W.C. Fields, who filmed two of his best comedies (and his last starring roles) at this time: *The Bank Dick* in 1940, and *Never Give a Sucker an Even Break* the following year. Critic James Agee said of Fields, "He was the toughest and most warmly human of all screen comedians, and *It's a Gift* and *The Bank Dick*, fiendishly funny and incisive white-collar comedies, rank high among the best comedies (and best films) ever made."

Fields, like Laurel & Hardy, had also been experiencing difficult creative battles with studio executives—who, most often, were themselves not creative at all. As Fields' health declined, his drinking habits did not ease, precipitating his worsening condition (after *Never Give a Sucker an Even Break*, he appeared only in cameo scenes in a handful of films). Eddie Cantor claimed that he had shared a moment with a somewhat sorrowful Fields at the end of Fields' life, in 1946. "'Eddie,' he said, 'I've often wondered how far I could have gone had I laid off the booze.' And, for the only time, I saw a tear drop off his face. Two days later he was dead."

Trade ad for *The Great Dictator*. Author's collection.

1940 AND BEYOND

As the 1940s began, a good portion of the globe was either at war, or on the verge of bloody conflict. Hitler's army invaded Poland in September of 1939, prompting Britain and France to declare war on the Third Reich (the U.S. continued its then-popular practice of isolationism until the Pearl Harbor attack on December 7, 1941).

Charlie Chaplin's sense of timing in 1940 can be viewed as either brilliant, or, with the benefit of hindsight, unfortunate. On October 15, he finally released his first true all-talking film, *The Great Dictator*, more than a decade after the rest of the motion picture industry had made the transition to sound.

Since the day of the film's release—and even before—there had been considerable controversy over its satire of the European fascism causing such upheaval. Here, Chaplin creates a fierce satire of Hitler and all that he represented (with Jack Oakie providing support as a faux Mussolini). By the film's release date, however, Hitler had drawn the world into its bloodiest war, and Chaplin's attempt to milk laughs from his Adenoid Hynkel character was met with some derision from critics. The film does conclude with a six-minute sequence in which Chaplin delivers an impassioned speech about how freedom must ultimately win over the evils of dictatorship.

After the revelation of the unspeakable genocide that had taken place in the concentration camps, Chaplin conceded in his autobiography, "Had I known of the actual horrors of the German concentration camps, I could not have made *The Great Dictator*, I could not have made fun of the homicidal insanity of the Nazis."

The Great Dictator proved popular with the public, despite the increasing weight of allegations by the U.S. government that Chaplin was a Communist sympathizer.

As the legendary comedians of the 1930s found themselves experiencing a downturn of their careers into the 1940s, a new batch enjoyed an upward trajectory. Abbott & Costello rode their radio and stage success into films, first appearing in 1940 as comic relief in *One Night in the Tropics* (starring Bob Cummings and Alan Jones), in which they performed several of the stage routines that had later made them such a smash on radio. The team released four films in 1941 alone, all of which did well at the box office, just in time to help save the struggling Universal Studios.

Of course, World War II made an impact on all aspects of American life, including entertainment, and just about every comedian or comedy team would make at least one military comedy, some peppered with none-too-subtle American propaganda, and most including musical stars and swing bands. Three of those four Abbott & Costello 1941 releases were military comedies, and all were fast-paced affairs, full of energy, music, and crammed with well-polished versions of their best stage routines.

Buck Privates led the pack of wartime-era musical comedies. Author's collection.

Buck Privates was their first and arguably best vehicle, showcasing them at the height of their talents. Filmed and released just before the U.S. formally entered WWII that December, it perfectly captures the stirring (and now corny) patriotism sweeping the nation at the time, and soon to be shamelessly exploited by Hollywood. The team's follow-ups, *In The Navy* (with its rousing musical refrain "We're in the Navy, watchdogs of liberty...") and *Keep 'em Flying*, were filmed and released in quick order. In fact, the second picture the team actually filmed that year, *Hold That Ghost*, had its release date delayed, allowing *In the Navy* to serve as a more suitable companion piece to *Buck Privates*.

In a curious bit of irony, the ceremony in which Bud and Lou placed their hand and footprints in front of Grauman's Chinese Theatre took place on December 8, the day after the Pearl Harbor attack.

In retrospect, it's surprising how much of a head start *Buck Privates* had on the other wartime musical comedies that followed. Hollywood didn't begin cranking out most of its major patriotic-themed productions until mid-1942. *Private Buckaroo*, featuring a cast of comic actors plus the Andrews Sisters and Harry James, was released in late May of that year. *Stage Door Canteen*, crammed with cameos by dozens of stars, wasn't released until June of 1943. *This is the Army*, based on the Broadway show from the previous year (and featuring Kate Smith's rendition of "God Bless America"), and *Reveille with Beverly* starring Ann Miller, were also both 1943 releases. A pair of bandleader Kay Kyser's vehicles, *Thousands Cheer*, and *Around the World* (fictionalizing the exploits of Kyser's band on its tour for the troops), were released in 1943 as well. Several top comedians, including Edgar Bergen, Joe E. Brown, Ed Wynn, and, most famously, Bob Hope, dedicated much of their work to entertaining the troops, both in the service, and recuperating in veterans hospitals.

Just as *Buck Privates* kicked off the wartime musical trend in 1941, its 1947 sequel, *Buck Privates Come Home*, pretty much closed-out the genre, serving as a matching bookend. As the horrors of war raged on two fronts half a world away from each other, Abbott & Costello proved to the be the perfect clowns to help Americans cheer, laugh, and even dance their way (if only for ninety minutes at a time) through what has been called our last "noble" war.

At the height of Bud and Lou's popularity, RKO brought comedians Wally Brown and Alan Carney together in 1943, with the hope of creating that studio's version of Abbott & Costello. Brown was the straight man (although he could deliver a gag line with ease), and Carney the Costello-like blunderer. The team, while pleasant enough to watch and good for a number of laughs, made fewer than ten comedies of varying quality before the studio gave up on them and terminated their contract.

On the airwaves, the public's favorite radio comedians and their programs continued to flourish, with no sign of flagging. Jack Benny, Fred Allen, and Burns & Allen, and Edgar Bergen continued to maintain a high degree of consistency in their programs, with Benny solidifying his cheap, vain character, as his supporting cast continued to increase their value to the program. Fred Allen added his most popular radio feature yet, "Allen's Alley," to his own program in 1942, a full decade after his debut on the air. Radio as a medium reached a peak of popularity and influence with the public during the war years, until, towards decade's end, the emergence of television as an affordable addition to the home changed things forever. The radio stars of the 1930s and '40s, who had grown so comfortable with their medium, found themselves with decisions to make in the post-war years.

Legacy

Looking back through the decades from today's vantage point, it's obvious that classic comedy didn't die with the end of the 1930s. The art's practitioners continued their own personal evolution with changing times, in order to extend their careers through the 1940s and into the television era, which presented new challenges to their careers, just as they had to make major adjustments from the stage to radio back at the dawn of the Golden Decade, and from radio to films. The fact that they are still remembered and celebrated today, considering all of the great comedians who have succeeded them, is testament to the quality and durability of their comedy.

As mentioned earlier, The Sons of the Desert organization still thrives around the world today and it pays ongoing tribute to Laurel & Hardy. The Stoogeum, a privately-owned museum just outside Philadelphia, offers thousands of items, and a movie theatre, for Three Stooges fans. Statues and plaques honor Stan Laurel and Oliver Hardy in their respective hometowns.

Even the United States Postal Service honored the comedians of the Golden Decade in 1991 with a set of commemorative stamps, featuring the caricature artwork of the great Al Hirschfeld. And, of course, both classic and obscure comedy film and radio performances from the 1930s can be found (sometimes requiring a bit of perseverance) on countless Internet sites.

U.S. Postal Service pamphlet announcing the commemorative set. Author's collection.

Many scholars of entertainment history have offered their own take on the comedians of the Golden Decade, and how some of them thrived by taunting authority, or by representing and speaking for the "common man" at a time of great social and political disruption, etc. Such assessments can get bogged down in the kind of gobbledegook that all too easily throws a wet blanket onto the sheer joy of experiencing comedy, and laughing at the results of those who create and perform it.

It's perhaps best to let one of the greatest comic geniuses of all, Stan

Laurel, get the last word on such high-minded, scholarly interpretations of both his own work, and the work of his comedy peers:

> "That kind of junk annoys the hell out of me. What people like that don't understand and never will understand is that what we were trying to do was to make people laugh in as many ways as we could, without trying to prove a point or show the world its troubles or get into some deep meaning. Why the hell do you have to explain why a thing is funny? We were trying to do a very simple thing, give people some laughs, and that's *all* we were trying to do."

Amen.

* * *

Notes

Introduction

"Unlike, as in most of the arts, greatness in comedy...": Steve Martin, introduction to *The Most of S.J. Perelman* (2000 edition).

1929

Thomas Edison quote about talkies: *The New York Times*, August 1, 1929, p.3.

Leonard Maltin on early Our Gang sound releases: "the original sound effects and discordant musical instruments..." *Our Gang-The Life and Times of the Little Rascals*, p.93.

Groucho on comedians going into films: *Photoplay*, July, 1929, p. 51.

Morrie Ryskind on writing *Cocoanuts* with George S. Kaufman: *The Marx Brothers Scrapbook* p. 78-79.

Charles LeMaire talking about clothing for sound films: *Photoplay*, July, 1929, p.86.

Stan Laurel discussing *Unaccustomed as We Are* gag: *Mr. Laurel & Mr. Hardy*, p.155.

Hal Roach discusses filming with sound, foreign language versions: *The New York Times*, Jan 19, 1930, sect. 8, p.6.

Mack Sennett, "I'm going back to the fundamentals of silent screen comedy...": *The New York Times*, November 30, 1930.

Jack Benny quote about Thalberg hiring him: *Sunday Nights at Seven*, p. 38.

Amos & Andy didn't rehearse before airtime. "We couldn't do that...": *Radio Digest*, October, 1929, p.15.

Jack Benny on Amos & Andy: *Sunday Nights at Seven*, p. 33.

Amos & Andy article, "In order to get material for their act...": *Radio Revue*, "Amos & Andy--Radio's First Comic Strip," December, 1929, p. 8.

"So fair and deft have been their characterizations...": *Radio Revue*, December 29, 1929, p.8.

"For the first time people didn't have to leave their homes...": George Burns describes stopping vaudeville show for *Amos & Andy* broadcast: *Gracie: A Love Story*, p.87.

Amos & Andy to get a quarter of a million dollars for talkie: *Photoplay*, June, 1930, p.32.

Wheeler & Woolsey incorporating themselves: *The New Movie Magazine*, January, 1933, p.12.

W.C. Fields on Will Rogers: After Rogers' death, Paramount Studios asked Fields to write about his friend, to be used in publicity for the Will Rogers Memorial Fund. His essay is reprinted on pages 152-154 in *W.C. Fields by Himself*, edited by his grandson, Ronald J. Fields.

"He'd added a monologue to his [rope trick] act...": Eddie Cantor's comments on Will Rogers, *The Way I see It*.

Photoplay review of *They Had to See Paris*, December, 1929, p.52

Variety review of *They Had to See Paris*: October 16, 1929, p.17.

Review of Beatrice Lillie at the Palace: *The New York Times*, September 23, 1929.

"When we first started, I had all the funny jokes...": George Burns interview for *The Great Comedians*, p. 137-140.

Burns & Allen filming "Lamb Chops" sketch, "Gracie didn't want to do it..." *Gracie--A Love Story*, p.89.

"Gracie and I were perfect for radio.": *All My Best Friends*, p. 86-87.

George and Gracie tour U.K., "In those days, radio stations would use five minutes of comedy...": *All My Best Friends*, p. 88.

Notes

Harold Lloyd quotes about Roach, *Welcome Danger: "Conversations with the Great Moviemakers of Hollywood's Golden Age*, pages 10, 12.

Welcome Danger review: *Photoplay* mag. December, 1929, p. 55.

Welcome Danger review: *Variety* October 23, 1929, p.17.

The Rise of the Goldbergs review: *The New York Times* May 4, 1930, sect. 12, p.16.

"It is gratifying that the peoples of every race liked it...: Gertrude Berg, Radio Guide, November 14, 1931, p.1.

1930

Strike Up the Band review: *The New York Times* Jan. 15, 1930.

Strike Up the Band review: *Variety*, January 22, 1930.

"Nothing is more fascinating and nothing more futile...": J. Brooks Atkinson, *The New York Times*, November 11, 1928.

"The Palace Theatre was the goal of every act in America...": *Much Ado About Me*, p. 120.

"To me, playing the Palace Theatre on Broadway meant you were a star.": *Gracie, A Love Story*, p.80

Variety review of Jack Benny at the Palace: January 1, 1930.

Billboard review of Benny, Burns & Allen, Jessel: January 11, 1930.

"Jessel is, beyond question, a smart and vaudeville-wise entertainer..." *The New York Times,* July 17, 1928.

"For every hickory-dickery dock..." Ed Wynn in *The New York Times*, February 23, 1930.

"It is Ed Wynn's field day... Review of *Simple Simon* by Brooks Atkinson, *The New York Times*, February 19, 1930, p.22.

Review of *Hold Everything* (film): *Variety*, March 26, 1930, p. 25.

"War broke out between two famous comedians not long ago.": *Photoplay*, June, 1930.

"New York stage directors, New York dialogue writers, and the musicians union all moved to Hollywood...": Buster Keaton, in a 1964 interview included in the documentary *A Hard Act to Follow*.

"It was Mack Sennett who took the first chance..." Article titled "Just Let Me Work" by Tom Ellis, *Photoplay*, March, 1930, p. 65.

Review of Harold Lloyd's *Feet First*: *Picture Play*, November, 1930, p. 65.

Radio-Keith-Orpheum chain announces it will discard the term "vaudeville": The New York Times, July 23, 1930, p.25.

"The great showplace found itself caught in a web of its own contradictions.": *Show Biz - Vaude to Video*, p. 72.

"W.C. Fields, noted stage comedy star, is another entrant in [RKO's] rush of short laughers...": *Photoplay*, September, 1930, p. 120.

Animal Crackers dialogue "reaches a level of literacy and wit that future Marx films can't hope to rival." *Groucho, Harpo, Chico, and Sometimes Zeppo*, p.105.

"Where six months ago it looked as though two-reel comedies would go out..." *Variety*, April 16, 1930.

"Players and directors need a table of statistics or some scientific basis for judging the comic content.": *The New York Times* editorial, November 1, 1930.

"I think as soon as the sponsors began allowing people to come into the studio to watch the broadcast, radio began changing.": *All My Best Friends*, p.133.

"You make them laugh, they will forget you, but if you make them cry, they will never forget you." Fannie Brice *The New Yorker*, April 20, 1929.

Sweet and Low review: *The New York Times*, November 18. 1930.

"When I was in vaudeville...": Fannie Brice *Liberty*, August 20, 1938.

"The piece seemed like a playground for all of W.C.'s wild antics...": Ronald J. Fields, *W.C. Fields: A Life on Film*, p. 77.

Review of Ballyhoo, starring W.C. Fields: *The New York Times*, December 22, 1930.

1931

"If Charlie Chaplin doesn't make talkies, he won't make anything.": *Motion Picture* magazine, "Al Jolson Answers Chaplin" by Cedric Belfrage, August, 1929.

"I was determined to continue making silent films…" Chaplin, *My Autobiography*, p. 366.

Erich von Stroheim on ZaSu Pitts: *Photoplay*, April 1931.

ZaSu Pitts on her hand waving: "I really don't know when I first began…" *Photoplay*, February, 1935.

Review of *Pajama Party*: *Variety*, November 3, 1931, p.17.

"He has stepped over to Broadway and brought in any number of shining names…" *Radio Digest*, February, 1933, p. 4

"There was no continuity to Eddie's character…" *All My Best Friends*, p. 88.

"A man with no talent…" Ed Wynn as quoted by his grandson, Ned, in Ned's book *We'll Always Live In Beverly Hills*.

"Eddie Cantor had to fight for his laughs.": Milton Berle, *B.S. I Love You*, p. 92.

"Eddie's a great performer…": Chico Marx quoted in *Growing Up with Chico*, p. 96.

Jerry Stiller on Cantor's radio performance: *Married to Laughter*, p. 32.

"Keeping an audience under glass was one thing…" *All My Best Friends*, p. 133.

"The audience is howling…": Cantor's memoirs, *The Way I See It*.

"We agreed, as long as he let me write her material." *All My Best Friends*, p. 89

"We were a hit. And when we left the studio that day…": Ibid., p. 90.

J. Brooks Atkinson review of *The Laugh Parade*: "Marshall of the Laugh Parade," *The New York Times*, November 16, 1931.

"Ed Wynn, King of Idiocy" by John Mason Brown, *Two on the Aisle*, p. 270.

1932

"They were quite a bit alike, Babe and Hal." Charley Rogers, *Mr. Laurel & Mr. Hardy*, p. 99.

"Perhaps in those days, the word used was not 'interfering' but 'collaborating'..." John McCabe, *Mr. Laurel & Mr. Hardy*, p. 122.

"It's amazing how much thought went into what on the surface looked like low-down stupidity." Leo McCarey, *Who The Devil Made it*.

"...but because he was doing twice as much work as Babe, and Babe agreed with him." *The Comedy World of Stan Laurel*, p. 62.

"I like to get a good reaction...I think I've earned my money." Oliver Hardy, as quoted in *Mr. Laurel & Mr. Hardy*.

"In addition to being two of the funniest men who ever lived...Patsy Kelly on Laurel & Hardy quoted in *Laurel & Hardy*, p. 9.

"I walked into the commissary in 1933..." Ed Wynn on Laurel & Hardy: *The Great Comedians*, p. 373.

"The big need was for ideas.": *Mr. Laurel and Mr. Hardy*, p. 137.

"...Getting the piano into the house...": *Film Daily*, February 28, 1932.

"The combination of more than a little slapstick..": *Motion Picture Herald*, March 12, 1932.

"A hilarious Laurel & Hardy comedy is the hit of the screen." *Hollywood Citizen News*, July 2, 1932.

"You couldn't pay me enough money to go on radio." Ed Wynn talked into doing his radio show: "This Business of Being Funny On Radio Is No Joke, Says Wynn" *The New York Times*, May 29, 1932.

"How can a man please twenty million people?": Ibid.

Review of first *Fire Chief* broadcast: *Variety*, April 27, 1932.

ZaSu Pitts on her hand waving: *Photoplay*, February, 1935.

"Radio was for performers who talked and sang...": *All My Best Friends*, p. 86.

"The three script writers never see each other..." *Radio Mirror*, November, 1938.

Notes

We got this idea of Gracie's brother..." *Playboy* interview, June, 1978.

"Like a pack of wolves, newspaper men descended upon George Allen...": *Radio Digest*, "The Comic Tragedy of Gracie Allen's Real Brother" by Pauline Swanson, June 1933, p.22-23.

Sennett interview, talks about W.C. Fields: *The New York Times*, April 20, 1959 p.20.

"Roscoe 'Fatty' Arbuckle is again hesitantly testing...": *Variety*, March 8, 1932, p.37.

"As I see it, there was no way to mesh, match, or blend Durante's talents with mine." *My Wonderful World of Slapstick*, p. 237.

"When you give me a Jimmy Durante..." Keaton 1964 interview, as included in the documentary *A Hard Act To Follow*.

"Buster Keaton is leaning over backwards..." *Photoplay*, February, 1932, p.96.

"Stan and I went abroad on what we thought would be...": Oliver Hardy, *The New Movie Magazine*, May, 1935, p.63.

"Nine persons went to hospitals and many others were less seriously hurt in a wild crush." : The New York Times, July 30, 1932, p. 16.

"As our train wasn't due in Glasgow till half-past ten at night..." *New Movie Magazine*, May, 1935.

"From the time Jimmy and I were teamed up I heard rumors..." *My Wonderful World of Slapstick*, p. 237.

"There was just no way of figuring out who would be good on the radio.": *All My Best Friends*, p.123

"I was in England on a vacation in August of 1932 when I received a cable from Billy Wells...": Jack Pearl, *Radioland*, April, 1934, p.28

"Jack had signed a contract to do thirteen weekly shows for a radio sponsor." *Radio Mirror*, January, 1936.

"Now the reason my character sustained over so many years...": clip on Jack Benny HBO documentary, *Love in Bloom*, 1992.

"It seemed to me that the bizarre-garbed, joke-telling funster was ogling extinction.": *Treadmill to Oblivion*, pp. 4-5.

"For a time veterans of the footlights fell back upon their old stage jokes…" *The New York Times*, October 2, 1932, sect. 8, p.6.

"In the theatre, the actor had uncertainly…" *Treadmill to Oblivion*, p. 3.

"Indeed, with the accelerated pace at which the entire entertainment world has come to speed of late…" *The New York Times*, October 9, 1932.

"Radio was new. It hadn't developed any comedy writers. *Treadmill to Oblivion*, p. 12.

"Fred Allen seems destined for the next ether comedy sensation honors…": *Variety*, November 1, 1932.

"He was a role model and still is…": Herman Wouk, *Fred Allen - His Life and Wit*, p. 257.

David Freedman understood the dilemma comedians faced: "In fifteen short minutes you play to forty million people. (*Radioland*. September, 1933, p. 42)

Wynn on old jokes: "The critics who belabor comedians for using old and stale material can't know much about comedy." *Radio Mirror*, January, 1934, p. 54).

"Benny in concocting the comedy, remains to write the continuity" : *Radio Mirror* November, 1935, p.9.

"In radio, I had two writers plus myself. Now this was in the thirties…" : Jack Benny interview, *The Marx Brothers Scrapbook*, pp. 45-46.

"Comedians certainly have had the spot during the past year.": *Radio Digest*, February, 1933, p.5.

"I work hard at being funny,"Jack Pearl says.": *Radio Stars*, March, 1933, p. 50.

George Burns credits the very nature of radio work, as opposed to that in films, for the healthy marriages: *Radio Stars*, December, 1936.

"Vaudeville, as we knew it, was dead.": *Milton Berle - An Autobiography*, p. 119.

"Vaudeville is singing its swansong…": *The New York Times*, November 14, 1932.

1933

"Have you noticed the frequent use of the expression 'a couple of laughs' during the past few months?" : *Radio Digest*, February, 1933.

"These media had hardened the theatregoers to the corn which was too often the stock in trade of vaudeville..." : *Show Biz*, p. 433.

Review of *She Done Him Wrong*: *The New Movie Magazine*, March, 1933.

Review of *She Done Him Wrong*: *Picture Play* magazine, May, 1933.

"This month may also mark the beginning of Mae West's slide down...": *The New Movie Magazine*, January, 1934, p. 33.

"Not one seems to have bothered about Mae as she really is. They all write about how hard-boiled she is." Mae West's sister Beverly interview, *The New Movie Magazine*, May, 1933, p.93

"The past year brought three overnight stars (Mae West, Katherine Hepburn, Bing Crosby).": *Variety*, January, 2, 1933, p. 27

"The two Mae West releases are credited as an important factor here.": *Variety*, January 2, 1934, p. 3.

"Well, it's quite an achievement, and you must hand it to Mae.": *The New Movie Magazine*, January, 1934, p.10.

"...another whose success has been built around one very definite type of character.": *Picture Play*, February, 1936.

Review of The Kid from Spain: "Listeners will, instead, remember a gorgeous production." *Picture Play* magazine, February, 1933.

Wheeler & Woolsey *Diplomaniacs* review: *New Movie Magazine*, June, 1933, p.112.

"No one has enjoyed Ed on stage and radio more than we have..." *Radio Digest*, June, 1933, p.3.

"...approximately 200 possibilities are discarded..." Wynn defending his material, *The New York Times*, "Playing For Laughs," April 23, 1933, section 9, p. 5

"We've been told that Gracie Allen's Dumb Dora character..." *Radio Digest*, June, 1933, p.5

Report of Roscoe Arbuckle's death: *The New York Times*, June 30, 1933, p.17. Funeral description printed in the *Times* on July 1, p. 13.

Review of *The Chief* film: *The New York Times*, December 2, 1933.

Ed Wynn's suspected conspiracy in Hollywood against radio comedians: interview with Max Wilk, August 9, 1960, The New York Public Library, American Jewish Committee Oral History Collection.

"Well, you know how these things go…" Jack Pearl, *Radioland* magazine, "You've Forced Jack Pearl to Tell the Truth," April, 1934, p.29.

"Probably the thing that almost all of the films we made…" George Burns, *All My Best Friends*, p. 159.

Fred Allen and Jack Benny on working in movies as well as on radio: *Radio Mirror*, November, 1935.

"Wollcott was a particularly good friend of Mrs. Roosevelt…": *Harpo Speaks*, p. 297.

"It sure as hell hadn't been easy to put my act together in Moscow." Ibid., p. 315.

"Harpo Marx received an ovation here tonight." *The New York Times*, December 19, 1933, p. 26.

"Maybe there is some obscure connection between the making of motion pictures and radio popularity." *Radioland*, February, 1934.

"The boys out on the [west] coast like to take anyone down a little.": Jack Pearl, *Radioland,* April, 1934.

"Jack Pearl has gradually built up an acceptance for…": *Radio Digest,* June, 1933 "Slipping and Gripping" column.

"To our mind the Baron failed because he was too much Baron.": *Radioland*, February, 1934.

"There is a vaudeville background to this framework which, even if it does resurrect a couple of familiars, is sturdy stuff.": *Variety*, November 11, 1936, p.45.

"The problem with relying on catchphrases is that they get very old while they're still new.": *All My Best Friends*, pp. 96-97.

"When listeners finally began getting tired of the line Jack Pearl had no insurance.": Ibid., p. 99.

"Again the four Marx Brothers crash through...": *Photoplay*, January, 1934.

"Practically everybody wants a good laugh right now and *Duck Soup* should make practically everybody laugh.": *Variety*, November 27, 1933.

"With each fresh appearance of the Four Marx Brothers..." *The New Movie Magazine,*
February, 1934, p.106.

1934

"Standing before a mike and hoping their effort were going over...": *Radio Mirror* June, 1934.

"In October, 1932, I said to several newspaper friends who were nice enough to quote me...":

"Radio Guy" *Variety* column by Eddie Cantor, Tuesday, January 2, 1934.

"Delivering a mere string of jokes is already a thing of the past in radio...": Eugene Conrad, *Radioland*, September, 1933, p.84.

"Despite the awful static coming from some radio editors to the effect that 'comedy is fading on the air...'" Eddie Cantor, *Variety*, Tuesday January 2, 1934.

"It would help...if George and Gracie had a studio audience to get the laughs started." *Radio Digest*, June, 1933, p.3.

"When I played in vaudeville...": Gracie Allen, *Radio Mirror*, March, 1935.

"Gracie never worked to the audience or, later, to the camera.": *Gracie, A Love Story*, p.53.

"We find it much easier to work before an audience..." George Burns, *The New York Times*, February 9, 1936.

Women in Burns & Allen audience miss the first Gracie jokes: *Radio Mirror* June, 1939.

"When asked what he considered the worst influence exerted on radio by the stage, he answered, 'The habit of playing before audiences.' *Radio Mirror*, June, 1934.

"With a bang-up entertainment in which practically all its big-name stars were represented...": *Radioland*, "The Editor's Opinion," April, 1934.

"...another whose success has been built around..." *Picture Play* on Mae West, February, 1936.

"This month may also mark the beginning of Mae West's slide down..." *The New Movie Magazine*, January, 1934, p.33.

"Miss Lombard, a tall, classic blonde...": *The New York Times*, September 14, 1934.

"His is a tough job..." Jack Benny on writer Harry Conn: *Radio Mirror*, November, 1938.

"All the comedians knew him." Jack Benny on Al Boasberg, *The Marx Brothers Scrapbook*, pp. 45-46.

"There they would be; one of the writers stretched out on the sofa..." Joan Benny, *Sunday Nights at Seven*, p. 69.

"Really, that's the only picture that Gable ever played himself." Frank Capra, *Conversations*...p.99.

"Mr. Burns writes all the dialogue for the team...": Burns & Allen in movies, *The New York Times*, May 6, 1934, sect. 9, p.4.

"The hell of it was he was basically so funny that I'd start to wail to the front office about how difficult he was, and I got no sympathy.": Leo McCarey, *Who the Devil Made it?*

Radio statistics: "The total number of radio sets in the United States is close to the 18,000,000 mark.": *The New York Times*, April 15, 1934.

"Miss West, in her own way, is excellent in the role Miss George created on the stage." *Variety*, November 25, 1936, p. 14.

"The Marx Brothers had been in a rut." *Harpo Speaks*, p. 374.

"After the lethargic welcome given to such pieces as Duck Soup...": *The New York Times*, October 20, 1934.

"Censorship, both official and unofficial, hangs like a storm cloud...": Eric Ergenbright, *The New Movie Magazine*, October, 1934.

Laurel & Hardy comment on each other: *The New Movie Magazine* May, 1935. p. 64.

Hal Roach speaks on purchasing *Babes in Toyland* for a film version: excerpt from *Films in Review*, date unknown, reprinted in *Pratfall* magazine vol. 1, #9, 1972.

Review of *Babes in Toyland*, "A musical fairy tale is unheard of in films...": *Picture Play* magazine, March, 1935.

Review of *Babes in Toyland* : *The New York Times*, December 13, 1934.

Review of *Babes in Toyland*: *Variety*, December 16, 1934.

Review of *It's A Gift*: *Photoplay*, February, 1935.

Review of *It's A Gift*: *The New York Times*, January 1, 1935.

"Howard and Shelton depend primarily upon ridiculous characterizations..." *Radio Digest*, February, 1933, p. 5.

"Two phases of W. C. Fields's remarkable talent are currently on view..." *Picture Play*, April, 1934.

"When sober, Ted was the essence of refinement...": *Moe Howard & the Three Stooges*, p. 103.

"We rehearsed a short three weeks before we shot it.": Larry Fine film interview, 1973.

"We all know it is easier to make an audience cry than laugh..." Hal Roach, *The New Movie Magazine*, November, 1934.

1935

"Radio was a medium, where, every week, more people would hear my jokes...": *Don't Shoot, It's Only Me*, p. 28-29.

"The Jordans are one of the few radio teams which bases its act upon the theory that its listeners have some intelligence.": *Radio Stars*, November, 1936.

"They told us Jack Benny and Fred Allen were setting the styles in comedy this year." *Radio Mirror* May, 1935.

"Forty-four of the forty-five RKO theatres in Greater New York will become double-feature houses tomorrow." *The New York Times*, September 6, 1935.

Review, The Man on the Flying Trapeze": *Picture Play*, October, 1935.

Stan Laurel fired, re-hired: *The New York Times*, March 16, April 5, 1935.

"Making comedy you have to go up; you can't do your funniest gag first or you die…" Roach on two-reelers (originally in *Films in Review*, reprinted in *Pratfall*, vol. 1, #9).

"I'll make a picture with you fellows with half as many laughs…" Groucho quoting Irving Thalberg, *Groucho and Me*, p. 235.

"I'd go to [Thalberg's] office with about seven pages of the script…": Morrie Ryskind, *The Marx Brothers Scrapbook*, p. 81.

"When asked after the tour what he thought of the process, Harpo gushed, 'Terrific.': *The New York Times*, November 17, 1935, sect. 9. p. 4.

Eddie Cantor tryouts for *The Kid from Spain*: *Variety*, March 1, 1932, p. 2.

"Working with the Marx Brothers was unlike anything…He did it over and over, till he finally came up with a good one and I burst out laughing.": Kitty Carlisle, *Kitty--An Autobiography*, p. 73.

Andre Sennwald's assessment of *A Night at the Opera*: *The New York Times*, December 15, 1935.

"Outside of that, however, the show's a comedy wow.": *Billboard* review of *Everything Goes*, December 21, 1935, p. 18.

1936

"There should be a law passed immediately requiring every revue to enlist the services of Messrs. Howard and Lahr.": *Billboard* review of *George White's Scandals*, January 4, 1936.

"[The] draw is Burns and Allen with their intimate revue…": *Billboard*, February 1, 1936.

"I was riding in my car one day and saw a mass of people coming out of a factory, punching time-clocks..." Chaplin in *The New York Times*, February 2, 1936.

Stan's comments on Chaplin's idea for *Modern Times*: intro, *The Comedy World of Stan Laurel*.

"The Roach lot, probably the most active single unit in town...": *The New York Times*, August 30, sect. 9. p.4

"While he didn't land a steady job, he and Charlie grew to be much in demand for special entertainments and parties...": *Radio Mirror*, September, 1938.

Review of Bergen's debut on Rudy Vallee's program: *Variety*, Dec. 30, 1936, p.36.

"Edgar Bergen did a thing no one thought possible in radio...": *Radio Mirror*, April, 1937.

"Imitation may be the sincerest form of flattery...": Rudy Vallee on Edgar Bergen, *The New York Times*, August 13, 1939, sect. 9, p. 10.

"Miss Brice is the personification of 'The Follies'.": *The New York Times*, September 15, 1936.

"A triumph of wit, humor, and goofy fun.": *Picture Play* review of *My Man Godfrey*, December, 1936.

"Broadcasters who study the various popularity polls report that Fred Allen..." *The New York Times*, December 6, 1936.

"Cantor believes the stage tryout [for] film comedy, to set laughs for timing, etc., is essential to a film reproduction.": *Variety* March. 1, 1932, p.2.

"B. L. are their initials. Beatrice Lillie and Bert Lahr are their names.": *The New York Times* review of *The Show Is On*: December 26, 1936.

Variety review of *The Show Is On*, Dec. 30, 1936, p.51.

1937

"I promise to remember I am performing for my listeners...": Ed Wynn *Radio Mirror*, February, 1937, p. 14.

"He worked himself to death…": Fred R. Sammis on Dave Freedman *Radio Mirror* March, 1937 p. 4.

"Surely, aside from the other comforts …": radio stars' salaries, *The New York Times*, March 14, 1937.

Henny Youngman at Lowe's State theatre vaudeville: *Billboard* March 20, 1937.

W.C. Fields letter to Jack Benny, "I listen to the program so assiduously every week…" May 6, 1941, *W.C. Fields, by Himself*.

"Now he is an institution…" *Picture Play* on W.C. Fields, September, 1936.

"When I had my own show I brought W.C. Fields in…": Edgar Bergen, *The Vaudevillians*, pp. 48-49.

"The Chase & Sanborn program is a multiple threat…": *Radio Mirror*, August, 1937.

Review of Bert Lahr as host: *Radio Mirror*, August. 1937.

"Never did a radio program whiz so quickly to top ranking…": *Radio Stars* editorial August, 1937.

"King Canute discovered he could not check the tide…" Frank S. Nugent on Chaplin retiring Little Tramp: *The New York Times*, September 19, 1937.

W. C. Fields comparing how performers are treated in various venues: *Radio Stars*, September, 1937, p. 76.

"I considered Al Boasberg one of the greatest gag men who ever lived--and in addition I considered him one of my very best friends.": Jack Benny, *Radio Stars*, October, 1937.

E. Bergen & McCarthy top poll: *The New York Times*, November 21, 1937, sec. XI, page 12.

"Freedman was, at the time, pursuing a lawsuit against his former employer, Eddie Cantor…" Fred R. Sammis in *Radio Mirror*, March, 1937.

"Reference to the name of Mae West, film actress, whose role in an 'Adam and Eve' sketch…": *The New York Times*, December 25, 1937.

"The scare thrown into the radio people by Mae West's recent broadcast has created…": *The New York Times*, December 26, 1937, sect. 10, p.5.

Rumor of Mae West on "The Kate Smith Hour": *Billboard*, January 22, 1938, p. 22.

Thalberg discusses *A Night at the Opera* with Marxes: *Groucho and Me*, p. 235.

Groucho on Thalberg's death: Ibid. p. 248.

1938

"An interesting phase of Bergen's career is the subjugation of his own personality...": Douglas W. Churchill in *The New York Times*, February 13, 1938, , sec. 10. p.5.

"Folks, it is going to be a little difficult to describe this one.": *The New York Times*, review of *Hellzapoppin'*, September 23, 1938.

"As no one needs to be told by now, *Hellzapoppin'* is one of the greatest moneymakers of all time.": *The New York Times*, May 7, 1938 sect. 10, p.1.

"All these comedy minds were necessary...": *Don't Shoot, It's Only Me*, p. 33.

I had misgivings about this..." Morrie Ryskind on writing the *Room Service* screenplay: *The Marx Brothers Scrapbook*, p. 82.

Year-end popularity poll of radio programs: *The New York Times*, December 4, 1938 sect. 10, p. 16.

"Despite the artificial studio atmosphere, lack of make-up...": *Radio Stars* December, 1938, p. 32.

1939

"They're talking about moving the whole *Your Hit Parade* program out to Hollywood." *Radio Mirror*, January, 1939, p. 52.

"[Producer] Mervyn LeRoy asked me to write a Marx Brothers film script .": Irving Brecher, *The Laugh Crafters*.

"The bring-W.C. Fields-back-to-Broadway movement...": *The New York Times*, May 7, 1939, sect. 10, p.1.

"It was an event when you can get all three of them on the set at the same time.": 1964 Keaton film interview, included in the documentary *A Hard Act To Follow*.

"It's a toss-up as to who provides the most fun, Abbott & Costello or Clark…" : *Streets of Paris* review, Variety, June 21, 1939, p. 50.

"Especially it is hard to find good comedians…": Rudy Vallee, *The New York Times*, August 13, 1939, sect. 10, p. 10.

"I got my biggest laughs when I did the warm-up before the show." *Milton Berle - An Autobiography*, p. 189.

"In view of the worrisome life most of us lead…": Milton Berle, *The New York Times*, December 31, 1939.

"In spite of the anti-Semitic propaganda…": *Radio Stars*, December, 1938, p.34.

1940

"Radio Rose of the Month goes to two new comedians, Bud Abbott and Lou Costello.": *Radio Mirror*, May, 1938, p. 55.

"Eddie, I've often wondered how far I could have gone had I laid off the booze.": W.C. Fields, quoted in *Take My Life*.

"Had I known of the actual horrors of the German concentration camps…" Chaplin, *My Autobiography*, p. 392.

"That kind of junk annoys the hell out of me." Stan Laurel, introduction to *The Comedy World of Stan Laurel.*, p. xii-xiii.

Bibliography

Allen, Fred. *Much Ado About Me*. Boston: Little, Brown and Company, 1956.

Allen, Fred. *Treadmill to Oblivion*. Boston: Little, Brown and Company, 1954.

Benny, Jack and Joan Benny. *Sunday Nights at Seven*. New York: Warner Books, 1990.

Berle, Milton with Haskel Frankel. *Milton Berle--An Autobiography*. New York: Delacorte Press, 1974.

Burns, George, with David Fisher. *All My Best Friends*. New York: G.P. Putnam's Sons, 1989.

Burns, George. *Gracie--A Love Story*. New York: G.P. Putnam's Sons, 1988.

Cantor, Eddie. *The Way I See It*. Englewood Cliffs, N.J.: Prentice-Hall, Inc., 1959.

Cassara, Bill. Edgar Kennedy: *Master of the Slow Burn*.: Bearmanor Media, 2005.

Chaplin, Charles. *My Autobiography*. Random House UK, 1964.

Curtis, James. *W.C. Fields*. New York: Alfred A. Knopf. 2003.

Deschner, Donald. *The Films of W.C. Fields*. Secaucus, N.J.: Citadel Press, 1966.

Edmonds, Andy. *Frame Up!* New York: Avon Books, 1991.

Everson, William. *The Films of Laurel & Hardy*. Secaucus, N.J.: Citadel Press, 1967.

Fields, Ronald. *W.C. Fields: A Life on Film*. New York: St. Martin's Press, 1984.

Fields, Ronald (editor) *W.C. Fields by Himself*. Englewood Cliffs, NJ: Prentiss-Hall, 1973.

Fleming, Michael. *The Three Stooges Illustrated History*. New York: Doubleday, 1999.

Furmanek, Bob and Ron Palumbo. *Abbott and Costello in Hollywood*. New York: Perigree Books/Putnam Publishing Group, 1991.

Grossman, Barbara. *Funny Woman: The Life and Times of Fanny Brice*. Bloomington: Indiana University Press, 1991.

Hope, Bob with Melville Shavelson. *Don't Shoot, It's Only Me*. New York: G.P. Putnam's Sons, 1990.

Howard, Moe. *Moe Howard & the Three Stooges*. Secaucus, NJ: Citadel Press, 1977.

Keaton, Buster and Charles Samuels. *My Wonderful World of Slapstick*. New York: Da Capo Press, 1960.

Marx, Groucho. *Groucho and Me*. New York: Bernard Geis Associates, 1959.

Marx, Groucho. *The Groucho Letters*. New York: Manor Books, 1967.

Marx, Groucho and Richard J. Anobile. *The Marx Brothers Scrapbook*. New York: Grosset & Dunlap, 1974.

Marx, Harpo with Rowland Barber. *Harpo Speaks*. New York: Freeway Press, 1974.

Marx, Maxine. *Growing Up With Chico*. Englewood Cliffs, N.J.: Prentice-Hall, 1980.

Maltin, Leonard. *Our Gang: The Life and Times of the Little Rascals*. New York: Crown Publishers, 1977.

McCabe, John. *Mr. Laurel & Mr. Hardy*. New York: Grosset & Dunlap, 1961, 1966.

McCabe, John and Al Kilgore and Richard W. Bann. *Laurel & Hardy*. New York: E.P. Dutton, 1975.

Morgan, Michelle. *The Ice Cream Blonde*. Chicago: Chicago Review Press Inc., 2016.

Oderman, Stuart. *Roscoe "Fatty" Arbuckle: A Biography of the Silent Film Comedian, 1887-1933*. Jefferson, North Carolina: McFarland & Company, Inc. 1994.

Ott, Frederick. *The Films of Carole Lombard*. Secaucus, N.J.: Citadel Press, 1972.

Parish, James Robert and William T. Leonard. *The Funsters*. New Rochelle, N.Y.: Arlington House, 1979.

Skretvedt, Randy. Laurel & Hardy--*The Magic Behind the Movies*.

Stein, Charles (editor). *American Vaudeville--As Seen by its Contemporaries*. New York: Alfred A. Knopf, 1984.

Stevens, George Jr. (editor). "*Conversations with the Great Moviemakers of Hollywood's Golden Age*. New York: Alfred A. Knopf, 2006.

Stiller, Jerry. *Married to Laughter*. New York: Random House, 2000.

The Vaudevillians" by Bill Smith, MacMillan Publishing Co. New York, 1976,

Wilde, Larry. *The Great Comedians*. Secaucus, N.J.: Citadel Press, 1968.

Wynn, Ned. *We'll Always Live In Beverly Hills*. New York: William Morrow & Company, Inc. 1990.

Index

Abbott, Bud xviii, xx
Abbott & Costello xvi, 256, 273-275, 289-291
Ace, Goodman and Jane 100-101
Albee, Edward Franklin 38
Allen, Fred x, xiii, xvi, xviii, xix, 18, 40, 80, 111-113, 116, 126, 148, 168-169, 235, 241, 260, 277, 292
Allen, Gracie xviii, 171
Arbuckle, Roscoe 54, 95-96, 124, 143, 286
Atkinson, J. Brooks 27, 37, 45, 86, 274
Barton, James 63, 65
Benchley, Robert 95
Benny, Jack x, xvi-xvii, xx, 17-18, 20, 29, 40-42, 62, 104-107, 113-114, 120-121, 149, 170, 235, 241, 243-246, 248, 277, 292
Berg, Gertrude 32-34, 264, 280
Bergen, Edgar xvi, 78, 232-235, 243-246, 249, 251, 255-256, 268, 292
Berle, Milton xx, 80, 125, 275, 279
Boasberg, Al 4, 30, 99, 120, 205, 248, 286
Bolton, Guy 44
Brice, Fanny xvi-xvii, xix, 63-67, 217, 225-227
Brecher, Irving 275
Brown, Joe E xvii, 46-50
Brown & Carney 291-292
Burns, George xviii, xx, 20, 28, 63, 80, 81, 107, 114-115, 127, 148, 151, 152, 168, 171

319

Burns & Allen x, xvi, 18, 28-31, 40-42, 78, 83, 98-100, 142, 145, 164, 216, 235, 241, 257, 278, 292
Byron, Marion 74
Cantor, Eddie xvi, xvii, xx, 3, 25, 78-83, 125, 144, 163, 164, 168-169, 205, 224, 235, 241, 273, 288
Capra, Frank 165-166
Carroll, Earl 18
Chaplin, Charlie xvii, 31, 71-73, 217-220, 288-289
Chase, Charley xv, xvii, xx, 74, 158, 286
Clark, Bobby xvii, 225, 273-275
Clark & McCullough xv, 36, 94, 128, 193, 200, 220-221
Colbert, Claudette 165
Conn, Harry 105, 117, 120, 230
Conrad, Eugene 99, 163
Costello, Lou xx
DeForest, Lee 3
DuMont, Margaret 60, 77, 206
Durante, Jimmy xvi, xvii, 42, 77, 97-98, 109-110, 145, 150, 170
Edison, Thomas 2
Errol, Leon 95
Fields, W.C. ix, xv, xvii, xix, 25, 58-59, 67-69, 128-129, 140, 145, 164, 176-177, 187, 194-195, 201, 202, 243, 265, 267, 287-288
Fine, Larry xviii
Freedman, David 66, 117-119, 231-232, 239, 240, 286
Gable, Clark 165, 184
Garvin, Anita 74, 77
Gershwin, George & Ira 37
Gilbert, Billy xviii, 77, 101
Gosden, Freeman, and Charles Correll (Amos & Andy) 19-22, 32, 278
Grant, Cary xvi, 135, 138
Hardy, Oliver xvii
Hays, Will (Hays Code) 181
Healy, Ted xx, 66, 145, 179, 282-284, 286
Hirschfeld, Al 293-294
Hoffa, Portland 112
Howard, Curly xviii
Howard, Moe xviii
Howard, Shemp xviii
Howard, Tom 121-122
Howard, Willie 215
Hope, Bob vxi, 197, 217, 261-262
Jessel, George xviii, 41, 63, 65
Johnson, Chic xvii
Jolson, Al xx, 41, 71, 168, 241
Jordan, Jim and Marion 198-200
Kaufman, George S. xvii, 5, 59, 204, 208, 271
Keaton, Buster xviii, xix, 17, 31, 50-54, 77, 96-98, 109-110, 220, 277

Keith, Benjamin Franklin 38-40
Kelly, Patsy 78, 91, 159, 225
Kennedy, Edgar xvii, 14, 94, 154
Langdon, Harry 57, 62
Lahr, Bert xvi, xviii, xx, 46-50, 143, 215, 238-240, 246
Laurel, Stan xvii, xix, 218, 225, 242, 295
Laurel & Hardy ix, xv, 9-11, 17, 24, 50, 77, 87, 101-102, 107-108, 150, 159, 160, 188-192, 286, 293
LeMaire, Charles 8
Lillie, Beatrice xvi, xcii, 26, 128, 238-240
Livingstone, Mary 106, 113
Lombard, Carole xvi, 145, 149, 166-167, 227-229, 249, 250
Lombardo, Guy 98
Lloyd, Harold xvii, xxiii, 3, 31-32, 50, 57, 286
March, Frederick 249
Marlow, June 14-15
Martin, Steve xxii
Marx Brothers, The ix, xv, xix, 5-8, 24, 59, 77, 83-85, 108-109, 123-124, 140, 154-156, 167, 203, 247, 262, 275, 287
Marx, Chico 80, 170
Marx, Groucho xvii, 5, 170, 173, 185
Marx. Harpo xvii, 156-158, 205
Marx, Zeppo 6
McCarey, Leo xviii, 9, 74, 89-90, 154, 164, 227
McCullough, Paul 220, 225, 286
Oboler, Arch 251
Olsen, Ole xvii
Olsen & Johnson 24, 78, 210, 257-260, 273
Our Gang (The Little Rascals) xv, 3, 14-16, 42-44, 225
Pearl, Jack xviii, xx, 110-111, 144-147, 150-152, 170
Penner, Joe xx, 78, 152-153, 230, 286
Perelman, S.J. 83, 128
Pitts, ZaSu xvii, 73, 75-78, 145, 225
Powell, William 227-229
Quinn, Don 199
Quirk, James R. 56
Ritz Brothers, The xv, xviii, xx, 178
Roach, Hal xvii, 3, 9-16, 31, 62, 73-78, 89, 92, 158, 188-192, 212, 224
Rogers, Charley 88
Rogers, Will xviii, 18, 25, 28, 175, 202, 286
Ryskind, Morrie xviii, 5, 37, 59, 204, 227, 263
Sennett, Mack 12, 54, 62, 92-93, 95, 128-129, 164, 286
Shelton, George 121-122
Skelton, Red 278
Smith, Kate xvi, 254, 256-257
Stiller, Jerry 80-81
Sullivan, Ed 104, 127

Thalberg, Irving 17, 52, 204, 247
Three Stooges, The ix, xv, xx, 145, 150, 179-181, 280-282, 293
Todd, Thelma xv, xviii, 14, 73-78, 83-84, 110, 155, 159, 185, 211, 286
Tugend, Harry 117
Vallee, Rudy xiii, xvi, 79, 152, 215, 234, 273
Walker, H.M. 10, 42
Weber & Fields 3, 18
Wells, Billy 110, 117, 119
West, Mae xv, xvii, xx, 132-140, 186, 251-254
Wheeler, Bert xviii, 143
Wheeler & Woolsey xv, 22-24, 54, 78, 94, 140-142, 155
Woolsey, Robert xvii, 186, 263, 286
Wouk, Herman 118
Wynn, Ed xvi, xviii, xx, 40, 44-46, 62, 74, 80, 83, 85-86, 91, 102-104, 116-118, 133, 142, 144-148, 163, 168, 221, 241, 268, 273
Youngman, Henny 257
Zeigfeld, Florenz 22, 44

www.ingramcontent.com/pod-product-compliance
Lightning Source LLC
Chambersburg PA
CBHW070307230426
43664CB00015B/2665